A LITTLE
DAM
PROBLEM!

JIM JONES

Claudia
Hope you
enjoy this
dam book.

J J

Caxton Press

This book is dedicated to five individuals who played a major role in preserving the State of Idaho's control of Snake River waters:

Former Governor Len B. Jordan
Former Governor John V. Evans
Rexburg Attorney Ray Rigby
Former Senator Laird Noh
Former Representative Vard Chatburn

Caxton Press

©2016 Jim Jones.

ISBN# 978-087004-602-5

Library of Congress Cataloging-in-Publication Data

Names: Jones, Jim, (Idaho Supreme Court Justice) author.
Title: A little dam problem / Jim Jones.
Description: Caldwell, Idaho : Caxton Press, 2016. | Includes bibliographical references and index.
Identifiers: LCCN 2016048255 | ISBN 9780870046025 (alk. paper)
Subjects: LCSH: Water rights--Idaho. | Snake River, South Fork, Watershed
   (Idaho) | Swan Falls (Idaho)
Classification: LCC KFI447.5.S66 J66 2016 | DDC 346.79604/691--dc23
LC record available at https://lccn.loc.gov/2016048255

Cover photo of Swan Falls Dam reprinted courtesy of Idaho Power Company.
Cover and book design by Jocelyn Robertson

Printed and bound in the United States of America

CAXTON PRESS
Caldwell, Idaho
195015

A LITTLE
DAM
PROBLEM!

JIM JONES

TABLE OF CONTENTS

INTRODUCTION

This book chronicles one of the most significant and contentious water battles in Idaho's history. Within a year of being elected as Idaho Attorney General in 1982, I found myself embroiled in a bitter fight with Idaho Power Company over control of the Snake River. In 1952, the Power Company made a deal with Len Jordan, who was then Governor of Idaho, and subsequently a U.S. Senator and my mentor, to subordinate all of its water rights on the Snake River to upstream consumptive uses. That meant Idaho Power could not complain if upstream farmers or others used and fully depleted the water rights at all of its hydropower dams on the Snake River. Thirty years later, I found myself trying to enforce that agreement against a powerful company that had supported my election.

On November 19, 1982, just two weeks after I was elected Attorney General, the Idaho Supreme Court issued a water rights decision that dumbfounded most Idaho water users. Almost everyone had assumed that the water rights for all of Idaho Power's dams on the Snake River were subordinate to consumptive uses—agriculture, industry, municipal, and domestic—because that was precisely what Governor Jordan and the Company agreed to in 1952. While the Supreme Court recognized that Idaho Power agreed to subordinate its water rights in order to gain Jordan's support to build three hydroelectric dams in Hells Canyon in lieu of one high federal dam, and that Jordan's support was essential for the success of its three-dam plan, the Court narrowly focused its decision on the subordination language in the federal license for the three Hells Canyon dams. Ignoring the broader scope of the Jordan-Idaho Power agreement, the Court ruled that the subordination condition in the license for the Hells Canyon complex applied only to those dams and did not affect any other Idaho Power dams upstream.

The Court went on to hold that Idaho Power had a priority right to practically the entire summer flow of the Snake River at the Swan Falls Dam near Kuna in southwest Idaho, the Power Company's next dam upstream from Hells Canyon. Those water rights dated back between 1900 and 1915 which gave the Company priority over a vast number of upstream water rights and a virtual stranglehold over Snake River water. The Hells Canyon dams produced about 85% of Idaho Power's hydroelectric power at that time, while the Swan Falls Dam produced about 1%. The Court's decision had the practical effect of negating the subordination of the Hells Canyon dams and handing control of the Snake River to Idaho Power by virtue of the water rights at the piddly little Swan Falls Dam.

Two months later, Idaho Power sought passage of legislation in the Idaho Legislature to consolidate its hold on the Snake River, while several upstream legislators sought to subordinate all of Idaho Power's water rights on the river. It also filed suit against somewhere around 7,500 upstream water right holders to ratchet up pressure on the legislators. The opposing forces fought to a draw in the 1983 legislative session.

When it became apparent that the State was losing the battle to Idaho Power, I teamed up with Governor John V. Evans to take the battle with the Power Company to the public arena. Thus, it was a Democrat governor and Republican attorney general, together with almost half of the Idaho Legislature, against Idaho Power, then regarded as the most potent political force in Idaho. The Power Company had strong support from several Republican legislative leaders, slightly more than half of the legislators of both parties in both houses, and a wide array of interest groups. The Power Company's forces were led by Logan Lanham, who was widely regarded as being the 800-pound gorilla of Idaho politics. The fight got very testy, with me attacking the Power Company for trying to usurp the State's control of the Snake River, and the Power Company contending that the Governor and I would drive everyone's electric power bills through the roof.

After heated debate and legislative maneuvering, the Idaho Power forces came out slightly ahead in the 1984 legislative session but made no real progress because Governor Evans vetoed both of the Power Company's bills. Two subordination bills that the Governor and I proposed were shot down, one by a rather unseemly legislative maneuver by Power Company forces.

Having failed to win the day in the Legislature, the Power Company then turned to the electoral process, launching a massive advertising campaign just before the May 22 primary election to oust some of our supporters in the Legislature and enhance the numbers of its friends. I recruited a second cousin to run against one of their champions and supported others who favored the Governor and me. Three of their supporters lost in the election and we sent a message to others that there would be a price to pay for siding with the Power Company.

Hostilities continued after the primary election, reaching a peak in the late summer. The Evans-Jones side of the fight had picked up substantial support across the spectrum in the southern part of the State using the bully pulpit. My argument was that the Power Company was intent on reaping hundreds of millions of dollars of profits for its stockholders by clinging to the water rights it had been gifted by the Idaho Supreme Court in violation of its agreement with former Governor Jordan. Governor Evans made it abundantly clear that Idaho Power would not win in the Legislature because of his veto power. Being stymied in the Legislature and by the electorate and having gotten a black eye in the public arena, the Power Company entered into negotiations with the State and we were able to reach a settlement that struck a good balance between and among the competing interests—a balance that continues to be the foundation of Snake River water management.

The settlement agreement required approval by the Federal Energy Regulatory Commission, which appeared to be a fairly routine matter. However, that also developed into a major fight. When FERC failed to act, we turned to Congress, which promptly gave its approval. Unfortunately, the legislation to which our measure was attached was vetoed by President Reagan. Further legislative action almost scuttled the settlement agreement, leading to a heated exchange with one of the most powerful men in the U.S. House of Representatives—Congressman John Dingell (D–Mich.). However, the bully pulpit again prevailed, Dingell backed down to save an Idaho colleague, the settlement was approved by Congress, and Governor Jordan's legacy was restored. The settlement resulted in new water allocation criteria for Idaho and a general adjudication of the Snake River Basin—one of the largest and most successful adjudications in U.S. history.

This book is not intended to be an analytical analysis of the dispute, weighing the merits of the claims and counterclaims made by the parties. Rather, it is an historical presentation of the fight from the standpoint of one of the combatants. In order to keep the presentation from being overly one-sided and to provide some neutrality and context, there are frequent references to, and quotes from, the print media.

It will not escape the reader's attention that I make substantial use of press releases and letters I wrote at the time in lieu of summarizing or restating arguments that were made contemporaneously. While I relied on staff members, particularly Pat Kole and Clive Strong, to develop my stance on the various issues and arguments, I personally wrote all of the press releases and all but a few of the letters that are quoted in the book. During my eight years as Attorney General I had no press assistant and therefore acted as my own press agent. Where a letter was prepared for my signature, I have endeavored to so indicate in a footnote.

Another reason for using the press releases and letters is to make it clear that the statements and arguments were those then made by Attorney General Jones. Some of the press releases are highly critical of Idaho Power, but they were a product of the time, issued in the heat of battle. They are an historical presentation, not reflective or representative of my current view of the Company or its posture on current issues. Idaho Power has been a good corporate citizen of the State of Idaho, has provided its citizens with some of the lowest-cost electricity in the country, and has contributed much to the growth of the State. Just because we fought it out on Swan Falls issues back in the 1980s does not change that fact. Idaho Power gained a substantial benefit from the Supreme Court's decision and can't be faulted for its dogged efforts to hang on to that unexpected benefit.

At this point, I should issue a word of warning. My spouse, an accomplished writer who knows little about water law, tells me that Chapter 1 is a tough slog for people without a background in water issues. The chapter has background that is necessary in order to understand the controversy. In doing so it uses some technical concepts. For those not versed on water issues, a short discussion of the basic concepts may be helpful.

Idaho follows the prior appropriation doctrine, which for shorthand purposes is sometimes referred to as first-in-time, first-in-right. When the water rights for Swan Falls Dam were acquired, one needed only to put the water to beneficial use in order to acquire a water right under the Idaho Constitution. Persons who put water from the same source to beneficial use at a later date, received a lower priority to use of the water. If Idaho Power had an unsubordinated water right of 8,400 cubic feet per second (cfs)[1] at Swan Falls Dam, anyone upstream with a later priority right would be junior and would have to allow the Power Company to utilize the full benefit of its 8,400 cfs before it could make use of its junior water right. If Idaho Power's Swan Falls water right was subordinated, upstream users who had junior water rights could fully deplete Idaho Power's Swan Falls water right without complaint by the Power Company.

The State of Idaho is the owner of waters within its boundaries and determines the allocation of water rights, which are property rights, as well as the management of those rights. The federal government, however, has responsibility for licensing of dams on navigable streams and rivers, such as the Snake River. Hydropower licenses issued by the pertinent federal agency, formerly the Federal Power Commission (FPC) and now the Federal Energy Regulatory Commission (FERC), contain conditions for operation of the particular dam, which may include a condition subordinating the use of waters at the dam. Thus, a federal license subordination condition could protect upstream water rights, even if there was no subordination condition in the state water right.

Idaho has another bedrock principle that goes in tandem with first-in-time, first-in-right: the water must be beneficially used—it can't be hoarded to deprive junior users of their rights. However, this concept did not figure prominently in the Swan Falls fight—just something to keep in mind.

---

1   Cubic foot per second means a cubic foot of water flowing past a given point in a second's time.

Consumptive uses of water include use for agricultural, industrial, municipal, and domestic purposes. Even though labeled as consumptive uses, some or all of the water for each type of use generally makes its way back into the Snake River system, either into the river itself or into the large underground aquifer that generally flows along the northerly side of the Snake River and in the same direction—the Eastern Snake River Plains Aquifer. Both surface and underground water were at issue in the Swan Falls dispute.

If Chapter 1 still seems to be difficult reading, all that one needs to know is that: (1) Idaho Power and Governor Jordan made an agreement in 1952 that the State would support Idaho Power's proposal to build three dams in Hells Canyon and oppose a federal plan to build a single high dam in Hells Canyon, but only if Idaho Power would subordinate all of its water rights on the Snake River to present and future upstream consumptive uses, (2) the Idaho Supreme Court held the subordination agreement did not apply to the Power Company's 8,400 cfs water right at Swan Falls, and (3) the ruling handed Idaho Power effective control of the Snake River's entire summer flow of water, unless we could take effective action to change that outcome.

This book has been simmering in my head since the mid-1980s, when Ray Marvin, who was then the executive director of the National Association of Attorneys General, suggested my subordination fight would be the good subject for a book. The idea has recurred many times since then but it was always put off to sometime in the future. In June of 2013, Dan Suhr, an old friend from Jerome, called to ask if I would speak to the Middle Snake Regional Water Resource Commission about the Swan Falls dispute. He and another old friend, Bob Muffley from Gooding, thought that some of the newer members of the Commission would benefit from learning about it. As Bob noted in a July 3 letter:

A few old-timers on the Commission, like Dan and I, started talking about the Swan Falls Agreement and we were met with blank stares from some of our Commission members. We discovered that younger people or those who hadn't been involved in water issues didn't know what it was all about and how it is extremely pertinent to our current short water year. Some of our region's legislators fit into that category. We think education is needed and who better to instruct them than the man who brokered the agreement.

I spoke to the group. There were a number of Magic Valley legislators present, including Senator Bert Brackett, an old friend from Three Creek, and Representative Scott Bedke, the Speaker of the Idaho House of Representatives, who is now one of the most knowledgeable members of the Legislature on water issues. During the question and answer session, Bert said I ought to write a book about the Swan Falls fight and I told him I thought I would do just that. Speaker Bedke asked me if I would make my presentation to a joint meeting of the House and Senate Resource Committees and I told him I would be glad to do so. I made the presentation during the 2014 legislative session. At that time, I noted that I intended to carry through with my statement to Senator Brackett to write a book on the subject.

Here it is.

A SUPREME COURT SURPRISE

Southern Idaho is semi-arid and highly dependent upon the waters of the Snake River. The river rises in western Wyoming, traverses the entire State of Idaho until it briefly exits into Oregon, and then flows in a northerly direction, forming the border between the two states. Most of the communities of any size in Southern Idaho were founded and grew up along the course of the Snake. Agriculture is the economic powerhouse of Idaho and this would not be the case without ample supplies of water, either in the Snake River or in the vast underground river that complements it in the Eastern Snake River Plains Aquifer. As John S. Gray, an Ada County delegate to Idaho's 1889 Constitutional Convention, said when commenting upon the arid public school land located along the Snake River, "Why, a man couldn't raise anything but jack rabbits on it, and a very poor crop of them."[2] Therefore, people in Idaho, particularly along the Snake, have always been vitally interested in water issues.

It came as a great surprise to the water community when the Idaho Supreme Court decided on November 19, 1982, that Idaho Power had an unsubordinated water right of 8,400 cubic feet per second at its Swan Falls Dam. That rate of flow essentially granted Idaho Power the entire flow of the river at that point during the agricultural growing season. The Company's water rights at the dam dated back to the early 1900s, so they had priority over a vast number of later upstream water rights. Almost everyone had previously assumed that all of Idaho Power's water rights on the Snake River were subordinated to consumptive uses and the river had been managed under that assumption for as long as anyone could remember. The Court's decision was a real

---

2   I.W. Hart, *Proceedings and Debates of the Constitutional Convention of Idaho*, Volume one, page 711 (1912).

shocker, sparking one of the most ferocious water battles in Idaho history.

In its decision, the Supreme Court laid out the following history of the Swan Falls dam:[3]

> The roots of this litigation stretch back to the early days of the state and the background must be set out in some considerable detail. The Trade Dollar Consolidated Mining Company constructed the first hydroelectric dam on the Snake River at the Swan Falls site in 1901. It originally provided power to the mines of the Silver City area, which service was later shifted to the towns which lay to the north. At that time there were a number of small scale companies supplying electric power in that region, and eventually five of those companies came to dominate the electric power supply market for southern Idaho. In 1915 those five companies merged to form Idaho Power Company, and in the merger Idaho Power acquired the Swan Falls dam and power plant, as well as others which had been built in the interim. *See* R. Sessions, *Idaho Power Co.*, 43–54 (1939).
>
> Idaho Power had secured a federal court decree which, together with state water licenses, granted Idaho Power water rights at Swan Falls of 9450 cfs with priority dates ranging from 1900 to 1919. However, it is undisputed that the Swan Falls power plant's hydroelectric capacity is 8400 cfs, and therefore, the water rights at Swan Falls are limited to 8400 cfs.

To put the Swan Falls hydro plant in context, the installed capacity of its entire hydro system at that time was 1,574.9 megawatts (MW) of which Swan Falls provided 10.3 MW or .7% of the capacity. Its actual production was about

---

3   *Idaho Power Co. v. State of Idaho*, 104 Idaho 575, 579, 661 P.2d 741, 745 (1983). The Court released its initial opinion on November 19, 1982. The State and other parties then petitioned for rehearing. The reported decision was issued upon denial of that petition on March 31, 1983.

1%. It was a small player in the system.

The litigation between the State and Idaho Power came about because of a petition filed against the Power Company in the Idaho Public Utilities Commission by a number of ratepayers, including Matt Mullaney and Senator John Peavey, who claimed that the Company failed to assert or protect its senior water rights at Swan Falls and thereby injured its ratepayers. According to the Supreme Court:[4]

> The genesis of the instant litigation was a complaint filed with the Idaho Public Utilities Commission by one Matthew Mullaney on behalf of himself and other ratepayers alleging that Idaho Power had failed to protect and preserve its Swan Falls water rights and that, by so doing, Idaho Power had wasted its assets and overstated its capital investment, thus resulting in overcharges to its ratepayers. Idaho Power sought to have that complaint dismissed for lack of jurisdiction. Idaho Power's motion to dismiss was denied, and Idaho Power answered the complaint indicating it would file an action in district court to protect those Swan Falls water rights. A large number of applications for water permits were then pending before the Idaho Department of Water Resources and Idaho Power filed protests against a large number of those applications. In the interim, and pending the outcome of this case, the Public Utilities Commission has retained jurisdiction over the Matthew Mullaney complaint.
>
> Idaho Power's action in the district court named as defendants the Public Utilities Commission, the Department of Water Resources, numerous canal and irrigation companies, and individuals involved with irrigation, together with the ratepayers who brought

---

4   104 Idaho at 582, 661 P.2d at 748.

the complaint before the Public Utilities Commission. Therein Idaho Power sought a decree that its Swan Falls rights were not subject to upstream depletion and that the state water plan was a taking of those rights. Idaho Power also sought to have the court identify those areas where its water rights were protected. The Department of Water Resources answered Idaho Power's complaint, claiming that the State Constitution allows the state to limit hydropower rights and that Idaho Power had lost those rights by adverse possession, forfeiture, and abandonment. Grandview Canal Co. in its answer added laches and subordination in the Hells Canyon and Strike licenses as affirmative defenses, and Nelda McAndrew added waiver and quasi-estoppel to the list of affirmative defenses.

This seemed to be a straightforward recitation of the facts leading to the action in district court. However, some of the defendants in the lawsuit began to suspect that Idaho Power had had a hand in bringing about the proceeding in the Public Utilities Commission after the Power Company inadvertently disclosed a memorandum from its attorney, Thomas G. Nelson, to Idaho Power CEO James Bruce, dated June 22, 1976, a year prior to the filing of the PUC complaint by Mullaney, Peavey, and others. The memorandum addressed "the discussion of the possibility of using the Swan Falls water right to prevent upstream depletion of the [Snake River] by irrigation projects and consequent diminution in power generation...." The memorandum noted that Idaho Power's three Hells Canyon dams, which were located downriver from Swan Falls, had a subordination condition in their federal power license and that the first Idaho Power dam upstream from Swan Falls, C.J. Strike, also had a subordination clause in its power license, inserted at the request of Idaho Power.

The memo concluded:

> If IPC was to attempt to use its Swan Falls water right to prevent further irrigation depletion above Strike, any benefit from stopping such depletion would, of course, redound to the benefit of flows at Strike, and potentially in Hells Canyon. Thus IPC would be doing indirectly what it cannot do directly, that is, protect its Strike and Hells Canyon projects from upstream depletion. In our judgment, the IPC license and state water license provisions above referred to would be construed to make the Swan Falls right subject also to depletion, since the IPC plants on the Snake are all co-ordinated for operation, and since the water license depletion provision in the Strike and some of the Hells Canyon licenses were inserted at the request of IPC.
>
> Additionally, a depletion provision similar to that in the license for Hells Canyon and the old American Falls plant will almost certainly be in any new license issued by the [Federal Power Commission] for the Swan Falls site…. Therefore, as a practical matter, even if the Swan Falls right could now be used as a basis for stopping development which would substantially impair that right, the issuance of a new FPC license for that site will prevent any such protection being derived from the Swan Falls water right.
>
> CONCLUSION: The Idaho Power Company's water rights for its Swan Falls plant cannot be used to prevent consumptive uses from depleting the flow of the Snake River above Swan Falls.

The memorandum was accidently disclosed by Idaho Power in discovery proceedings in the district court and it was a confidential attorney-client communication so it was given no weight in the proceedings. However, some of the parties pointed to it as evidence that the PUC proceeding was not something that came entirely out of the blue by ratepayers but that the Power Company, which was obviously interested in the issue, may have played some part in getting the proceeding going or, at the least, encouraging those who initiated it. From Idaho Power's standpoint, a proceeding initiated in the PUC would have advantages over one initiated in the courts because at that time the PUC was receptive to arguments that appeared to favor the ratepayers. Any PUC ruling would eventually be decided by the courts on appeal, but a favorable PUC ruling would certainly be advantageous. However, without proof one way or the other as to whether the Power Company had some involvement in initiating or encouraging the PUC proceeding, that issue is merely in the realm of speculation and beyond the scope of this book.

In its decision, the Supreme Court recognized that the Power Company's license for the C.J. Strike hydro project, located just upstream from Swan Falls, contained a subordination clause.[5] It then addressed the events leading up to the construction and licensing of the Power Company's three-dam Hells Canyon hydroelectric complex:[6]

Len Jordan had been elected governor of Idaho, taking office in 1951, and a major controversy was under way between the federal government and Idaho Power regarding the development of the Hells Canyon stretch of the Snake River (lying northerly along a portion of the western boundary of Idaho). Jordan sought to apply pressure to Idaho Power by insisting upon subordination clauses being inserted in the licenses for the proposed Hells Canyon project.

Faced with Jordan's attitude, which was reflected by his administrative department charged with issu-

5   104 Idaho at 579–80, 661 P.2d at 745–46.
6   104 Idaho at 580–81, 661 P.2d at 746–47.

ing state water right licenses, Idaho Power agreed to subordinate their state water right license at C.J. Strike to future upstream depletion. That water license was issued in 1953 and contained the first unrestricted subordination language on record.

As to the Hells Canyon stretch of the Snake River, two competing proposals had been put forward. One, a single massive structure to be known as High Hells Canyon project, was to be constructed and operated by the federal government. The second was the proposal of Idaho Power to build three smaller dams on the same portion of the river. Legislation authorizing the federal project was introduced in Congress and contained a subordination clause, but attached certain conditions giving the federal government limited control over the reasonableness of future upstream depletions. *Hells Canyon Dam: Hearings on H.R. 5743, Before the Subcomm. on Irrigation and Reclamation of the House Comm. on Interior and Insular Affairs,* 82d Cong., 2d Sess. 510 (1952) (statement of Rep. Engle).

To obtain the influence of Jordan and the irrigators, then as now a powerful political force in the state, for its Hells Canyon three-dam project, Idaho Power proposed that the FPC license for the Hells Canyon project contain a clause subordinating its rights to future upstream depletion without condition. That distinction between the two projects appears to be one of the major factors in gaining Jordan's support for Idaho Power's proposal. *Id.* at 501 (statement of Gov. Jordan). By the time of the senate hearings on the Hells Canyon project in 1955, Robert E. Smylie was governor of Idaho. Smylie also reiterated the state's interest in full unconditional subordination of Idaho Power's water rights in the Hells Canyon project to future upstream diversion.

*Hells Canyon Project: Hearings on S. 1333 Before the Sub-
comm. on Irrigation and Reclamation of the Senate Comm.
on Interior and Insular Affairs*, 84th Cong. 1st Sess., 6
(1955) (statement of Gov. Smylie).

Idaho Power asserts that its economic survival was
dependent upon the Hells Canyon project and that it
thus agreed to subordinate its water rights at Hells Canyon in return for the support of state government and
the agricultural irrigators. While such might be regarded as an overstatement, nevertheless, the Hells Canyon
dams remains today one of the more important parts
of Idaho Power's rate base. Another factor, although
unarticulated, may well be that a single high federal
dam would have been administered by the Bonneville
Power Administration, and historically, Idaho Power
has actively opposed efforts to extend Bonneville Power's authority into this portion of the Northwest. *See* G.
Young & F. Cochrane, *Hydro Era: The History of Idaho
Power Co.,* 64 (1978); Idaho Evening Statesman, May 30,
1963, p. 8 (full page advertisement by Idaho Power).

At the time of the pendency of congressional action
authorizing the federal High Hells Canyon project,
Idaho Power had initiated and was engaged in proceedings before the FPC to obtain a license for its three-
dam project. In 1955 the FPC issued a single license to
Idaho Power for the construction of three dams (Low
Hells Canyon, Oxbow and Brownlee), stating that the
dams should be treated for the purposes of that license
as "one complete project." Consistent with the request
of Idaho Power, that license contained a subordination
provision with no conditions attached. In another portion of the Hells Canyon license, minimum flows were
required at specific points on that reach of the river in
accordance with the federal governments' navigation-

al servitude. (Hells Canyon Project FPC license, Article 43). The FPC order granting the license to Idaho Power was appealed by proponents of the federal High Hells Canyon dam to the D.C. Circuit of the United States Court of Appeals. That Court held that the FPC was not required to approve a potential federal project over an available private project and that the FPC was not required to measure a federal project it had just rejected against the remaining private project to determine which of the two was the "best adapted" plan for developing the waterway. *National Hells Canyon Ass'n v. Federal Power Comm'n,* 237 F.2d 777 (D.C. Cir. 1956), *cert. denied,* 353 U.S. 924, 77 S.Ct. 681, 1 L.Ed2d 720 (1957). The subordination clause, its validity or scope, was neither challenged nor considered on that appeal.

The Court correctly stated the history that resulted in the construction of the three Hells Canyon dams and how Idaho Power's use of Snake River water for generating hydropower became unconditionally subordinated to depletion by upstream consumptive uses. Unless the Power Company had agreed to subordinate to upstream uses, then-Governor Jordan would not have supported its project and there would likely have been one high federal dam instead of three Idaho Power dams in Hells Canyon.

The Hells Canyon issue was hotly contested in Idaho, but also around the nation. It was essentially a fight between public power, which had been a feature of President Roosevelt's New Deal, and private power, which was then being championed by Idaho Power Company. In his book *Public Power, Private Dams — The Hell's Canyon High Dam Controversy,* Karl Brooks, a former Idaho legislator, documents the struggle between public and private power. Brooks notes at page 174 that Dwight Eisenhower made the Hells Canyon controversy a national issue when he appeared in Boise in August of 1952 to address the Hells Canyon issue in "his first formal speech of his first campaign trip."[7] Eisenhower undoubtedly appeared and supported private power at the urging of Governor Jordan.

Even though I was ten years old at the time, the Hells Canyon controversy made an impression on me. My father, Henry Jones, was a strong supporter of the Idaho Power three-dam plan and made his position known to the family and many others throughout the community. I don't recall the issue of subordination having been mentioned, but it was clear to me that Henry Jones supported Governor Jordan's position and I assumed he was right in doing so.

The parties in the district court filed motions and cross motions for summary judgment. The district judge, Jesse Walters, reached essentially the same conclusion that Idaho Power's attorney, Tom Nelson, had reached in his 1976 memo to Jim Bruce—that the subordination of Idaho Power's water rights extended from the three Hells Canyon dams all of the way up the Snake River. Judge Walters ruled that the provision in the federal license subordinating Idaho Power's water rights at its Hells Canyon dams was lawful and that the effect of the license provision[8]

> had subordinated all of Idaho Power's water rights used in hydropower production at all of its facilities on the entire Snake River watershed. In reaching that result the district court relied on federal preemption under the Federal Power Act. The court focused on language in Article 41 subordinating water rights at the Hells Canyon project to future upstream depletion "on the Snake River and its tributaries," from which the court reasoned that this meant the entire river up-

---

7   *See also, Idaho Statesman* (Boise), Aug. 20, 1952.
8   104 Idaho at 583, 661 P.2d at 749.

stream could be depleted, including any water rights at any other dam upstream from Hells Canyon. The court reasoned that since the entire river is one hydropower system, with Idaho Power operating its dams in a coordinated manner, such system could not be subordinated in bits and pieces.

All the Supreme Court had to do was affirm the district court's rational decision and put an end to the dispute. However, in defiance of logic and common sense, the Court concluded that the subordination of the Hells Canyon dams only applied to those three dams and did not extend to any of Idaho Power's upstream dams. Having acknowledged that the first dam upstream from Swan Falls, C.J. Strike, had been fully subordinated and that the three Hells Canyon dams immediately downstream from Swan Falls had been fully subordinated, it seemed a matter of logic and common sense that Swan Falls was also subordinated. There was very little inflow to, or outflow from, the Snake River between C.J. Strike and Hells Canyon so it made absolutely no sense for Governor Jordan to seek subordination of the Hells Canyon complex if it didn't apply all of the way up the Snake River. What would be the point of insisting that only the Hells Canyon dams be subordinated? The State would receive absolutely no benefit from that.

In order to reach its conclusion, the Court seemingly concluded that Governor Jordan was clueless and that a river system can be managed on a completely segmented basis with the flow at any of several dams on the river being increased and decreased as if by magic. As Tom Nelson said in his memo to Jim Bruce, and as Judge Walters ruled, Idaho Power operated its dams in a coordinated manner as one system. If the river could be depleted to the state-mandated minimum flow at C.J. Strike above Swan Falls and at the Hells

Canyon complex below Swan Falls, it made no sense to hold that Idaho Power was entitled to demand almost all of the summer flow of the river, at least to 8,400 cfs, at Swan Falls.

The Court remanded the case for consideration of other defenses asserted against Idaho Power such as abandonment, forfeiture, estoppel, and the like, which gave the State a toehold to seek what was essentially the "resubordination" of the Power Company's Snake River water rights. However, the decision set in motion a highly contentious fight that would take years to resolve.

THE CAST OF CHARACTERS

The person who played the most important role in the Swan Falls fight was Governor Len Jordan, who laid the predicate in 1952 by insisting that Idaho Power subordinate its Snake River water rights as a condition for obtaining the right to build its three Hells Canyon dams in lieu of the single high federal dam. Jordan was the perfect candidate to make a Hells Canyon deal because he and his family lived on a remote ranch along the Snake River below Hells Canyon from 1933 to 1941. Life on the Jordan sheep ranch is documented by his wife, Grace, in her book, *Home Below Hells Canyon.*

Jordan was born in Mt. Pleasant, Utah, on May 15, 1899, and grew up in Enterprise, Oregon. He enlisted in the U.S. Army during World War I and was commissioned as a second lieutenant. After the war, he attended the University of Oregon on a football scholarship. Jordan graduated with a bachelor's degree in business administration in 1923, earning a Phi Beta Kappa key in the process. He married Grace Edington of Hood River, Oregon, on December 30, 1924. She was also a University of Oregon graduate (1916) and Phi Beta Kappa key recipient. Jordan became foreman of a large ranching operation on the west side of the Snake River which fell on hard times during the depression. By 1932, he was earning $100 a month plus room and board, when the bank holding his savings failed. At that point he received an offer from a Portland bank that had repossessed a Hells Canyon sheep ranch when the owner defaulted on a $50,000 indebtedness. Jordan was told he could have the ranch if he went in, operated it, and paid the bank's money back with interest. The Jordans took the deal, moved onto the isolated ranch, worked it productively for eight years, paid the bank its

$50,000 plus interest, and received title to the ranch. In 1941, the Jordans and their three children moved to Grangeville. There, he farmed, managed a string of grain elevators on the Camas Prairie, and established a farm implement business, a real estate agency, and an automobile dealership.

Jordan ran for the Legislature in 1946 and won the election, representing Idaho County in the Idaho House for two years. He lost a reelection effort in 1948 but came back to win the governorship in 1950. He served four years as Idaho's governor. At that time the office was limited to one four-year term. Following his service as Governor, President Dwight Eisenhower appointed Jordan to head the United States delegation to the International Joint Commission, where he helped negotiate agreements with Canada for the St. Lawrence Seaway, the Columbia River Basin Treaty, and Libby Dam. He was appointed to the U.S. Senate in August of 1962 following the death of Senator Henry Dworshak, elected to a four-year term in a 1962 special election, and reelected to a six-year term in 1966. His appointment to, and service in, the Senate was the subject of another Grace Jordan book, *The Unintentional Senator*. Jordan retired from the Senate at the end of his term in January 1973 and died on June 30, 1983. Grace Jordan died on September 17, 1985.

Len Jordan was very knowledgeable about water issues, being among the first prominent Idahoans to recognize, as early as the late 1950s, that water was a finite resource in Idaho and that steps needed to be taken to preserve and enhance the resource, such as recharging the Snake River Plains Aquifer. Jordan's knowledge of water issues became apparent early in his Senate tenure, as reported by the Chicago Tribune:[9]

> The sheep rancher had a gift for simple logic and clarity not often displayed in the Senate. He demonstrated

---

9   Edwards, Willard, Chicago Tribune Press Service, "Sen. Len Jordan Got Start on Sheep Ranch in Idaho." *The Spokesman-Review (Spokane), Nov. 3, 1963.*

it, even more remarkably, in an analysis this week of a complex issue—federal verses state jurisdiction in water development. This is a subject of vital interest to the West. Jordan stripped it down to the bare bones of comprehensibility for those to whom it had hitherto been a dull and mystifying dispute.

Jordan played a major part in passage of the Wild and Scenic Rivers Act and legislation to establish the Sawtooth National Recreation Area, as well as other legislation protecting Idaho's scenic wonders. Except for the wild rivers legislation, he insisted on legislative language calling for any federal reserved water rights for such protected areas to be established under Idaho law. With regard to the Hells Canyon controversy, long-time Idaho Statesman political editor John Corlett observed that Jordan "opposed the federally funded high Hells Canyon Dam on the middle Snake River.... I heard him testify at congressional and other hearings that if Idaho Power Co.'s three dams were to be built, the water for power there must be subordinated to upstream domestic and irrigation purposes. His request prevailed."[10]

The Jordans were warm, intelligent, and genuine people. I worked as an intern in Senator Jordan's Washington office during the summers of 1965 and 1966 and then returned as a full-time employee for his last three years in office. During that time and after he retired, I looked to him as a friend and mentor. Although the Senator did not live to see the fierce fight that developed between myself and Idaho Power in 1984, I thought it an odd coincidence that I would be in a position to try to force Idaho Power to live with the deal he had struck with the Company more than 30 years previously to subordinate its Snake River water rights.

Governor John V. Evans was a stalwart partner in the

---

10   Corlett, John. "Jordan remembered for integrity, courage." *Idaho Statesman, July 2, 1983.*

Swan Falls fight. Being of Idaho pioneer stock in southeast Idaho, he understood the critical role of Idaho's water, both in its history and for its future. Evans was born in Malad on January 18, 1925, and graduated from Malad High School in 1943. He served as an infantryman in the U.S. Army during World War II. He attended Stanford University after the war and, in 1951, graduated with a degree in business and economics. He married his high school sweetheart, Lola Daniels, in Malad on April 29, 1945. After graduating college, Evans engaged in farming, ranching, and business in Malad.

Evans became interested in politics in the late 1940s, when Democrats stood a chance of being elected in Idaho. The family's eulogy said:

> Following in the footsteps of his grandfather, D.L. Evans, who served as Idaho House Speaker at the turn of the 20th century, Evans spent thirty-three years in public service. His service was almost continuous from 1953 to 1987 when he finished his term as the 27th Governor of the State of Idaho. He served three terms in the Idaho Senate from 1953 to 1958, serving as Majority Leader of the Idaho Senate in 1957-1958. Mr. Evans left the legislature and was elected Mayor of Malad and served from 1960 to 1966. Mr. Evans returned to the Senate in 1967 (Minority Leader from 1969-1974) and served four more terms, until his election as Lieutenant Governor in 1974.

When Governor Cecil Andrus was appointed as Secretary of the Interior by President Jimmy Carter, Evans succeeded to the office of governor on January 24, 1977. He was elected to a term in his own right in November of 1978 and reelected in 1982, serving until January 1987. Upon completing his service, the Governor joined the family banking business, D.L. Evans Bank in Burley, serving as President until his death on July 8, 2014. During that period of time, the bank expanded practically the entire reach of the Snake River through southern Idaho from Idaho Falls to Caldwell.

Governor Evans' background in agriculture and banking in southeast Idaho prepared him to deal with important water issues. According to the family's eulogy:

> Being a farmer and understanding the importance of Idaho's water, Governor Evans guided Idaho in the resolution of one of the most troubling water issues of the century. Governor Evans, along with then Attorney General Jim Jones, negotiated a settlement with Idaho Power on the Swan Falls Decision, which established minimum flow for power generation and required a basin wide adjudication of the Snake River Water Rights.

A Republican Attorney General and a Democrat Governor may have been unlikely allies in the Swan Falls fight, but politics had to take a back seat because of the importance of the issue. I must say that Governor Evans and I had any number of issues on which we disagreed and things became testy from time to time. However, I never questioned his sincerity or his honesty. He was not a showboater but, rather, a genuine good person, trying to do what he thought was right. My view of Governor Evans was reflected in a letter I wrote to the Idaho print media following his death on July 8, 2014:

> In 1983, an epic battle erupted between the State of Idaho and Idaho Power Company over the company's water right at its Swan Falls dam. That resulted from a November 1982 decision of the Idaho Supreme Court,

which appeared to give the power company control of the full flow of the river at that location.

Former Governor John Evans vigorously defended the State's interests in that fight, contending that the outcome would affect the interest of every Idahoan, as well as the future development of the State. Governor Evans exercised leadership and statesmanship, standing firm for the benefit of Idaho's citizens, vetoing two legislative measures in the process.

After two stormy legislative sessions, substantial litigation efforts, and heated debate on both sides, Governor Evans suggested the matter be negotiated. A resolution was reached in October 1984 that addressed the valid interests of all concerned, resulting in water policies that have stood the test of 30 years' time.

One of the measures that Governor Evans insisted upon was a full adjudication of water rights in the Snake River Basin. The adjudication was designed to quantify and prioritize all water rights along the Snake River, both surface and groundwater, so that water users knew where they stood and that they had protected rights. A management system has been put into place to ensure the efficient and wise use of Snake River water under the bedrock principles of first in time is first in right, and beneficial use.

After 27 years, the adjudication is almost complete. The Snake River Basin Adjudication has been recognized as a model for its conduct and efficiency. Governor Evans did not live to participate in the celebration of the conclusion of the adjudication that took place in the latter part of August 2014. However, it is an important part of his legacy and Idahoans should be thankful for his faithful stewardship of our important water resources.

I wish he could have been present at the celebration commemorating the virtual conclusion of the adjudication. Lola Evans passed away on May 19, 2015.

Pat Costello, a graduate of Boston College Law School, acted as Governor Evans' legal counsel and point man on Swan Falls. Pat, who originated from Kansas and received his undergraduate degree from the University of Kansas, worked closely with my staff and was one of the principal players in negotiating the settlement agreement and then selling it to the Legislature. He did a good job for the Governor, although we did have a bit of a dust-up toward the end of the settlement negotiations, which will be discussed later. At the end of Governor Evans' term of office, Pat engaged in private law practice, served seven years as a magistrate judge, directed clinical programs at the University of Idaho College of Law, and now serves as a mediator, arbitrator, and negotiator, advocating peaceful resolution of legal disputes. He certainly earned his peaceful resolution stripes in the Swan Falls fight.

Ray Rigby did not hold any elective office during the Swan Falls battle, but he played a major part in its outcome. Ray became interested in water law during his service in the Idaho State Senate (1965–1973) and by the time of the 1982 Supreme Court decision had become one of Idaho's premier water lawyers.

Ray was born April 16, 1923, on a ranch in Rexburg. He started thinking about the law based on his experience in public speaking and debate during his senior year at Madison High School in 1941:[11]

Rigby was elected as the student body president while at MHS and while serving in that capacity was approached by a friend who suggested they could become lawyers if they got into debate.

11   "'Equal justice for all' is lawyer's creed." *Standard Journal (Rexburg)*, Feb. 2, 2009.

"We were encouraged to take debate, because my friend said we ought to be lawyers. Of course, when I heard the name I didn't even know what a lawyer meant. I took debate, and we won the district championship and took second in the state tournament. (In that tournament) they picked the 10 top debaters, and I was one of them."

His experience with public speaking and debate convinced him that he could study law and still live on a ranch in Rexburg. As a child, Rigby had always dreamed of having his own ranch.

Ray graduated from high school in 1941 and began studies at the University of Idaho that fall. When Pearl Harbor was bombed and war broke out, he enlisted in the Army Air Corps. While on leave from the military, he married Lola Cook from Idaho Falls on December 8, 1944. After the war Ray returned to the University of Idaho. He obtained his law degree and passed the State Bar in 1950. Ray was elected as Madison County Prosecuting Attorney that year and served as such for the next 14 years. During that time, he established his private law practice in Rexburg.

Rigby served as a Democrat State Senator from January 1965 to January 1973 and gained the respect of legislators from both sides of the aisle. Because of his water rights expertise, Ray served on the Interstate Conference on Water Problems for 12 years, with two terms as chairman, and was Idaho's representative on the Western States Water Council for 14 years. He was appointed by the U.S. State Department as a delegate to the United Nations World Conference on Water in Argentina in 1977.

In recognition of his water expertise, on May 10, 1983, Governor Evans appointed Ray as chairman of his Swan Falls Task Force, which was charged with the responsibility of determining what course of action the State should pursue, both in response to the Supreme Court's decision and in mapping out a sound strategy for Idaho's water future. During the course of the Swan Falls fight, Ray was frequently consulted by both the Governor and me on a variety of issues involving substance, strategy, and procedure. He also played a major role in educating legislators and the public at large as to the substance of the issues and the need for corrective action.

Lola passed away in 2002. Since then, Ray has had the comfort of his seven children with more than 100 grandchildren and great-grandchildren. He continued his law practice for over ten more years. As of this writing, Ray has retired from the active practice of law but his legal opinion, particularly on water issues, is still sought and valued. His colleagues in the legal profession have expressed their appreciation of Ray's knowledge, expertise, and collegiality—he has received the Idaho State Bar's Professionalism Award, as well as its Distinguished Lawyer Award. And aside from all that, he is an outstanding human being and a good friend.

Laird Noh was the leader of the subordination effort in the Idaho Senate during the 1983 and 1984 legislative sessions. Laird, a Twin Falls Republican, was elected to the Senate in 1980 and became chairman of the Senate Resources and Environment Committee two years later, serving in that capacity for 22 years. Laird quickly became a knowledgeable and effective spokesman on the water rights issue, which was extremely helpful because the Senate was almost evenly divided on the issue but slightly inclined toward the Power Company's point of view.

Laird was born in Twin Falls on September 28, 1938. After graduating from Kimberly High School, he attended the University of Idaho, graduating in 1960 with a Bachelor of Science degree in business and agriculture. He served as U of I student body president during his last year. He then attended the University of Chicago, receiving an MBA in 1963. He was an assistant professor of economics at Boise Junior College (now Boise State University) from 1963 to 1965. He then returned to the family sheep business in Magic Valley and since 1965 has been president of the Noh Sheep Company. He and his wife, Kathleen, have two children.

The Noh family arrived in the Magic Valley in 1908, when they began their sheep ranching and farming business. As a result, Laird was well acquainted with agriculture and water issues when he began his service in the State Senate. In 1931, the family owned a farm at the mouth of Dry Creek at Artesian, south of Murtaugh, where they drilled two of the first irrigation wells in Idaho. He relates that when some adjoining landowners, the Stoners, subsequently drilled a larger well in the vicinity, the water level of the Noh wells immediately declined. The Nohs sued and obtained an injunction against the Stoners based on their priority of right. The Stoners appealed to the Idaho Supreme Court, which ruled in favor of the Nohs, holding that a prior appropriator of groundwater was protected in his historic pumping level.[12]

During his career, Laird has received numerous awards, including the Water Statesman Award (2005) from the Idaho Water Users Association, Legislator of the Year Award (2004) from the Idaho Association of Soil Conservation Districts, the Lifetime Wildlife Service Award (2004) from the Idaho Fish and Game Advisory Council, and the Silver Ram Award (1977) for his contributions to the American sheep industry. He has been deeply involved in conservation issues, serving as a trustee of the Idaho Nature Conservancy from 1986 to 2009. He received the Lifetime Achievement Award from the national organization in 2005. Laird could be properly described as an intellectual, but he was a down-to-

---

12   *Noh v. Stoner*, 53 Idaho 651, 26 P.2d 1112 (1933). The *Noh* holding was subsequently modified in substantial respects by Idaho Code section 42-226, as explained in *Baker v. Ore-Ida Foods, Inc.*, 95 Idaho 575, 581–83, 513 P.2d 627, 633–35 (1973).

earth legislator who looked for practical solutions and he has acted similarly in his personal life. He is a downright good person.

Vard Chatburn of Albion was the leader of the subordination effort in the Idaho House. Vard was born on the family ranch in Albion on August 7, 1908. He attended school in Albion, having to ride horseback two and a half miles back and forth from the ranch as a first grader. Later, he and his six siblings drove a buggy to school. After graduation, Vard attended Albion State Normal School where he received a teaching degree in 1927. During a two-year teaching stint in Rigby, he married Eva Lemmon on June 3, 1929. He taught school in several other locations (Victor, Hammett, Minidoka, and Boise) until 1937, when he returned to Albion to resume ranching.

Vard's grandfather was one of the first settlers in the Albion Valley, moving there in 1880. As a member of a pioneer family, he understood the importance of water issues. His grandfather built a water-powered grist mill at the lower end of the valley. When farmers moved into the valley, established farmsteads, and diverted water upstream for irrigation, the source of power for the mill dried up and the family moved to the family ranch.

In 1956, Vard was elected on the Republican ticket to serve Cassia County in the Idaho House of Representatives. He served in the House for 30 years, retiring in 1986.

During his service in the House, Vard chaired the House Resources and Conservation Committee, where he presided over the contentious Swan Falls legislation. Although the House was about evenly divided on the issue, it inclined slightly toward the subordination point of view. That didn't make Vard's work any easier because the issue was hotly contested, particularly in the 1984 session.

During his years of service to the State, Vard received

numerous awards: Idaho Grassman (1964), Legislative Conservation Award (1966 and 1979), Idaho Working Conservationist (1976), and Idaho Water Users Hall of Fame (1978). Shortly after his retirement in 1986, a new Idaho Fish and Game Department building in Boise was named the J. Vard Chatburn Building in his honor. Vard passed away on April 9, 1995, at 86 years of age, and Eva passed away shortly thereafter, on July 15, 1995.

Two people from the Attorney General's office played a critical role on the Swan Falls issue—Pat Kole and Clive Strong. Pat came on board in May of 1983 as Chief of the Natural Resource Division. He received his undergraduate degree from the University of Michigan in 1973 and a Juris Doctor degree from the University of Denver law school in 1975. Following graduation from Law school, Pat served as a law clerk for Judge Joseph Quinn in the Second Judicial District, a short time in the Attorney General's office, as a Deputy Ada County Prosecutor from November of 1976 through September of 1979, and with the Caldwell law firm of Gigray, Miller, Downen & Weston, until May 1983. Pat is a personable and outgoing individual and he did a good job of speaking on the issue before legislators and the public. When I was unable to attend legislative hearings, Pat made presentations to legislative committees on my behalf. Because of his handling of legislative matters, in 1985 he was made Chief of Legislative Affairs. When negotiations toward settlement began in 1984, he acted as chief negotiator on behalf of the Attorney General's office.

Clive Strong joined the office in August of 1983 and quickly became my go-to guy on issues of substance and strategy on Swan Falls. Clive received a BS in forest business management from the University of Idaho in 1974, a Juris Doctor degree from the U of I in 1977, and a masters of law from the University of Michigan in 1983. After receiving his JD, he worked in a law office for one year, taught at the University of Puget Sound Law School for two years, and then went to the University of Michigan. When Pat assumed the Legislative Affairs position, Clive succeeded him as Chief of the Natural Resources Division. It did not take long to learn that when Clive provided advice on an issue of substance, he was always 100% right. Before taking action on any of the Swan Falls issues, I made sure to run it by Clive and get his advice and concurrence. He was one of the best hires I made during my eight years in office.

Our chief adversary was Jim Bruce, who was Idaho Power's CEO from 1976 until his retirement in 1985. Throughout the water rights battle, I never had ill feelings toward Jim Bruce because he was a gentleman who did not engage in unsportsmanlike conduct.

Jim was born in Boise on June 23, 1920. He attended St. Joseph's School and St. Teresa's Academy in Boise, Columbia Prep in Portland, the University of Portland, and then obtained his bachelor's degree from the College of Idaho. He began law school at Georgetown University in Washington, D.C., enlisted in the Army when World War II broke out, and completed his legal studies at the University of Idaho School of Law in 1947. He married Lois Stevens of Twin Falls on August 25, 1946. After spending a couple of years in the Ada County Prosecuting Attorney's Office and a brief time in private practice, Jim went to work as an attorney for Idaho Power in 1951 and spent the next 34 years working for the Power Company.

Jim served on the boards of a number of companies, including Albertsons, First Security Bank and Blue Cross of Idaho. He served on the board of St. Alphonsus Hospital, Bishop Kelly High School, and the College of Idaho. Jim died on February 20, 2014, just six months before the celebration of the winding down of the Snake River Basin Adjudication.

Jim Bruce had been a strong supporter of conducting an adjudication of the Snake River and was also committed to negotiations towards settlement of the Swan Falls fight. Pat Costello recalled that Jim "was instrumental in keeping Idaho Power at the negotiating table during times in the process when it appeared no agreement could be reached." At the time of his retirement in 1985, Jim reportedly said, "Any time you go into a lawsuit, you can lose. If you can make a compromise settlement, one that gives everybody an acceptable solution, that's the way to go."[13]

Idaho Power's lead attorney during the Swan Falls dispute was Tom Nelson, a principal partner at the Twin Falls law firm of Nelson, Rosholt, Robertson, Tolman & Tucker. Tom received his law degree from the University of Idaho College of Law in 1962. He served in the Idaho Attorney General's office as a deputy and then chief deputy from 1963 to 1965. During Tom's tenure in office, Allan Shepard, who went on to serve on the Idaho Supreme Court and who wrote the Swan Falls opinion, was the State's Attorney General. Tom was a respected and accomplished attorney and considered to be one of the best water lawyers in the State. The conclusion in his 1976 memorandum to Jim Bruce — that Idaho Power could not use the Swan Falls water rights to prevent consumptive uses from depleting the Snake River above Swan Falls — was based on sound legal analysis. Unfortunately the Supreme Court gave it no heed. Tom was nominated on July 18, 1990, by President George H.W. Bush to fill a seat on the U.S. Ninth Circuit Court of Appeals. He was confirmed by the Senate and received his commission on October 17, 1990. He passed away on May 4, 2011, leaving behind his wife, Sharon, and four children. Tom was a worthy adversary during the Swan Falls fight and, after it was settled, he was a straightforward advocate for implementing and upholding the terms of the

---

13   Sowell, John. "Former Idaho Power CEO James E. Bruce dies." *Idaho Statesman*, Feb. 22, 2014.

agreement.

The person most involved in handling the Power Company's public relations and lobbying efforts throughout the Swan Falls dispute was Logan Lanham. Logan was widely regarded as being the 800-pound gorilla of Idaho politics. It was largely because of Logan that people joked the State had acquired its name by adopting the Idaho from Idaho Power. In a 1987 survey conducted by the Idaho Statesman, Logan topped the list of behind-the-scenes power brokers in the State. He and Jim Goller, the chief of staff for Senator McClure, "were mentioned slightly more frequently than any other Idahoans in a statewide survey of influential persons who were asked to identify people who would wield substantial power behind the scenes but are not well-known by the public to do so."[14]

I first met Logan when I was working for Senator Jordan in the early 1970s. Sometime in the fall of 1970, Logan stopped by the office for one of his periodic visits. He was preceded by what smelled like a lilac-scented aftershave, which was kind of popular in those days. When Logan walked into the room, you didn't think of aftershave, however, but that he could probably beat you to a pulp. I don't mean to imply that he had an evil presence, but he certainly had a presence — you knew immediately when Logan walked into the room. He was just a little bit frightening. He had a congenial manner, but you knew that this was a person you did not want to mess with. Logan had a firm jaw, a strong handshake, and a manner of projecting that left a definite impression.

Logan was not only tough but he knew the ropes. By virtue of his position as Vice President of Public Affairs for Idaho Power, he obviously had a relationship with every member of the Idaho Legislature, whether they were friend or foe on an issue. He had a good deal of influence because he

---

14   Etlinger, Charles. "Waiting in the wings." *Idaho Statesman,* July 23, 1987.

decided who got campaign contributions and who didn't. He was widely acquainted with those in administrative agencies who had dealings with the Power Company. During the Swan Falls dispute, we learned to our distress that he also had great influence within the halls of Congress, on both sides of the aisle, and within the administrative agencies, particularly the Department of Interior and Federal Energy Regulatory Commission. It seemed like every time we made a move during the Swan Falls fight, Logan had already been on the scene and had been able to get his foot in the right door.[15]

Logan's principal assistant was Greg Panter, who grew up on a ranch near Thatcher. He fit the typical stereotype of a trusty sidekick. During the Swan Falls hostilities, I generally referred to Logan as Br'er Fox and Greg as Br'er Bear, although Logan was the larger of the two but with the craftiness of Br'er Fox. Laird Noh made a note of a conversation he overheard in his Senate office on April 11, 1983, that he felt was typical of what some people around the Legislature thought of Greg. He reported Greg telling Senator Reed Budge that he "could have sold [the Legislature] a truck load of snake oil on whatever."

As for myself, I was born on May 13, 1942, and grew up on a farming and cattle-feeding operation west of Eden. My father, Henry Jones, was somewhat a legend in the Magic Valley. He had come to Idaho in the early 1930s with just a few dollars in his pocket and eventually operated the largest cattle-feeding operation in southern Idaho. He was a man of his word who made thousands of contracts — buying and selling cattle, cattle feed, crops, and so on — based solely on his word. I recall one instance where a cattle buyer from California backed out on a purchase when the price dropped. The man's name is emblazoned in my memory — Danny Reitman — because it was such an unusual happening and my Dad made sure that everyone in the cattle business knew about it. That

---

15   Logan died on April 16, 2015, at 88 years of age. For a man who wielded a great deal of power in Idaho for over two decades, it is odd and somewhat sad that nary a mention was made of his passing in the media. All that appeared was a bare death notice.

had a substantial effect on how I view interpersonal dealings: that your word is your bond, with or without a writing. That outlook probably had a lot to do with my approach to the Swan Falls fight—when you give your word, you keep it.

I can't say I was a particularly studious kid in high school. The subjects came easy so I did not put out a great deal of effort. However, right at the start of my senior year, I accidentally collided with an electric pole while driving my Dad's 1958 Chevrolet much too fast. That caused two broken legs, a 14-week stay in Magic Valley Memorial Hospital, and additional months of recovery at home. From that point on, I became a serious person with big aspirations.

After graduating from Valley High School in 1960, I went to Idaho State University to learn how to be an engineer. However, engineering drawing seemed like drudgery and President Kennedy was urging young people to serve their country. At that time, I decided to be a United States Senator, which was probably not the ideal career choice for an introvert like me, but one learns to adapt. So, I transferred to the University of Oregon, got a degree in political science in 1964 along with an Army ROTC commission, and then got my Juris Doctor degree from Northwestern University School of Law in Chicago in 1967. After passing the bar in Idaho in 1967, I started service in the Army as a first lieutenant in the field artillery branch. After artillery school at Fort Sill, Oklahoma, I spent about three months in Okinawa, whereupon I requested reassignment to Vietnam. The Army graciously provided me a 408-day visit there with a battalion of 8-inch and 175-mm guns. Most of my tour was spent living amongst the Vietnamese military at Tay Ninh Province headquarters in charge of a small liaison group tasked with the responsibility of obtaining Vietnamese clearance for artillery and air strikes in the Province. I also acted as an artillery spotter, flying in small, two-seater "Bird Dog" airplanes of fairly ancient vintage and directing 200 and 146-pound projectiles to various locations in War Zones C and D, but that is an entirely different story.

After leaving the Army, I went to work for Senator Jordan from January of 1970 through December of 1972. When he retired, I moved back to Idaho and set up a law office practice in Jerome. When Congressman George Hansen got into legal trouble, I called Len Jordan to see whether he thought I should throw my hat into the ring against George in the 1978 Republican primary. He said it was not a good idea since George had a strong and dedicated following. That was in January. When George got some additional bad press toward the end of March, I threw my hat into the ring 45 days before the May primary, which was not a very sound move but I ended up with about 44.5% of the vote. After licking a few wounds, I started thinking that if I had a year to get myself better known, I could win the next time around. I ran again in 1980, but actually fell back to about 41%. When an opening came up in the Attorney General's office, I figured I could do that type of work. After a tough primary and tough general election, I won the position in the 1982 election. About two weeks after election day, the Supreme Court issued its Swan Falls decision. While I shared in the shock that reverberated around the southern part of the State, there were other pressing matters weighing on me, such as getting the office organized, learning the ropes, and so on. I had no idea how the Swan Falls issue would play out or that it would become such a big part of my life.

SEARCHING FOR A QUICK FIX

A meeting was held in Boise on December 30, 1982, to consider the implications of the Supreme Court's Swan Falls decision and what might be done about it in the 1983 legislative session. Attendees included members of the House and Senate resource committees, representatives of the Governor's office, governmental water experts and a variety of water users. Idaho Power's attorney, Tom Nelson, advised the group that about 7,200 irrigators upstream from Swan Falls were likely infringing on the Company's water rights for the Swan Falls Dam and that Idaho Power was contemplating legal action against them.[16] Ken Dunn, Director of the Idaho Department of Water Resources, said that his office and Idaho Power might be able to agree on a contract that would guarantee the water rights of about 5,000 farmers who had already been using water from the Snake River or the Snake River Plains Aquifer before the issuance of the Supreme Court decision. Nelson indicated that the Power Company might be willing to dismiss the contemplated litigation as to those alleged infringers of its water rights, as well as to existing water right applicants who had made substantial investment toward developing their farming operations.

The group was advised that quick resolution could not be expected for the legal and technical questions raised by the Swan Falls case and that a technical committee appointed by the Legislature to consider various aspects of the issue could take up to three years to answer the most pressing questions. It was reported that some eastern Idaho farmers were unable to obtain bank loans because of the cloud cast

---

16   Zellar, Ron. "Some Swan Falls questions may take years to answer." *Idaho Statesman, Jan. 1, 1983.*

over the validity of their water rights by the court decision, giving some urgency to the quest for an answer.

While the Supreme Court had sent the case back to district court for consideration of a variety of defenses to Idaho Power's priority claims, that would obviously take years to resolve. Interested parties began floating a number of proposals to bring about a quicker fix than could be expected in the court proceedings. Tom Nelson unveiled what would become the Power Company's proposal: legislation authorizing a contract that would essentially grandfather in existing users and immunize Idaho Power against the type of claims being asserted in the PUC by Mullaney and Peavey. The Idaho Water Resource Board was looking into the possibility of condemning the unsubordinated Swan Falls water right that the Supreme Court had discovered. Senator Noh was giving thought to legislating a higher minimum streamflow in the Swan Falls stretch of the Snake River and both he and Representative Chatburn were considering the possibility of legislation to subordinate (or resubordinate) the Snake River dams upstream from Hells Canyon.

I took office on January 7, 1983, and was aware of the fact that various parties were developing solutions to short circuit the litigation but expected that the court proceedings would produce the ultimate answer. I have to admit that the Swan Falls issue was not then at the top of my agenda, as there were plenty of other issues to deal with, not the least of which was taking over the reins at the Attorney General's office.

Before taking over, I interviewed key staff members and let them know that there would be no turnover. However, several decided to move on to greener pastures (attorneys at the office were among the lowest paid around the entire country at that time), so we needed to fill positions. The State was in a financial crisis because of a rather depressed national economy, requiring attention to budgetary considerations. In addition to my own budget woes, as a member of the Board of Examiners, I had to decide how much to cut from other agency funds to balance the State budget. The Board also included the Governor and Secretary of State. We held a number of hearings to cut millions in spending authority, and that took a good deal of time.

Also, during my first few weeks in office, I received notification from the United States Supreme Court that a long-standing case brought by my predecessors against the States of Oregon and Washington over salmon and steelhead was scheduled for argument before the Court on March 23, requiring a crash course in anadromous fish issues. I spent two weeks in Washington, D.C., with Deputy Attorney General Steve Goddard, fish biologist John Coon, and the massive record compiled in proceedings before a Supreme Court special master, learning about the migration and spawning habits of various runs of salmon and steelhead, the fishing practices of our downstream neighbors, and the like. Preparing for and arguing the case was the focus of my attention for a good part of the 1983 legislative session.[17]

On January 19, Senator Noh and Representative Chatburn got their committees together for a joint meeting on Swan Falls issues. Perry Swisher, who was then the President of the Public Utilities Commission, told the legislators that development of additional farm land above Swan Falls Dam could cost Idaho Power $53.8 million per year in lost power revenues. That would supposedly result in a 17 percent across-

---

17   *Idaho ex rel. Evans v. Oregon*, 462 U.S. 1017, 103 S. Ct. 2817, 77 L. Ed. 2d 387, 13 Envtl. L. Rep. 20,658 (1983). The Supreme Court ultimately decided that the doctrine of equitable apportionment applied to a multi-state natural resource such as anadromous fish and that each of such states had a responsibility to conserve and augment the resource, but a majority held the record before the special master did not contain clear and convincing evidence that Oregon and Washington had mismanaged the resource. The case gave me a greater appreciation for Idaho-origin anadromous fish and a strong commitment to do what I could do to protect and enhance their runs.

the-board rate increase for the Company's customers.[18] This was apparently based on a study thrown together by PUC staff members using worst-case scenarios. On the other hand, Ken Dunn said that "full protection of the Swan Falls water rights could mean pulling the plug on 250,000 acres of existing irrigated farmland." Ken also mentioned that the State could request the Federal Energy Regulatory Commission (FERC) to insert a subordination condition into the FERC power license for Swan Falls. FERC had reissued the license for the plant during the previous month but had agreed to retain jurisdiction to allow the State an opportunity to intervene and seek reconsideration. Subsequently, the State did just that. Logan Lanham told the committees that Idaho Power did not intend to block water development for residential uses and was considering similar treatment for commercial and light industrial purposes.

One of the attorneys in my Natural Resources Division provided me a memorandum on January 20, summarizing developments since the Supreme Court's decision, including the January 19 legislative hearing. There was no indication at that time of a problem in the handling of the litigation, other than the unfortunate decision by the Court.

The Idaho Water Resource Board held its initial hearing on the Swan Falls issue on March 4 to consider, among other things, acquisition of Idaho Power's Swan Falls water rights by condemnation. Idaho Power submitted a written statement for the record essentially saying that there was no need for concern because it did not intend to block economic development and had no desire to control the future of Idaho. It argued that future agricultural development above Swan Falls would deplete the water supplies for its hydropower dams, resulting in increased power costs for ratepayers and that it should be compensated for any reduction in its water

---

18   Zellar, Ron. "Hearing opens Snake water-rights debate." *Idaho Statesman*, Jan. 20, 1983.

rights. While much of what the Company said was debatable, it hit the nail on the head in one respect by saying, "There is no practical risk of meaningful depletion below Swan Falls, so an acre-foot of water passing Swan Falls will reach the dams in Hells Canyon." In other words, negligible amounts of water are removed from the Snake River between Swan Falls and Idaho Power's Hells Canyon complex. So, Swan Falls, which produced an insignificant amount of power for ratepayers, was essentially being used to unsubordinate the three Hells Canyon dams, which produced the lion's share of the Company's hydropower. Thus, a fairly small dam posed a very large problem. By insisting that it receive its full 8,400 cfs flow at the Swan Falls dam, Idaho Power could effectively shut down all pumping of irrigation water from the Snake River Plains Aquifer because its right had an earlier priority date than the ground water irrigation rights.

The Senate and House resource committees began consideration of various proposals to address the Swan Falls decision. Both Laird and Vard were working hard to educate their fellow legislators on the ramifications of the decision and to line up support for subordination of Idaho Power's hydropower rights. Vard's committee acted first, approving a memorial to Idaho's U.S. Congressional delegation, urging that its members "use their influence to seek subordination of Idaho Power's water right at Swan Falls (and other Snake River hydrogenerating facilities) as a condition to relicensure [of Swan Falls] by the Federal Energy Regulatory Commission." The memorial, House Joint Memorial No. 7, passed the House on March 8.

Vard was also able to get a subordination bill sent to the House floor in early March. The bill authorized the State to subordinate water for power purposes and stripped the PUC of authority to deal with allegations that a utility had failed to protect its water rights. The latter provision also called for protecting existing water users from Idaho Power's claim of priority under the Supreme Court decision. In essence, the bill sought to accomplish both sides' legislative objectives. The bill came up for consideration by the House on March 14 but ran into a snag. Representative Gary Montgomery of Boise argued that the bill should be put on hold until my office could give an opinion on its constitutionality, asserting that the subordination provision might constitute a taking of property without due process of law. On a 38-30 vote, the House put the legislation on hold for two days pending my opinion.

In response to the request from the House, Robie Russell, one of my deputies, opined that the bill was probably constitutional but that it might be prudent to separate the two provisions so as to not run afoul of a constitutional provision limiting legislative acts to a single subject.[19] Robie indicated that a court would have to decide whether compensation was owed to a utility whose water rights were subordinated under the bill. Representative Walt Little, a Republican from New Plymouth, who chaired the House Affairs Committee, said the committee would rewrite and act upon new legislation as soon as possible.

At the same time, Laird was able to get the Senate to act upon the House Joint Memorial. The Senate first voted to defeat the Memorial, then voted to reconsider the vote, and then passed it on a 19-14 vote. Governor Evans' intervention with Senate Democrats was instrumental in the Memorial's reversal of fortune.

Representative Chatburn got his new subordination bill introduced in the House State Affairs Committee on March 18. The new legislation, House Bill 304, was almost identical to the bill that had been held on the House floor, except that the subordination and PUC provisions were both limited to

---

19   Idaho Const. Art. III, § 16 states, "[e]very act shall embrace but one subject and matter properly connected therewith...."

amending Title 42 of the Idaho Code, which deals with water rights. Because Logan questioned the constitutionality of the subordination provision and threatened legal action if it was enacted by the Legislature, H.B. 304 contained additional language making both of the provisions void if one were subsequently struck down in court action. The House acted favorably on the bill, leaving it up to the Senate to act. The bill went to Laird's committee on March 24 but no action was ever taken on it. Logan managed to sandbag it.

In an apparent attempt to add fuel to the legislative fires, Idaho Power carried through with its threat to sue the water right holders who it alleged were infringing upon its Swan Falls water right. The number of prospective defendants was now rumored to be 7,500. The lawsuit, dubbed Swan Falls II[20], or the 7,500 Suit, was filed in Ada County District Court on March 29. This certainly appeared to be designed to create some momentum in favor of the Power Company's legislation.

Senator Noh was having difficulties with his committee members. Now that the legislative focus was on the Senate, Logan and his troops were lobbying furiously against subordination legislation. The committee voted on April 4 to split the H.B. 304 issues into two separate bills. The committee sent the Idaho Power bill, Senate Bill 1180, to the floor of the Senate. The committee killed a motion to send Laird's preferred bill, Senate Bill 1188, to the floor. That bill, much like H.B. 304, called for subordination of Idaho Power's Snake River water rights and also for protection of existing upstream water users. The committee also sent a third bill, Senate Bill 1189, to the Senate floor. That bill provided for subordination of hydropower rights. After the committee meeting, Laird said, "Idaho Power won that round. Never in the history of the Legislature has Idaho Power ever failed on

---

20   Idaho Power's initial action against the State, which resulted in the Supreme Court decision, is hereafter called "Swan Falls I".

an issue on which it has an interest."[21]

The committee separated the two issues on a 6–4 vote. Earlier, Laird contemplated amending H.B. 304 to increase the minimum streamflow at Swan Falls from 3,300 cfs to 5,400 cfs during the summer months. However, on March 30 the Idaho Supreme Court issued a decision that eliminated that possibility. The Court ruled that the Idaho Constitution did not permit the Legislature to establish minimum streamflows different than those contained in the State Water Plan developed by the Idaho Water Resource Board.[22] Laird noted, "If we can't change the state water plan, then we cannot increase the minimum streamflow to 5,400 cubic feet per second at Swan Falls."[23]

Logan was pleased with the committee's separation of the two issues. He said, "That's as it should have been all along. Let's take care of these people whose water rights are in jeopardy right now. Then, let's take the appropriate time needed to address future uses." On the other hand, Laird said that "by splitting the legislation, we are taking away the leverage of protecting existing water users that we needed for passing subordination. If we don't pass subordination, we're saying that a single public utility will control all the water that supports 70 percent of Idaho's population. And by the action we took today, we've greatly increased that possibility."[24]

That wasn't the end of the issue in the Senate, however. On April 8 the Senate voted down S.B. 1189 by an 18–17 vote. It approved S.B. 1180, sending it to the House. The following day, Vard's committee approved a new subordination bill, sending it to the House floor in an unusual Saturday session. The House approved the new bill, House Bill 367, on April

21   Gramer, Rod. "Bills on Swan Falls rights sent to Senate floor." *Idaho Statesman,* April 5, 1983.
22   *Idaho Power Co. v. Dept. of Water Res.,* 104 Idaho 570, 661 P.2d 736 (1983).
23   Hammond, Bruce. "Senate panel drops Swan Falls plan." *Times-News (Twin Falls),* April 5, 1983.
24   Hammond, Bruce. "Senate panel drops Swan Falls plan." *Times-News,* April 5, 1983.

11 by a vote of 41–29 and also passed S.B. 1180, the Power Company bill.

Governor Evans expressed disappointment with the Senate's failure to approve subordination legislation, saying it was important that the State retain control over its water. The Governor and his staff had been lobbying in favor of the various subordination bills among the Democrat members of the Legislature. His party members, particularly in the Senate, were skeptical about subordination and a number had contributed to the defeat of both S.B. 1188 and S.B. 1189. After the House approved H.B. 367, the Governor weighed in heavily to get it to the Senate floor. Laird tried to get the bill approved for floor action on April 11 but had not been able to garner the necessary votes. The following day, he and Senator John Barker, a Republican from Buhl, "carefully engineered a method for calling the bill directly out of committee—a move that resulted in a parliamentary fight and a halting of Senate proceedings. To resolve the deadlock, the rest of Noh's committee finally agreed to release the bill from committee."[25]

H.B. 367 finally came up for a vote on April 12, but was defeated on a tally of 16–19, which Laird attributed to a change of position by two senators, Dane Watkins of Idaho Falls, and Terry Sverdsten of Cataldo. The previous subordination legislation had been defeated in the Senate, primarily because of Democrat opposition. But, as the Times-News reported, "intense, personal lobbying by Governor John Evans, who favors subordination, apparently swayed some of his fellow Democrats when the vote was taken on April 12. 'The Governor stuffed us in a barrel, and sent us over Swan Falls,' quipped one Democratic senator after leaving a meeting that morning with Evans." Laird said, "I believe this is the end of it for now," and he was correct.[26] The Legislature adjourned having handed Idaho Power a victory with the

25   Hammond, Bruce. "Idaho Power's water rights not subordinated." *Times-News,* April 13, 1983.
26   Hammond, Bruce. "Idaho Power's water rights not subordinated." *Times-News,* April 13, 1983.

passage of S.B. 1180, while the subordination proponents were not able to achieve any success. This was due primarily to Logan's effective efforts, particularly in changing the two votes in the Senate.

In recognition that many issues remained unresolved, the Legislature approved a Senate Concurrent Resolution (SCR No. 110) on April 14, establishing an interim committee of legislators "to undertake and complete a study of the status of existing water rights and future water needs for the waters of the Snake River, its tributaries and the aquifer." Laird and Vard would thus have the responsibility of examining the Swan Falls issues and providing guidance to the members of the 1984 legislative session.

With the adjournment of the Legislature, the focus shifted to the Idaho Water Resource Board, which voted on April 15 to pursue the condemnation and purchase of the Swan Falls Dam. However, Idaho Power's President, Bob O'Connor, said the dam was not for sale and was "a very valuable piece of property in our plans." Senator Noh indicated his first choice would be to subordinate the Power Company's Swan Falls water rights but "barring that, state ownership of the dam would guarantee 'the public hearing process and the legislative process in determining where and how that water would be used.'"[27]

The interim legislative committee appointed by the Legislature to consider Swan Falls issues met on May 10 and, among other things, approved a study of the Snake River system to determine the impact of subordination on water flows, as well as the relationship between surface and underground water.[28] Idaho Power agreed to pay $35,000 to fund the study. Senator Terry Reilly, a Nampa Democrat, was the sole committee member to oppose Power Company funding, arguing that it could give "the appearance of

---

27   Stevenson, Mary. Associated *Press.* "*Swan Falls controversy: What Now?*" *Idaho State Journal* (Pocatello), *April 17, 1983.*
28   Hammond, Bruce. "Panel approves study of Swan Falls dispute." *Times-News,* May 11, 1983.

impropriety, and thereby destroy the study's credibility."
During the meeting, Logan Lanham told the committee that
Idaho Power was drafting the contract called for by S.B. 1180
with the intent of removing about 5,000 people as defendants
in Swan Falls II.

On the same day of the interim committee meeting,
Governor Evans announced the formation of his Swan Falls
Task Force, which was to be chaired by Ray Rigby. He said,
"It is imperative that the state maintain its responsibility and
authority to protect and manage our water resources."[29]

On May 12, 1983, Former Governor Cecil Andrus had
the opportunity to weigh in on the Idaho Water Resource
Board proposal to buy Swan Falls at an appearance before
the Idaho Press Club. When asked whether he thought the
purchase of the dam was the proper course to pursue, he
responded, "No. I do not.... I do not think we need to buy
that facility. What we need to do is to look at minimum flows
in the Snake River, make it possible for the farmers who have
water rights in the state to continue to have those rights and
to have a tangible personal property, not something that is
preempted. So, I, my personal opinion is that we don't need
to own that, and that the, I do not believe that the agricultural
rights should be eminent over, preeminent over all of it, the
uses."

Meanwhile, the Federal Energy Regulatory Commission
was still mulling over the State's request to intervene in the
Swan Falls relicensing proceeding for the purpose of inserting
a subordination clause into the FERC license. According
to a UPI wire story, a FERC staff attorney observed, "It's a
fairly extraordinary situation where a state has requested to
subordinate the water rights of a licensee of a project."[30] The
attorney said Commission "members were 'well aware' of
the water rights controversy brewing in Idaho, but they have

29   Hammond, Bruce. "Panel approves study of Swan Falls dispute." *Times-News*, May 11, 1983.
30   United Press International (UPI). "Swan Falls dam license process stalled." *Coeur d'Alene Press*, May 14, 1983.

not indicated whether they will continue postponing action until the problems are resolved. 'It could take some time. It's something that requires serious deliberations by the staff and the commission.'"

The Water Resource Board met on June 3 to consider again the possibility of taking over the Swan Falls Dam. Darcy Frownfelter, one of my deputies, advised the Board that it had the authority to condemn and purchase the facility for fair market value. Logan was present at the meeting and put on a bit of a performance. He made a show of recording the proceedings and then took the opportunity to hold an impromptu press conference. According to the Times-News, "Frownfelter's report to the board was filmed by an Idaho Power camera crew. It also was digested carefully by two Idaho Power officials who gained a glimpse of the court strategies that the state someday may use against the company to try to win takeover approval."[31] Logan "told reporters at the meeting that his company would fight any takeover action all the way to the U.S. Supreme Court." Nevertheless, the Board agreed to continue researching a possible takeover of the dam.

Work on the various Swan Falls issues continued apace during the summer. The Governor's Swan Falls Task Force held periodic meetings, as did the interim legislative committee. Also, representatives of the State and Idaho Power were negotiating the contract called for by S.B. 1180, which became known as the 1180 Contract. The negotiators announced on July 14 that they had reached tentative agreement on the terms of the contract. As had previously been envisioned, about 5,000 irrigators would be dropped as defendants in Swan Falls II upon signing of the contract. Those would be water users who were using their water rights at the time of the Supreme Court's decision, as well as those who

---

31   Bernton, Hal. "State board reviews Snake River dispute." *Times-News, June 4, 1983.*

had made substantial investment toward that end.[32] About 2,200 defendants would remain in the lawsuit.

Idaho Power released a slick brochure in July, giving its side of the various Swan Falls issues. The brochure reported that its customers would lose if the State were to take over the Swan Falls dam or subordinate the Company's water rights at the dam. According to the brochure, subordination would cost "Idaho Power ratepayers more than $53.8 million annually." The Company disclaimed wanting to be the State's watermaster and said it had "no interest in running farmers out of business." The publication said that although Swan Falls is "a very small dam," its condemnation would lead to condemnation of its power plants at Bliss, Lower Salmon, and Upper Salmon. According to the Company, any future consumptive water uses upstream of Swan Falls would require compensation to the Power Company.

Although it did not seem to be a big deal at the time, I hired Clive Strong during the summer. Clive started working as a deputy in the Natural Resources Division of the office on August 1. Clive had seemed a bit stiff when I interviewed him, but he had great qualifications for the job. Little did I realize at the time that he would play such a major role in the Swan Falls fight, not to mention the numerous accomplishments that he achieved for the State throughout his tenure with the Attorney General's office.

For the most part, the press went into hibernation on the Swan Falls issue during the summer. A notable exception was a series of articles written by Ron Zellar of the Statesman. He had two articles in the August 14 issue. The first, titled "No water, no money: Swan Falls water decision leaves many high and dry," spoke to the impact of the Swan Falls decision on businesses supporting agriculture, particularly well drillers and irrigation equipment dealers. The second,

---

32   Associated Press. "Swan Falls agreement reached." *Idaho States-man,* July 15, 1983.

which began a three-part series, was titled "Swan Falls: Ruling stymies farmers who want to drill wells," and dealt with the moratorium on water permits and the fact that it had stymied new agricultural development. The second article in the series, published on August 15, contained interviews with four of the individuals who had signed the PUC complaint prompting Swan Falls I. Bud Purdy of Picabo expressed regret about becoming involved in the effort. However, the other three—John Faulkner of Gooding, Gerald Tews of Filer, and Senator John Peavey of Carey—said that it had been beneficial for Idaho's interests in that it would keep electric rates from increasing. All three opposed subordination of Idaho Power's water rights. The third article in the series, published on August 16, dealt with the 1180 Contract. The articles were even-handed and well written.

After receiving a copy of the draft 1180 Contract, Governor Evans circulated it and sought public input. The response was not overwhelming. By the August 25 deadline, only 11 people had submitted written comments. Laird Noh was one of the commentators. He asserted that the criteria for releasing water right holders as defendants in the Swan Falls II were too narrow in several respects. He indicated that it was not clear whether Idaho Power actually needed protection from ratepayers in proceedings before the PUC because, as he understood it, land and water, including the Power Company's Swan Falls water right, are the property of the Company's stockholders, rather than its ratepayers. He said the issue needed to be explored to see whether Idaho Power had actually given up anything as a quid pro quo for the benefit it was to receive under the 1180 Contract. Laird also made an interesting comment on a publicity campaign that the Power Company had been conducting during the negotiations:

While this summer Idaho Power Company has launched a major effort to sign on Idaho ratepayer-stockholders and enhance the public image of Idaho stockholders in the Company, we must remember that 95% of the equity ownership of Idaho Power is beyond the boundaries of Idaho. This strong divergence of interests between Idaho Power stockholders and the citizens of our state mandates a very tough bargaining position which will minimize as much as possible the financial damage to innocent Idaho citizens.

Ray Rigby urged that the Governor postpone approval of the contract until the district court decided in Swan Falls I whether Idaho Power had forfeited its Swan Falls water right. He also urged that the State seek subordination in the FERC proceeding. He said:[33]

"Once [water users] become cognizant of the fact that the future development of southern Idaho is going to be controlled in essence by the Idaho Power Company and that the governor.... has negotiated away...one of their most valuable rights without having the matter first tried, I think there will be severe criticism."

It should be mentioned that Ray's comment was strictly hypothetical, as the Governor had given absolutely no indication that he intended to sign the contract.

On the other hand, Tom Stivers, the Speaker of the House, a strong supporter of Idaho Power, urged the Governor to sign the contract. The muted response to the Governor's request for comment demonstrated that the Power Company had done a fairly good job of convincing existing water users that the 1180 Contract was the best way

---

33   UPI. "Stivers: State should sign Idaho Power's water right contract." *Idaho Press-Tribune (Nampa), Aug. 26, 1983.*

to protect their interests. Many people were not aware of the stakes involved or simply resigned to the fact that the Power Company's proposed solution was the only game in town. That would soon change

THE AWAKENING

On September 1, a major wakeup call in the form of Clive J. Strong came bounding into my office. Clive had just attended a meeting of the Governor's Swan Falls Task Force. He handed me a memo summarizing the deliberations and recommendations of the Task Force.

The Task Force recommended that the Governor seek an Attorney General's opinion as to the constitutionality of the Senate Bill 1180 scheme. The Task Force generally agreed that the 1180 Contract should not be signed without further review, particularly of its effect on Swan Falls I. Kent Foster, a water lawyer from Idaho Falls, argued that the legislation violated Idaho's constitutional prohibition against special legislation. Pat Costello, the Governor's legal counsel, requested that consideration of the contract be held in abeyance pending the AG's opinion on the contract and its authorizing legislation. The Task Force agreed.

Task Force members questioned the advisability of entering into a contract prior to pursuing the Swan Falls litigation to a conclusion on its merits. They were concerned about the Water Resources Department's approach, which supported approval of the contract prior to resolution of the litigation. Several members stated that Idaho Power had waived its claim of priority over the many water users who it had encouraged to settle and develop farms that were dependent upon its electricity for pumping irrigation water. Approval of the contract would jeopardize the State's litigation posture in Swan Falls I. Ray Rigby emphasized that Idaho Power clearly agreed to subordinate all of its upstream claims of priority as a specific condition to getting the State's approval of its three Hells Canyon dams.

Ray expressed concern that many water users who were defendants in Swan Falls II did not have adequate notice of the provisions of the proposed contract and were not aware that it would not result in a waiver of Idaho Power's priority right at Swan Falls. The Company would retain its priority, but just not assert it against the released defendants. He contended that the State could not enter into a contract that affected the individual property rights of so many water users. There was discussion among Task Force members as to the possibility of consolidating Swan Falls I and II into a class action suit to resolve the matter, instead of pursuing a contract.

During the meeting, it was brought out that Idaho Power developed a slide show that was being presented to civic groups and school children throughout its service area to support its take on the Supreme Court's decision, its favorable effects for ratepayers, and the advisability of adopting the Company's proposed solution. Essentially, Idaho Power was the only voice being heard by the public, which was swaying opinion in its favor even among water user defendants in Swan Falls II. What was more unsettling were comments that Ray made to Clive following the meeting. Ray had been closely involved with the litigation leading up to the Supreme Court's decision and stated his opinion that the State's attorneys were simply being overpowered by Idaho Power's legal team. The attorneys assigned to the Water Resources Department were spread thin, having to deal with the Department's regular business, while also trying to do justice to this extremely important litigation. On the other hand, the Power Company had a sizeable legal team consisting of both in-house and outside counsel. Tom Nelson, who would go on to be appointed to the Ninth Circuit Court of Appeals, was an experienced litigator and had a particular rapport with the Idaho Supreme Court, having served as a deputy Attorney General for Chief Justice Allan Shepard when he was the State's Attorney General. Ray asserted that the State needed to substantially up its game in the litigation and recommended that the case be removed from the agency and taken over by the Attorney General's central office. He was concerned that the agency's support for the contract would influence its litigation posture in Swan Falls I.

This highlighted problems that were becoming increasingly apparent to me about the way legal services were provided to State agencies. Agencies on occasion influenced the legal posture of their in-house attorneys in a manner that I felt was legally unsupportable. Further, the office was often unable to effectively supervise and support attorneys working for the agencies. About a third of the attorneys in the office were central office attorneys who answered directly to the Attorney General. The remaining two-thirds were assigned to, housed at, and paid by the agencies. They bore the title of Deputy Attorney General but essentially had two bosses. Our relationship with the attorneys working at the Water Resources Department was good, as opposed to some other agencies where the arrangement was sometimes strained and far from ideal. Attorneys assigned to an agency were expected to provide the full range of attorney services—legal advice, litigation expertise, and the like. This did not always work out because an attorney experienced in the agency's specialty might not have courtroom experience. And, sometimes captive agency attorneys might not be willing to speak out when the agency wants to pursue a wrongheaded legal agenda. This problem arose in the late 1950s, when the voters elected an Attorney General who was clearly incompetent. When that Attorney General sought to prevent a State agency from hiring its own counsel, the matter came before the Supreme Court. The Court, recognizing the folly of turning the agency's business over to the elected Attorney General, allowed the agency to keep its attorney. From that point forward, there had been a division between central office attorneys and agency attorneys.

Acting upon Ray's recommendation, the case was taken over by the central office for pursuit by the Natural Resources Division. Their instructions were to move forward expeditiously with Swan Falls I, particularly focusing on the State's affirmative defenses of estoppel, waiver, forfeiture, abandonment and the like.

The same day the Task Force met, the interim study committee of legislators held a meeting to consider the proposed contract authorized by S.B. 1180. The Legislative Council Committee on Water Rights, co-chaired by Senator Noh and Representative Chatburn, focused on the provisions of the contract—whether it protected enough water rights claimants and whether it was advisable policy. Senator Peavey, who supported the contract, recommended that its coverage be expanded to include defendants who obtained their water right prior to the Supreme Court decision, whether or not they had made a substantial investment in an irrigation system. Greg Panter, the Power Company's representative at the meeting, argued against any expansion, claiming expansion might result in further lawsuits from ratepayers or company stockholders.

Both Senator Noh and Representative Chatburn expressed concern about moving forward with the   contract. Senator Noh "feared water users might be robbed of legal remedies if they dropped out of the lawsuits and the contract was later ruled unconstitutional."[34] He contended that water users simply did not have enough information to decide whether or not to support the contract. Representative Chatburn agreed, saying "contract talks should be delayed so all concerned parties can see whether they are jumping from

---

34   Botka, Bruce. UPI. "Swan Falls panel wants users shielded." *Times News,* Sept. 2, 1983.

the frying pan into the fire."

The Water Resources Department head, Ken Dunn, expressed guarded support for the contract, indicating that the litigation would continue forward but that approval of the contract would only reduce the number of defendants. Greg Panter agreed, saying "all you are doing in this contract is removing a whole lot of people from this lawsuit and giving them the right to go ahead and farm while the other issues are cleared up."[35]

Following up on the Task Force recommendation, Governor Evans sent a request to my office to review the constitutionality of the contract and its authorizing legislation. Our offices worked together to word his opinion request and we thus began close coordination of a strategy to bypass the contract and have the matter resolved favorable to the State either through the legislative process or in judicial proceedings. Our concern was that Idaho Power was pursuing a divide-and-conquer strategy. That is, by giving relief to those water users who had already developed their property or made a substantial investment toward that end, support for an overall resolution of the dispute in the State's favor would be substantially weakened. While we certainly sympathized with the plight of the 5,000 or so defendants who would benefit by execution of the contract, approval would substantially strengthen the Power Company's hand going forward in the Legislature and weaken the State's ability to achieve a successful outcome in that arena and perhaps even in the ongoing litigation.

When the opinion request was disclosed in the press on September 11,[36] my office received an urgent call from Logan Lanham. Logan wanted to meet with me to discuss what legal advice might be forthcoming in the opinion. When Logan walked into the office, he was somewhat agitated and

---

35   Botka, Bruce. UPI. "Swan Falls panel wants users shielded." *Times News*, Sept. 2, 1983.
36   UPI. "AG asked to review Swan Falls contract." *Idaho Press-Tribune*, Sept. 11, 1983.

gave the clear impression of being on a mission. He first mentioned the opinion request and then expressed hope, possibly expectation, that the opinion would come out fairly, which I interpreted to be in favor of the constitutionality of the legislation and contract. Logan reminded me of the Power Company's contribution to my campaign during the general election contest in 1982. I recalled that a contribution in the amount of $500 had been made and wondered if that was expected to be the price of my fairness in the opinion. In any event, after a fairly short discussion I assured Logan that I would carefully monitor the project and make sure that the end product was legally sound. As Logan left, I had the feeling that there would soon be a parting of the ways.

I think it is fair to say that Logan misjudged me. I've had that happen occasionally because I'm not a naturally out-going person, don't have an imposing presence, and am a certifiable introvert. While Logan might be one of the first people you would notice when entering a crowded room, I would fall into the mid or lower range of noticeability. I think Logan had the impression he could push me around. However, I have a steely resolve and when I think I am right I will pursue it to the bitter end. Logan could not have influenced me away from my course of action even if he had applied rigorous waterboarding.

Four days later, Idaho Power tightened the screws on the defendants in Swan Falls II, sending them a letter urging that they contact Governor Evans to support the contract. The letter noted that as a result of the Supreme Court's decision, "the water rights of approximately 7,500 present and potential Snake River Basin water users have been placed under a cloud. These are individuals and groups whose water rights or potential water use are junior to and intrude upon Idaho Power's water rights." The letter indicated that the Company had filed Swan Falls II with the "greatest reluctance" in order to safeguard its Swan Falls water rights. It said that "to avoid just this sort of situation, Idaho Power asked for a law passed in the last Legislature that would protect you and other jeopardized water users." The law allowed for a contract that would protect existing water users, as well as protecting Idaho Power against complaints by ratepayers that it was not protecting its own water rights. The letter went on to say that "if Governor Evans signs the contract, your water right...will be protected and we will dismiss any challenge to that water right from our lawsuit. If the governor does not sign the contract, however, Idaho Power will have no choice but to proceed with its legal action." The letter warned that "some people for reasons of their own are urging the governor to delay signing the contract. We believe delay poses the prospect that you and Idaho Power will be in lengthy and expensive litigation during which our mutual water rights will be in jeopardy." The letter was a fairly persuasive call to action and it resulted in a number of pleas to the Governor to sign the proposed contract.

The next move came from Kent Foster, who filed a lawsuit on behalf of two water user families in eastern Idaho, challenging the constitutionality of Senate Bill 1180 and the 1180 Contract. He said the suit was filed because his clients were "worried that the signing of the contract would potentially adversely affect some of their water rights."[37] He claimed the Legislature had no authority to sanction the contract and that "the determination of water rights should lie with the judicial, not legislative branch."[38] We sent copies of the complaint to members of the Legislature on November 14, as well as to Idaho Power and Tom Nelson. I advised the Governor that in view of the litigation, it may not be proper for my office to proceed with the opinion.[39]

---

37   Anderson, Cindy. "Swan Falls suit may block Idaho Power contract." *Post-Register (Idaho Falls)*. Nov. 15, 1983.
38   Christensen, Steven. UPI. "Jones won't rule on water dispute." *Times News*, Nov. 15, 1983.
39   Christensen, Steven. UPI. "Jones won't rule on water dispute." *Times News*, Nov. 15, 1983.

The following day, I sent a letter to Governor Evans indicating that after considering the lawsuit, we concluded it would be inappropriate to issue an opinion on the contract since the matter was now squarely before the courts for determination. The letter said that because of the pending lawsuit "a constitutional cloud hangs over the Swan Falls contract and the authorizing legislation. It would be my advice that you refrain from taking any further action with respect to the contract until such time as the recently-instituted lawsuit is concluded." I suspected that Logan was thinking his $500 campaign contribution was misspent money.

On November 16 I told the press that my office intended to move forward with the litigation of Swan Falls I since the constitutional challenge effectively stymied a legislative solution for the time being. That same day Governor Evans said he would halt negotiations on the contract proposal, agreeing that no action should be taken while the lawsuit was pending.[40] The Governor indicated that the matter would be in the hands of the courts for at least a year.

At the same time the State was moving forward with the litigation in State court, the Water Resources attorneys were seeking relief in the federal arena. Since all of Idaho Power's dams on the Snake River were licensed by the Federal Energy Regulatory Commission, it was thought that the State could achieve its goal by inserting or retaining subordination conditions in the licenses for all of those dams. Some of the Company's power licenses did contain subordination conditions but others did not. As a result of the deal struck with regard to the Hells Canyon dams, the federal licenses for all of the dams upstream from the Hells Canyon complex should have contained subordination language. Either the Water Resources people had fallen down on the job or just thought that a hand-shake deal was all that was needed.

One of the FERC licenses that did not have a subordination condition was for Idaho Power's generating

40   Botka, Bruce. UPI. "Suit tangles water dispute." *Times News,* Nov. 17, 1983.

facility at Twin Falls, the falls after which the City of Twin Falls was named. That facility was up for relicensing and the Water Resources attorneys were petitioning for intervention in the FERC relicensing proceeding in order to pursue a subordination condition. On November 18, I notified Governor Evans of that fact and of the fact that Idaho Power was opposing the State's petition. The Company was telling FERC that water rights at the dam, including priority, should be handled and decided under State law, rather than by Federal action.

The subordination issue heated up as the 1984 session of the Legislature approached. In addition to the public education effort being pursued by Idaho Power, groups of water users, particularly defendants in Swan Falls II, were meeting to discuss their options. Elaine Martin of Jerome, one of about 200 defendants at a meeting in Idaho Falls, characterized the Swan Falls II suit as "good politics," devised to minimize opposition to the Power Company in the court proceedings.[41] Martin said that she and her husband had mailed letters to other defendants and could find only 4,000 who might be affected by the suit, some of whom owned less than an acre of irrigated land. Her contention was that the contract was only a band-aid and not an effective cure.

At the same time, Logan Lanham announced that the Power Company had a new legislative fix that would supersede that contained in S.B. 1180. The new proposal would provide protection to Idaho Power from complaints by ratepayers that it was not protecting its water rights, which would then result in Idaho Power dismissing its claim against the 5,000 defendants without the necessity for a contract with the State. Logan contended that the new measure would avert three years or more of litigation, during which "irrigators will be held hostage by the dispute, unable to get bank loans

---

41   Zellar, Ron. "Idaho Power plan called way to end water-rights case." *Idaho Statesman,* Nov. 30, 1983.

or sell their farms."[42] The obvious intent was to bypass the requirement for the Governor's approval that was contained in S.B. 1180.

In the lead-up to the new legislative session, Idaho Power stoked up a public relations campaign contending that subordination of its Swan Falls water right would result in substantial rate increases for its customers. It cited the previously-mentioned preliminary study prepared by a staff member of the Public Utilities Commission, estimating a potential annual rate increase of $54 million, requiring a 17 percent across-the-board rate increase. My response was that we had all assumed since the Hells Canyon deal in the mid-50s that the Company's water rights at Swan Falls were fully subordinated and that this had not had any apparent effect on power rates for about 30 years. Why would there be a change on into the future? The Power Company also indicated that with a steadily increasingly need for power, cheap hydropower was essential for keeping its rates down. If the State limited the Company's use of water to generate power, it would have to build more expensive coal-fired plants to serve the increased demand for electricity. Fortuitously, however, just at that time a representative of the Bonneville Power Administration advised a group of Pacific Northwest energy experts meeting at Washington State University that the area was "confronted with energy surpluses well into the next decade." He said, "It's a very unsettling bit of information to the people in the business of load forecasting."[43] So much for the need of more coal-fired plants and higher rates.

For his part, Governor Evans was laying out the need for water users and the general public to support comprehensive water planning. He told a meeting of the Idaho Water Users Association in Idaho Falls that, "We must accept the fact that increased water management is absolutely necessary."

---

42   Zellar, Ron. "Idaho Power plan called way to end water-rights case." *Idaho Statesman*, Nov. 30, 1983.
43   Beck, Janet Parker. "Surplus energy creates problem for forecasting Northwest needs." *Lewiston Tribune*, Dec. 1, 1983.

He said the 1180 Contract "only addresses existing uses and does not address the problem of new consumptive uses."[44] In order to better manage Idaho's water resources, the Governor recommended "an adjudication study to be undertaken to fully define all existing water rights in the Snake River drainage. The study will be a monumental task but one that will only become more difficult and less accurate if delayed." He said it was important to address "the critical issue of ground water administration, as more and more wells are drilled and water levels in the aquifer will drop affecting both ground water and surface water supplies...and to evaluate the levels of efficiency of the systems using water."[45] These comments presaged the subsequent Snake River Basin Adjudication and the State's decision to conjunctively manage ground and surface water.

My public comments were addressed primarily to getting the Swan Falls dispute resolved through court proceedings, rather than the Legislature. It was apparent that Idaho Power was preparing for a legislative fight in hopes of limiting the scope of any further court proceedings. Governor Evans and I were working on our own legislative fix but we were inclined to keep our powder dry until the Legislature went into session in January.

In addressing the Idaho Water Users Association convention in Idaho Falls, I said that the only way a truly definitive resolution could be reached was through aggressive pursuit of Swan Falls I and that I would be seeking funding for two additional lawyers and a paralegal during the next session to work on the litigation.[46]

At that same meeting Ken Dunn picked up the Governor's theme about the necessity for an adjudication of Snake River water rights, asserting that "we are dealing

44   "Water issues vital to state, Evans says." *Post-Register,* Dec. 8, 1983.
45   "Water issues vital to state, Evans says." *Post-Register,* Dec. 8, 1983.
46   Retallic, Ken. "State gets aggressive on Swan Falls resolution." *Post-Register,* Dec. 9, 1983.

with a finite supply of water." He indicated that "improved water management, better use of existing storage, and a better knowledge of the Snake River watershed is the future of Idaho."[47]

Meanwhile, Clive prepared talking points for Pat Kole on Swan Falls litigation for presentation to a December 12 meeting of the Legislature's interim study committee. The talking points were designed to derail Idaho Power's legislative fix—S.B. 1180 and the recently-announced new version. The talking points noted that the legislation was a poorly conceived band-aid for a complex issue and that it mislead citizens into believing that it resolved the Swan Falls dispute, giving them a false sense of security. More importantly, he argued:

> By dismissing those individuals with the strongest claim from the pending litigation, the state may be throwing out the baby with the bathwater. As noted previously, the contract does not resolve the controversy. There remains an issue as to individuals who have not made a substantial investment in their permits and as to future development. Under the contract, future use of Snake River water is largely left unresolved. Thus, if the state is to gain any control over the water for future generations, the remand case must be successful. Yet as mentioned, if only weak defendants are left, this will be impossible. Idaho Power would then control the future for our state. This is in direct conflict with the mandate of the constitution, which requires that the waters of the state be made available to all citizens for beneficial use.

On the other hand, pursuing Swan Falls I would provide a basis for resolving the dispute in its entirety. The

---

47   Retallic, Ken. "State gets aggressive on Swan Falls resolution." *Post-Register, Dec. 9, 1983.*

Supreme Court introduced unacceptable uncertainty into the matter by holding that the Power Company's water right was not subordinated. Numerous defenses had been presented by the State and they held a good deal of promise for success. In fact, in his 1976 memorandum to the Power Company brass, Tom Nelson had opined that the junior water users would likely prevail on the estoppel issue — that because Idaho Power had long acquiesced in the use by upstream junior water right holders of waters it now claimed under the Supreme Court's decision, it may well be precluded from asserting a priority claim.

The problem with the estoppel defense is that it would not apply to new water users — new agricultural users, companies needing water for industrial uses, municipalities needing expanded supplies, and so on. Without a subordination decision in favor of the State, those issues would have to be addressed by subsequent legislation. Another thing that caused concern regarding the litigation was the fact that the Supreme Court would be the ultimate decider. Where it had gone so far afield in its Swan Falls I decision, there was concern that it would do likewise with respect to any appeal of a district court decision on the remand. However, that is something we would only have to worry about if we could not obtain a victory in our favor in the Legislature.

The interim study committee also heard from the Twin Falls City manager, who said that Twin Falls and other cities upstream would have difficulty recruiting industries until the Swan Falls dispute was resolved. He said the Swan Falls conflict prevented the City of Twin Falls from obtaining a crucial water permit that was needed to help convince Stouffer Food Corporation to build a major plant in Twin Falls. The city manager said that when the City could not get the permit, the Governor's office urged that the City negotiate an agreement with Idaho Power but that the utility would not sign any written agreement.[48]

Apparently, I had not yet been written off as a lost cause by Idaho Power because I received a nice box of tasty Lee's Chocolates from the Company for Christmas. On December 20, I dropped a note to Greg Panter thanking him for his thoughtfulness. That would be my last Christmas gift from Logan.

The Christmas cheer apparently wore off in a matter of ten days because on December 30 I informed the press that Idaho Power quietly applied to almost double its water right at the Swan Falls Dam as part of an effort to expand the dam's generating capacity. The application for 16,000 cubic feet of water per second at the dam, almost double the 8,400 cfs discovered in the Swan Falls decision, had been filed in March of 1982. My staff learned of the filing around the first of December while researching the Swan Falls issue. We were concerned that Idaho Power said nothing about this significant expansion in the 1983 legislative session. Logan told the press that the failure to mention the filing "wasn't intentional." I remarked, "It's something that's a little large to slip somebody's mind." I noted that had the legislators been made aware of the application during the 1983 session, "It could have had some influence on how people looked at the subordination issue." Senator Noh agreed that the application "should have been called to legislative attention." He said the application "indicates Idaho Power probably does intend to move as quickly as it can and as efficiently as it can to sew up all the additional water in the river."[49]

The Idaho Statesman did a nice wrap-up of the Swan Falls issue in an end-of-the-year piece published on December 31:[50]

The complex legal battle over water in the Snake

---

48   Bernton, Hal. "Issue clouded Stouffer bid." *Times News*, Dec. 13, 1983.

49   Stevenson, Mary. Associated Press. "Jones raps silence on Swan Falls application." *Idaho Statesman*, Dec. 31, 1983.

50   "Water-rights battle rages on." *Idaho Statesman*. Dec. 31, 1983.

River became even more complicated in 1983, when lawyers started numbering the cases Swan Falls I, Swan Falls II, Swan Falls III.

Attorney General Jim Jones was up to Swan Falls V at last count. New cases seemed to be sprouting like branches from a tree recently trimmed.

The Idaho Legislature approved a compromise in April to narrow the scope of the dispute by removing several thousand defendants. But the legislation itself became the subject of a suit in November.

The case started in 1977 when a group of Idaho Power customers asked the Idaho Public Utilities Commission for damages, contending that the utility raised its rates to build coal-fueled generating plants while failing to protect the water rights for cheaper hydroelectric plants.

An Idaho Power suit filed in response to the challenge named 29 defendants, prompting lawyers to refer to the case as "Idaho Power against the world."

But the number of people involved grew since an Idaho Supreme Court ruling Nov. 19, 1982. The court said Idaho Power did not give up its water rights in the 1950s when the utility agreed to allow water for other uses to gain the right to build three power dams in Hells Canyon.

In response, Idaho Power filed suit in April against an estimated 7,500 water permits, arguing that the irrigators, municipalities and businesses all use water that belongs to the utility.

Gov. John Evans said he will ask the 1984 Legislature for $796,000 for the first year of a multiyear study to settle who owns how much water in the Snake River Basin.

Even so, the case is likely to keep lawyers busy for

at least a few more years, Jones said.

Things were just getting warmed up.

A HOT JANUARY IN BOISE

1984 started with a bang. On January 3, I wrote Governor Evans to advise him that the Power Company caused the removal of a subordination provision from the FERC license for the Upper Salmon Project located on the Snake River upstream from Swan Falls just two years before the Supreme Court's Swan Falls decision. The letter informed the Governor:

> You should be aware that one of my staff attorneys has recently made a surprising and disconcerting discovery with regard to the Snake River water rights issue. As you know, my central office assumed responsibility for all Swan Falls and related water litigation several months ago. In connection with our assumption of that responsibility, my staff has devoted considerable time to the issue of subordinating non-consumptive power company water rights to up-stream commercial, industrial, domestic and agricultural usages. Certainly there is no issue which has greater implications for the future development of all of southern Idaho.
>
> During the research effort, one of my attorneys has learned that Idaho Power Company was successful in quietly removing a subordination provision from the Upper Salmon Project license. A renewal license for the Upper Salmon Project was issued to Idaho Power Company on June 13, 1979. Article 29 of the license provided as follows:
>
> > The project shall be operated in a manner that will not conflict with the future depletion in flow of the wa-

ters of Snake River and its tributaries, or prevent or interfere with the future upstream diversion and use of such water, above the backwater created by the project, for the irrigation of lands and other beneficial consumptive uses in the Snake River watershed.

Sometime after the license was issued, Idaho Power Company filed an application for rehearing seeking, among other things, the deletion of Article 29. The Federal Energy Regulatory Commission took the matter under advisement and on July 24, 1981, issued an amended license which deleted the subordination clause in Article 29.

It is surprising that the subordination clause was deleted and especially so because FERC did not have the benefit of the State's input on the matter. We are currently trying to determine why the State did not intervene in the proceeding—whether notice of the application for amendment was not received or whether the State's interests were not represented through inadvertence. We are exploring the options the State may have with respect to obtaining some redress or remedial action. We are also checking to see whether the power company has taken similar action with respect to other projects on the Snake River. When there is additional information to report, I shall be in touch with you again.

We circulated copies of the letter to the press, resulting in an article headlined "Discovery of IP water-use clause deletion stuns AG."[51] I'm not sure that I was stunned, but certainly disconcerted. The article referenced my letter to Governor Evans and said the Attorney General "was considering taking action to have the clause reinstated

---

51   UPI. "Discovery of IP water-use clause deletion stuns AG." *Idaho Press-Tribune*, Jan. 5, 1984.

because he believes water for power-generating purposes should be subordinated to allow for multiple water uses." It included my quote: "I think that as a policy matter, all power-generating facilities should have their water rights subordinated. We should have multiple use of the water— for farms, industry. That's the way it always has been." The article continued, "Larry Taylor, an Idaho Power spokesman, said the clause was deleted from the FERC license to prevent a technical conflict with another provision of the detailed permit. And he said the subordination clause had no affect on any action the State may take on subordinating water rights." This was certainly an interesting take on the matter.

Governor Evans and I met on January 4, to discuss legislation that we would jointly propose to subordinate Idaho Power's Swan Falls water right. Based on the almost evenly divided votes on competing Swan Falls proposals in the last session, we thought that there was a reasonable chance of success for our side. Now that the water user community had had an opportunity to consider the flaws in S.B. 1180, they might call upon their respective legislators to join the subordination effort. We agreed to finalize our legislative proposal for announcement later in the month. Laird and Vard were on board with this approach and would be sponsoring the legislation in their respective chambers.

Senator Noh was busy spreading the word about the Power Company's efforts to free their dams upstream of Swan Falls from any hint of subordination language. Days before the start of the 1984 legislative session, he spoke to an agribusiness seminar in Idaho Falls, urging attendees to get involved in the political process.[52] According to the newspaper report, after addressing the need to move forward with the Swan Falls I case, Laird said "Idaho Power is making other moves concerning permits and rights at its Upper Salmon and

52   Menser, Paul. "Eastern Idaho farmers told representation begins at home." *Post-Register*, Jan. 6, 1984.

Shoshone Falls dams. New federal permits have no language concerning subordination." The article continues:

> "They're obviously moving very rapidly to consolidate their power in the Snake River drainage," he added. "The Federal Energy Regulatory Commission has done nothing."
>
> Noh said he feels Idaho Power wants rights to all the water in the Snake River. "I personally believe that Idaho Power means to get power over the water, derive the maximum amount of profit from a scarce commodity. . .then pass that profit on to its board of directors, who can then move to build a coal-fired plant, and pass the cost on to the ratepayers." He said whether or not that happens, "eventually we're going to run out of water in the river. We've got to know how to manage it."

During his presentation, Laird addressed another problem for our side of the issue—lack of awareness of the implications of the Swan Falls fight outside of the agricultural community, particularly in the urban areas. According to the Post-Register article:[53]

> The Idaho Water Resource Board held six hearings last summer, and while interest grew steadily as they progressed downriver, "people in the urban areas didn't even understand. The Idaho Statesman was reluctant to run stories on it, simply because it was an issue its readers wouldn't understand," Noh said.
>
> Noh said 20 percent of the state's population now lives in Ada County, and if they don't understand the issue, their representation in the legislature will be as

---

53   Menser, Paul. "Eastern Idaho farmers told representation begins at home." *Post-Register,* Jan. 6, 1984.

vague. If farmers want their interests represented, they
will have to define and push for them.

"You can see here the importance of politics in agriculture...how times change much more than how
crops grow. It's frustrating when legislators say 'I
don't know how to vote, so many of the teams have
shifted.'"

Laird correctly noted that for an issue of such importance
to the future of the State there had not been a great deal of
press coverage about it. That was largely a function of the
complicated nature of the dispute. The press coverage to date
had largely played it as a fight between farmers on the one
hand and the Power Company and its ratepayers on the other.
Those outside of the agriculture community were generally
unaware that the outcome of the fight might well affect them.
If Idaho Power gained effective control of the Snake River,
the State would not be in a position to properly plan for the
future development of farms, businesses, and communities
in the Snake River Basin. The Power Company could object
to any new application for a water right for any purpose, be
it agricultural, domestic, municipal, or governmental, all the
way up to Milner Dam near Murtaugh and perhaps beyond.
In order to move forward, any water right applicant would
have to reach an accommodation with the Power Company,
which would certainly be profitable from its standpoint. But
that would not be to the State's benefit. It was important
to get this message across and to let people know that the
State would do a better job of overseeing the development of
southern Idaho than a privately-owned entity, motivated by
profit rather than the public interest. If the voters were not
happy with the manner in which the State operated the river,
they could throw the bums out. That would not happen with
a private entity, even a public utility.

Even those in the water community did not fully understand the implications of the dispute or the necessity to become involved to affect its outcome. Ray Rigby was also busy on the speaking circuit, urging water users to "get their feet wet" and lobby for water rights.[54] He said the Swan Falls dispute is "challenging rights of all water users up and down the Snake River plain," and that they all needed to get involved to resolve the issue.

On January 6 the Water Users Association directors met to consider the Swan Falls issue. Logan Lanham and Greg Panter urged support for the new legislation that would provide relief for the 5,000 or so defendants in Swan Falls II, without the necessity of a contract. They advised that the bill would be presented during the first week of the legislative session. I, of course, urged opposition to the legislation, indicating that it would not be in the State's best interests and that the only viable solution was allowing the matter to be resolved in further court proceedings in Swan Falls I. The directors endorsed the Power Company's proposal by a 6-4 vote.[55] We hoped for a strong majority of the directors to oppose the new legislation. The outcome was a disappointment and an indication that it would be an uphill fight to win the hearts and minds of the water using community.

Governor Evans kicked off the start of the 1984 legislative session with an announcement that he would support the recommendations made by his Swan Falls Task Force, including: moving forward expeditiously with Swan Falls I; seeking additional appropriations to fund legal and technical expertise to litigate that case; retaining subordination as a viable option; not signing the contract and supporting the repeal of S.B. 1180; and supporting an adjudication of the Snake River, funded by water user fees.

For my part, I held a press conference to announce

54   Anderson, Cindy. "Irrigators told to fight for rights in Swan Falls case." *Post-Register,* Jan. 4, 1984.
55   Gallagher, Susan. Associated Press. "Water plan backed." *Times-News,* Jan. 7, 1984.

that my staff learned of another FERC license from which the Power Company had successfully deleted a subordination provision. At a press conference in my office on January 11, I announced "that Idaho Power Company quietly removed a subordination provision from the Shoshone Falls Project license in 1981." The Shoshone Falls Project is located on a spectacular waterfall several miles upstream from the City of Twin Falls.

My press release said, "It appears that this is a part of a coordinated effort by the utility to consolidate its control of Snake River water rights. Idaho Power has been quite successful in frustrating the State's policy of subordinating water rights for power generation to up-stream consumptive uses of water such as industrial, agriculture, and domestic."

The renewal license for the Shoshone Falls project was issued to Idaho Power on June 13, 1979. Article 39 of the license provided:

> The project shall be operated in a manner that will not conflict with the future deletion in flow of the waters of Snake River and its tributaries, or prevent or interfere with the future upstream diversion and use of such water, above the backwater created by the project, for the irrigation of land and other beneficial consumptive uses in the Snake River watershed.

Sometime after the license was issued, Idaho Power filed an application for rehearing seeking, among other things, the deletion of Article 39. FERC took the matter under advisement and on January 23, 1981, issued an amended license that deleted the subordination clause in Article 39. I mentioned that the State had no apparent notice of the rehearing, that the State had not had the opportunity to give its input, and that we were exploring options the State may have with respect to obtaining remedial action. I also let the press know that my office was drafting legislation to address the Swan Falls issue.

This press conference initiated a new procedure on the part of Idaho Power. From this point on, a power company representative, generally Logan Lanham or Greg Panter, would attend my press conferences on the Swan Falls issue, listen attentively, sometimes record my remarks on tape, and then take the floor afterwards to give their side of the issue. I felt I was being dogged by a flying "truth" squad, but it was just becoming part of a day's work. An attorney from the Company attended the Shoshone Falls press conference and, immediately following my presentation, took the floor to give the company's side of the issues. Although it was my office, the lawyer was a nice fellow, a competent lawyer, and entitled to present his company's position in a public building, so I didn't throw him out.

The in-house attorney, Nick Ysursa, said the Company's actions in the FERC proceedings were proper and that the subordination conditions were removed because "the State—not the federal government—has jurisdiction over water rights, and that the deleted clauses would have contradicted other portions of the licenses."[56] Here, Ysursa was speaking of both the Shoshone Falls and Upper Salmon Project licenses.

I made my budget presentation to the Joint Finance-Appropriations Committee on January 11. In addition to asking for $100,000 for two additional lawyers and a paralegal starting in the upcoming fiscal year, I asked for immediate funding for the attorneys so that we could build up our Swan Falls litigation team. This brought a torrent of questions from the Senate co-chair of the Committee, Senator David Little of Emmett, a Power Company supporter. He questioned why the State should put up money to fund a

56   Zellar, Ron. "Attorney general to draft Swan Falls legislation." *Idaho Statesman*, Jan. 12, 1984.

litigation effort that would primarily benefit irrigators above Swan Falls. He contended that the State's litigation posture did not protect the rights of many western Idaho water users and taxpayers below Swan Falls.[57] My response was that Idaho Power had substantially more financial resources available to litigate Swan Falls I and that the State's efforts were hampered by limited research and personnel funds. "You can debate the merits of the issue, but no one should debate that the state should be fairly represented in its efforts to fight Idaho Power's (attempt) to take over the river." The exchange became somewhat heated, but there were a number of committee members who appeared to be supportive. I was told that Logan and Greg Panter were working hard behind the scenes to generate opposition to the funding request.

I also made an appearance before the Senate Resources and Environment Committee on January 11 and warned that failure to subordinate the Swan Falls water right would not only hurt agriculture but also impede upstream development of industries dependent on adequate water sources. I pointed out that this applied to a new nuclear project that people in Idaho Falls were attempting to get located at the Idaho National Engineering Laboratory, the large and sprawling nuclear facility located west of Idaho Falls.[58]

That same day, Ken Dunn said that his department was unaware of Idaho Power's requests to remove the subordination conditions from the Shoshone Falls and Upper Salmon Project FERC licenses because the State was not on the notice list, not having been a party to the original licensing proceedings. Ken correctly stated that, had those provisions not been deleted from the licenses, they would have effectively acted to subordinate Idaho Power's water rights for those projects to upstream uses. Idaho Power's spokesman, Larry Taylor, responded that since the two projects obtained vested

---

57   Marks, Ellen. UPI. "Jim Jones' 52% budget-hike request questioned." *Idaho Statesman*, Jan. 14, 1984.
58   Associated Press. "Jones Says Swan Falls Flap Could Affect NPR." *Idaho State Journal*, Jan. 12, 1984.

State water rights before they came under federal licensing requirements, the FERC licensing subordination clauses didn't apply.[59] This contention, however, did not take into the account the deal that Governor Jordan made with Idaho Power to subordinate all of its water rights upstream of the Hells Canyon dams.

Like the City of Twin Falls, the City of Jerome encountered difficulty in expanding its municipal water supply for domestic and business purposes. A Times-News reporter, Bonnie Baird Jones, wrote that the City applied for pumping rights for additional water for an upgrade to the City's water system and drilled a well for that purpose, but had been unable to get a water permit because of the moratorium imposed as a result of the Supreme Court's Swan Falls decision.[60] The moratorium affected municipal as well as agricultural and industrial uses.

With the Legislature now in session, practically each day brought a new wrinkle to the fight. On January 13, Senator Noh wrote me to say that Idaho Power had imposed a deadline for the enactment of a potential legislative solution to the Swan Falls problem. Mark Thompson, the chief of my Administrative Law and Litigation Division, responded to Laird with remarkable dispatch that same day, saying "As I understand the Company's position, it is claiming that, in order to avoid dismissal of its complaint, it must obtain service of process on all of the parties in the Swan Falls II litigation, and incur substantial attendant costs, before the end of February. Idaho Power has, therefore, indicated that any legislative action must occur before February 1."

Mark noted that although a civil procedure rule called for dismissal of cases where no action had taken for a period of one year, any dismissal would be without prejudice and dismissal could be avoided if the plaintiff demonstrated good

59   Kenyon, Quane. Associated Press. "Legislature Resumes Action on Planned Swan Falls Measures." *Idaho State Journal,* Jan. 12, 1984.
60   Jones, Bonnie Baird. "City has new well, but no water right." *Times-News,* Jan. 11, 1984.

cause. He opined that with the exceptionally large number of defendants and the attendant cost of serving them with process, "it appears likely that Idaho Power would have little difficulty in convincing the district court that there is sufficient cause for its delay in pursuing service of process." He concluded: "In view of the nature of this action and the ongoing efforts to reach a legislative resolution, it is highly unlikely that the district court would dismiss the matter for want of prosecution. However, even should such a dismissal take place, the Company could then refile the same lawsuit with little inconvenience." This was just another effort to tighten the screws, both on the Legislature and on the defendants in Swan Falls II. Despite our letter to Senator Noh, the Power Company continued to use the threat of serving the 7,500 defendants and requiring them to come into court to defend as a means of promoting its legislation.

That same day, the Idaho Statesman published an article wherein Governor Evans accused Idaho Power of "deceiving the state by secretly asking the Federal Energy Regulatory Commission to remove a restrictive clause from the license on two of its Snake River power plants."[61] Rod Gramer reported that, "Evans said it appeared to him that Idaho Power was attempting to tighten its control over water rights on the Snake River." Those remarks were made at a January 12, meeting of the Idaho Press Club. The Governor criticized FERC for not notifying the State about Idaho Power's request to remove the subordination conditions from the licenses and for not notifying Idaho's congressional delegation. Larry Taylor, responding on behalf of Idaho Power, said that the Company followed FERC's procedures in asking for the elimination of the clauses and that "the company could have put up billboards and bought television ads announcing its intentions, but people would not have cared because they

---

61   Gramer, Rod. "Evans accuses Idaho Power on Snake rights." *Idaho Statesman,* Jan. 13, 1984.

were not interested in water rights at the time. 'I don't know how much more we could be expected to do.'"

My thought was that billboards and television ads were not particularly necessary but that a one-page document might have sufficed to provide notice to the State that the licenses were to be denuded of any vestige of subordination.

Also during his Press Club presentation, Governor Evans expressed support for my pursuit of the water rights fight in the courts, calling it "the most appropriate and proper direction."[62] He said, "I don't think there is any way in the world Idaho Power can [support] its position of not subordinating its interest to upstream development. In the end we'll see those rights subordinated to upstream development. It can't happen any other way."

An editorial that appeared that same day in the Idaho State Journal exemplified the problem that the Governor and I were facing.[63] The Journal had the impression that the fight was only between Idaho Power and its ratepayers and a few fat cat farmers. The editor wrote:

> Attorney General Jim Jones was right — up to a point. He was right when he said earlier this week Idaho Power has acted properly in protecting its interests in the battle over water rights at the Swan Falls Dam; the company, according to recent court decisions, owns both the rights and the dam.
>
> He was also on target when he said the water rights of current water users — including farmers and municipalities — below the dam must be protected, and that legislation is needed to accomplish that. Even Idaho Power doesn't quarrel with that.
>
> But then he said Idaho Power's interests in protecting its water rights conflict with public need of water

62   Associated Press. "Evans vows to win Swan Falls battle." *Post-Register*, Jan. 13, 1984.

63   "In Whose Interest?" *Idaho State Journal*, Jan. 13, 1984.

for many uses…

Wait a minute.

The real conflict, in practice if not necessarily in theory, is between Idaho Power — including its rate-payers throughout Southern Idaho, who would pay drastically higher power bills if the utility lost its water rights — and a few people who want to develop additional irrigated agricultural acreage, which would tie up vast amounts of precious water.

Jones should bear that in mind and take a second look at where the state's real interest lies.

As the editor noted, I said the Power Company was acting properly in protecting its interests. If a court had given me a wonderful gift like the Snake River, I would certainly have felt justified in fighting hard to keep it. That did not mean, however, that I approved of the Power Company's attempt to wriggle out of the deal it struck with Governor Jordan to subordinate all of its water rights above the Hells Canyon complex. The second paragraph of the editorial was dead wrong in assuming that the Swan Falls fight involved protection of current water users below Swan Falls. The fight had nothing to do with water rights held by those below Swan Falls. It had everything to do with those holding water rights upstream from Swan Falls. It was fairly clear to me that the editor lacked a basic understanding of what was at issue in the fight.

Not being one to bypass the opportunity to respond to a wrong-headed editorial, I fired back with a guest opinion that the Journal was kind enough to print.[64]

Your editorial of January 13 evidenced a serious misconception of the Swan Falls issue. The issue is

---

64   The guest opinion was sent to the Journal on January 18 and appeared in its January 29 issue.

whether the State of Idaho or Idaho Power Company is going to control the Snake River. This is not a fight between irrigators and rate payers but, rather, a dispute between Idaho Power Company and the people of Idaho as to who will control Idaho's future development.

If Idaho Power Company has the right to an undiminished flow of 8400 cubic feet per second through its Swan Falls generating facility, industrial, agricultural and commercial development in southern Idaho will be effectively stymied. The state's long-standing policy of using its water resources for multiple purposes will have been frustrated. A single company will have been allowed to essentially lock up one of Idaho's most valuable resources — the Snake River.

The stakes are huge, both for the state's economic wellbeing and for Idaho Power's economic fortunes. Your December 13 issue reported the difficulties which the City of Twin Falls had encountered in attracting a very desirable industry. Stouffer's Food Corp. had been looking at Twin Falls as a potential site for a food processing plant which would employ 1500 people. Twin Falls City manager Tom Courtney told a legislative committee that Stouffers decided to locate in Springville, Utah, in part because of better water availability. Idaho Power's apparent control over the Snake River was an important factor in discouraging this plant which would have provided much employment, tax base, and income and sales tax revenue to the people of Idaho. Stouffers would have been a perfect industry for location in Idaho so that we could turn raw agricultural products into finished food products through the labors of many Idaho workers. Because of the Swan Falls problem we can expect a similar fate for other industries which may wish to locate in Idaho but which may be discouraged because of the non-availability of water.

The power company has been painting the most dismal picture possible for rate payers in order to bolster its case. However, there is no assurance that electric rates will be substantially boosted if Idaho Power ultimately loses the Swan Falls case. Idaho Power's assertion that there would be a $57 million rate increase in the event that it loses its apparent unsubordinated rights at Swan Falls assumes that there would be some increase in demand for electricity. If the industrial and agricultural development of southern Idaho is brought to a standstill because of the unavailability of water, there will be no need for additional electricity to serve Idahoans and no need for a rate increase. Further, there is no reason why future applications for water rights should not take into account their potential impact on availability of water for generation of hydropower. In other words, a balanced approach to utilization of our water resources can and should be enacted through the legislative process and such appropriate action would prevent unwarranted impact on electrical rates.

The fact is that it is in the benefit of all persons in the state to have a balanced program for utilization of our water resources. To lock up a substantial portion of our water solely for generation of electricity makes no sense. If 8400 cubic feet per second of water were to be run through the generators at Swan Falls it would flow out of the State of Idaho to be pounced on by downstream states or possibly California. Idaho would become a no-growth state with no water to allow expansion of cities and towns or to allow growth of industry which would provide jobs and tax base or to allow additional (but orderly) enhancement of agri-

cultural production. The State of Idaho must win the
battle with Idaho Power Company so that the multiple
use concept can be continued with respect to our vitally important Snake River.

Channel 7 in Boise (KTVB) interviewed me on January
13 for its Viewpoint program that would run the following
Sunday. The program was a favorite of political junkies in
the State Capitol and provided an opportunity to do some
educational work. I said that if there was not enough water
in Southern Idaho for both hydroelectric generation and
future farm and industrial development, the use of water for
electricity should take a back seat. "We can't find alternatives
to having drinking water, water for irrigation, or to run
our processing plants. But Idaho Power has alternatives for
generating power. The question is, should we let the utility
run the southern half of the state of Idaho, or should we let
the state run it? It is in our best interests to have a growing,
robust economy, not one directed by Idaho Power."[65]
    Little brushfires of conflict continued to break out in
a variety of places. On January 16, Kent Foster announced
that he had resigned from the Governor's Swan Falls Task
Force on January 2, two days after Jim Bruce sent a letter to
the Governor questioning Kent's participation because of a
conflict of interest. The letter also questioned Ray Rigby's
chairmanship of the Task Force on the same grounds. The
letter asked "whether lawyers hired to represent litigants in
the pending lawsuits can render effective, unbiased advice,
given their monetary and professional ties to the point of view
of their clients."[66] Foster contended Idaho Power's stand was
"a little bit like the pot trying to call the kettle black," noting
that the Power Company saw nothing wrong with exerting
its influence at State meetings and hearings on the Swan Falls

65   Associated Press. "Development More Important Than Electricity, Says Jones." *Idaho State Journal,* Jan. 13, 1984.
66   Associated Press. "Utility's Stand 'Like Pot Calling Kettle Black'
– Foster." *Idaho State Journal,* Jan. 17, 1984.

issue and even funded a technical study for the State's use. The Governor's attorney, Pat Costello, indicated he thought Foster's position on the task force might give the appearance of impropriety but he saw no problem with regard to Ray Rigby's position.

Idaho Power's new legislation gained approval in the House State Affairs Committee on January 19. Normally, the legislation would have gone to Representative Chatburn's House Resources and Conservation Committee. Vard mentioned that the bill probably would not have been approved had it been brought to his committee.[67] Vard said the proposal was not acceptable to him because it did not subordinate the Swan Falls water right to upstream consumptive uses. "I hope we have a better piece of legislation that will take this bill's place. The bill I'm hopeful will be presented will include a benefit for ratepayers and subordination."

In addition to granting Idaho Power protection from ratepayer actions in Public Utilities Commission proceedings, and dismissing water users from Swan Falls II who began using water before the Supreme Court decision as well as those who had made substantial investments toward that end, the new legislation would exempt domestic and non-consumptive commercial, industrial and municipal uses from Idaho Power's priority claims.

My comments on the bill were that it was vague, that it inappropriately tried to establish legislative intent with a letter written by the Power Company, and that language in the legislation attempted to establish as a fact that the Swan Falls right had priority over upstream water users—a matter that was yet to be determined in Swan Falls I. I mentioned that an Evans-Jones proposal was being drafted to deal with the question of the conflicting water needs of power generators and irrigators. "What we're working on...offers a solution to

67   Shaughnessy, Rick. "Bill may free Idaho Power from Swan Falls litigation." *Times-News*, Jan. 19, 1984.

get this entire matter resolved and not have loopholes and strings hanging out that might come back to haunt us."[68]

The hostilities between my office and the Power Company were taking a toll on my relationship with some of my political supporters. On January 19, I wrote a letter to Barbara Panter in Thatcher, Idaho, who wrote to question why I would side with Governor Evans, a Democrat, in opposing the Power Company where her son worked. Her son was Greg Panter, Logan's sidekick. I said that the Governor was on the right side of the issue, a position shared by former Senator Len Jordan, a Republican. "I suspect a part of my strong feelings on the issue were fostered by my association with Len Jordan. He, also, strongly believed that the State, and not a utility, should control the destiny of Idaho. It was only after he thought he had extracted that agreement that he allowed Idaho Power Company to build the three Hells Canyon dams. I find it rather ironic that I should be one of the people involved in the effort to carry out the deal that he thought he made with the power company." Barbara and her husband, Ron, had been good supporters in my campaign for Attorney General. They rounded up a horse for me to ride through a parade in the City of Grace during the campaign. It was one of the few parade horses people provided me that was not skittish and inclined to buck. They were good people. Barbara later wrote a more pointed letter saying that I was treating Greg unfairly, to which I made a more pointed response that permanently severed any relationship.

That evening, I drove down to Bliss to deliver a broadside against the Power Company. I told the Gooding County Farm Bureau that, "They (Idaho Power) are going to use every legal means at their disposal to gain a stranglehold on the Snake River," and that the fight is not between customers of the utility and irrigators but, rather, "a struggle between Idaho Power and the people of Idaho for control over the

---

68   Stevenson, Mary. Associated Press. "Idaho Power plan would drop some Swan Falls defendants." *Idaho Statesman,* Jan. 19, 1984.

Snake River."[69] According to the newspaper report, I "painted a picture of a quiet—and somewhat sinister—effort by Idaho Power to flaunt state policy by obtaining unrestricted water rights for many of its power plants in southern Idaho," and said that "to date, Idaho Power is winning its battle against the state, but...the battle is just beginning."

The article reported another aspect of the dispute that my office was considering:

> Jones also said that he may have discovered a new legal bargaining chip to use in his battle against Idaho Power.
>
> According to the attorney general, the state has been granted ownership of the riverbeds of all navigable waters in Idaho by the federal government. Thus, he views the state government as a landlord who has allowed Idaho Power the use of the Snake River's bottom without asking for any rent or imposing any restrictions.
>
> "If they have put dams on our property without first obtaining our permission, they may just be in a world of hurt," Jones said.
>
> Idaho Power might decide that it is better to agree to restrict its water rights rather than risk possible eviction from the state-owned riverbed, he said.

I have to admit that my office had not spent a lot of time working on this theory of relief, but it did have some surface appeal and gave the Power Company an additional problem to think about. The article said that Logan responded by lashing out at me for "trying to use the police powers of the state" to restrict Idaho Power's water rights. "If the state will take our property away, what are they going to do to yours?"

---

69   Bernton, Hal. "Jones: Utility wants a stranglehold on river." *Times-News*, Jan. 21, 1984.

The concerns being raised by the Governor and myself appeared to have had some effect on Idaho Power because Jim Bruce spoke with a well-regarded Associated Press political reporter, Quane Kenyon. He said he was "surprised" and "upset" by claims the two of us had made that Idaho Power was trying to take over the Snake River.[70] He said the Power Company had not acted secretly in causing subordination clauses to be removed from the FERC licenses for two of its facilities and that the Company had no aim to be a "water czar" for the State, but rather wanted to ensure an adequate supply of low-cost of hydroelectric power to supply its customer needs.

The following day, the Post-Register reported that a grass roots organization of individual water users and agribusiness interests had formed to return water rights control to the State.[71] The organization, Idaho Water Rights Defense, adopted the theme "Idaho water for Idaho citizens, for now and forever." The group was chaired by an old friend and supporter, William Lanting of Hollister, a former speaker of the Idaho House of Representatives. The group had three vice chairs, Lowell Moore of Roberts, Verl Andrew of Idaho Falls, and another old friend, Forrest Hymas of Jerome. Bob Hammond of Idaho Falls was head of the legislative committee and Elaine Martin of Jerome was executive secretary. Andrew said Idaho Power's legislation to withhold priority claims against 5000 of the Swan Falls II defendants was a "smoke screen" because Idaho Power would still have control over future development of the State. He said, "We are not willing to let a large corporation walk off with the future of this state." He said the organization's "current efforts are being directed toward assisting Attorney General Jim Jones 'write a bill to supersede Idaho Power's latest attempt, which is to by-pass the governor's signature on a contract.'" This was just

---

70   Kenyon, Quane. Associated Press. "Idaho Power executive upset by new barbs." *Lewiston Tribune*, Jan. 22, 1984.
71   Retallic, Ken. "Group seeks state control of water rights." *Post-Register*, Jan. 23, 1984.

the kind of grassroots support we needed.

That same day, Governor Evans and I announced our proposal to resolve the Swan Falls dispute. We revealed in a joint statement that "Vard Chatburn and Laird Noh, chairmen of the House and Senate Natural Resources Committees, assisted in the drafting of the legislation and are jointly sponsoring it" and that it had the support of "the members of the Idaho Water Resource Board and the Governor's Advisory Task Force on Swan Falls."

In our statement, we said the legislation "reinstates Idaho's long-standing policy of subordinating hydropower usage of water to consumptive uses for industry, agriculture and drinking. However, it provides that all future water applications take into account the effect on hydropower. This will allow us to make better balanced use of our water resources and to protect rate payers from unreasonable rate increases." The bill called for subordination of hydropower uses to upstream consumptive uses, consideration of the effect of new water permit applications on hydropower generation, and protection of electric utilities from action by the Public Utilities Commission for failure to protect their water rights. Governor Evans said the legislation would "put the state back in control of Snake water rights" and is superior to "the Idaho Power piecemeal proposal."[72]

The provision protecting Idaho Power from claims that it failed to protect its water rights was, of course, based on a similar provision in the Power Company bill. The Governor and I wanted to portray this as compromise legislation. The provision requiring new water rights to be evaluated for their effect on hydropower generation was included for two reasons. First, it was simply good public policy. We recognized that there needed to be a balance between inexpensive and abundant hydropower, on the one hand, and the availability

---

72   Associated Press. "Evans, Jones write measure to settle Swan Falls matter." *Post-Register,* Jan. 23, 1984.

of water to support additional agricultural development, growing communities, and industrial needs on the other. Second, we recognized that Idaho Power's most potent argument was that subordination would result in an increase in power rates. If we were to prevail, we needed to show that this was not the case and that we were conscious of the need to keep power rates low.

Senator Peavey expressed his opposition to the bill, saying it "would not alter the pattern of the 1960s and early 1970s, when development of large blocks of land for farming lowered the amount of water in the Snake River."[73] He said, "Most of the recent farm development has been by wealthy investors seeking tax shelters. We give them free water and free land and they come out very well when they sell their land after it is developed."

Jim Bruce said the Water Resources Department "would be ineffective in protecting the interests of power users because no single water application would be large enough to cause a significant reduction in power generation." He continued, "Any one of them in and of itself is not a problem. The problem is the accumulation of many. And that is what's been happening."[74] He indicated that the company had not discussed whether it would "challenge the Jones-Evans proposal in court if it passes."

One report touched on the bipartisan angle. The Idaho Press-Tribune said, "Gov. John Evans and Attorney General Jim Jones are putting partisan concerns in the background to promote a plan they say would resolve a bitter dispute with Idaho Power Co. over Snake River water rights."[75] The article also mentioned, "The attorney general said the bill, if it became law, would render essentially meaningless two current lawsuits stemming from the controversy over Idaho

---

73   Zellar, Ron. "Evans, Jones announce Swan Falls legislation." *Idaho Statesman,* Jan. 24, 1984.
74   Zellar, Ron. "Evans, Jones announce Swan Falls legislation." *Idaho Statesman,* Jan. 24, 1984.
75   UPI. "Swan Falls water fight unites Evans, Jones." *Press-Tribune,* Jan. 24, 1984.

Power's water rights at Swan Falls Dam."

The Evans-Jones bill came up for hearing before a joint meeting of the Senate and House resource committees on January 25. Since Idaho Power's main contention was that subordination would cause power rates to skyrocket, I told the committees, "There is no assurance that power rates will go up if Idaho Power Company loses the Swan Falls water rights battle and there is no assurance that power rates will not go up if Idaho Power wins." I said the Evans-Jones bill,

> will prevent the substantial rate increases which Power Company officials have threatened would result from subordination of their Swan Falls water rights. These dire predictions are based on a worst case scenario where upstream water permits would be handed out willy-nilly without any consideration of the effect on hydropower generation. That simply will not happen. In fact, our legislation mandates consideration of the effect of all subsequent applications for water permits on hydropower generation and on all <u>existing</u> undeveloped permits. If a permit would significantly impact hydropower production contrary to the public interest, the application would be subject to denial. This assures a balanced use approach toward our important water resources. It gives assurance of reasonable electric rates while making water available for industrial growth, increased domestic consumption and cost-effective agricultural development. Growth and development of our communities can and must go hand-in-hand with low-cost electricity.

The most compelling evidence to deflate the Power Company's dire predictions is the past experience in Idaho. From statehood until the Supreme Court's Swan Falls decision in 1982, we operated on the premise that hydropower production was subordinate to consumptive uses necessary for a growing economy. In other words, we have had subordination for all these many years. Yet, Idahoans pay the lowest electrical power rates in the country. If subordination would result in astronomical rate increases, it would already have happened.

There is no assurance that power rates would not increase if the Power Company won the subordination issue both in the courts and in the Legislature. The benefits of the unsubordinated water rights could well go to the Power Company's stockholders, as opposed to the rate payers. Our research shows that if the Power Company were to sell or lease its water (which it could do with an approved change of use), the stockholders could well end up receiving the benefit of the resulting revenues. The Boise Water Corporation [99 Idaho 158] case decided in 1978, indicates that the stockholders, not the rate payers, can receive the revenues from the sale of utility property. If this were to hold true for the sale or lease of Power Company water, the money from the sale would go into the stockholders' pockets. It could become profitable for the Power Company to sell the water for upstream development, thereby depleting the flows through its generators and necessitating rate increases. The only way to preclude this potential windfall to stockholders is to subordinate the water rights.

The only way to assure protection of Idaho's future taxpayers and rate payers is to place Idaho's future in the hands of its people and elected representatives instead of placing it in the hands of the Power Company's stockholders and board of directors who are not obligated to account to the people. This is the system we have had and this is the system which Governor Len Jordan thought he was assuring in the early 1950s when he allowed Idaho Power Company to build their three dams on the Hells Canyon. He believed that he had secured the agreement of the Power Company to subordinate their water rights to upstream development and we all operated on that premise until just recently. A deal was struck and the Power Company should live by it.

The Governor and I also issued a fact sheet, debunking Power Company claims that electric rates would increase $52 to $57 million per year if subordination legislation passed. We focused on a study funded by Idaho Power that estimated power rates could increase by $52 million per year by the end of the century if the Legislature approved our subordination legislation. We noted this would not occur with the requirement in our bill that new water rights could not be granted without consideration of the effect on hydropower production. We pointed out that more than 81% of the Power Company's hydropower production occurred at dams that were fully subordinated. Less than 19% of the power was generated at unsubordinated dams and about a fourth of that was from the Upper Salmon and Shoshone Falls Projects. We particularly focused on Swan Falls Dam, which produced only .003% of the total projected yearly loss of generation. That would result in lost revenue from annual power production of only $42,600 by the end of the century.

We concluded:

It also becomes clear that the power company, through the Swan Falls controversy, is attempting to control 100 percent of the mainstream flow of the Snake River even though it holds only a small percentage of "unsubordinated" water rights. The strategic location of the Swan Falls facility would allow the power company to set by fiat a minimum streamflow of 8400 cubic feet per second. That flow would generate an additional $42,600 per year (compared to a subordinated scenario), while preventing the state from upstream development which would generate hundreds of millions of dollars of economic activity. It would, however, allow the company to accomplish indirectly what it cannot accomplish directly, i.e. achieving unsubordinated status for the Hells Canyon complex—something which it specifically gave up in 1953. Thus, one of the least important power facilities on the Snake River is being used as a lever to gain control of an 8400 CFS right to the very life blood of Idaho.

The fact sheet highlighted that the Supreme Court's decision allowed the water right at one of Idaho Power's least productive facilities to give it almost full control of the Snake River. Although not spelled out in the fact sheet, it had always been understood that Idaho Power was not entitled to any water above Milner Dam, which is located near the city of Hazelton about 150 miles upstream from the Swan Falls Dam.[76] The Company's water rights for its dams located downstream of Milner, including Swan Falls, came from inflows into the river from the Snake River Plains Aquifer. Some of the power licenses for those dams had subordination clauses, while others did not. The three Hells Canyon dams, which were the subject of the agreement between Governor Jordan and Idaho Power, produced the lion's share of the Power Company's electricity. Subordination of those water rights would have little value to the State because only a comparatively small amount of water was diverted for consumptive uses between Swan Falls and

76   My office was receiving troubling information that some of the defendants in Swan Falls II held water rights located above Milner, indicating that Idaho Power might be planning to challenge the long-establish understanding that it had no claim to waters above Milner.

the Hells Canyon complex. Once the water went through the generators of the Hells Canyon dams, there was little or no diversion for consumptive uses until the water flowed out of state. There would be little point in subordinating the water rights for the Hells Canyon dams unless the subordination were to apply all the way upstream to Milner.

Ray Rigby and Kent Foster also appeared before the House and Senate committees to express support for the Evans-Jones proposal. Although I had learned during the past year that many of the legislators discounted much of what they heard from lawyers, water lawyers like Ray and Kent usually had more credibility, particularly for legislators from areas east of Boise. Plus, Ray had served in the Senate for eight years and established a solid reputation for honesty and a thorough understanding of Idaho's water law. Vard's committee voted to introduce the bill, but that didn't mean a majority of committee members were committed to approving its substance.

On that same day, the Public Utilities Commission lifted a six-year moratorium on new requests by irrigators to hook up to Idaho Power's system. The Commission had imposed the moratorium after the 1977 complaint was filed against Idaho Power for not protecting its Swan Falls water rights. A spokesman for the Commission said the moratorium was intended as a temporary measure—"to preserve Idaho Power's water rights at Swan Falls until the state Supreme Court ruled on their validity."[77] The Commission determined the moratorium was no longer necessary because Idaho Power had been able to assert its claims in court. Larry Taylor responded that the Power Company would probably "seek court injunctions to block any new power hook-up requests from southern Idaho irrigators," and "if an irrigator does manage to obtain a new power hook-up, he may find himself

---

77   Bernton, Hal. "State regulators raise ban on irrigation-pump hook-ups." *Times-News,* Jan. 26, 1984.

burdened with new legal problems as well."[78]

Two days later, Jim Bruce penned a letter to Power Company employees apparently to assuage concerns among some employees as to the Company's actions. He said, "No doubt you have heard a lot of allegations recently about Idaho Power and water rights. Although I am not sure what is motivating the Governor, Attorney General, and some legislators, I can tell you with certainty their charges have no basis in fact." He sent along a fact sheet "prepared for legislators and the news media regarding some of the issues." The fact sheet stated that Idaho Power had not been trying to gain control of the Snake River, had not secretly removed subordination clauses from two of its federal licenses, had not secretly applied for additional water rights at Swan Falls, that subordination would result in significant rate increases, that Stouffers' decision not to relocate their plant in Twin Falls was not influenced by a lack of available water, and that Idaho Power's shareholders would not benefit from Idaho Power's position in the subordination fight. With regard to the claim that Idaho Power violated the Hells Canyon agreement it made with Governor Jordan, the fact sheet answer was notably terse. It did not focus on what was agreed to by the principals involved but merely said, "The Supreme Court decided that Hells Canyon subordination applies only as far up the river as the company's first vested water right, which is at Swan Falls." That was correct. However, the fact sheet did not address the broader and more important issue—what the substance of the Hells Canyon agreement actually was and whether the Power Company had violated the agreement. The Governor and I took this as another sign that our comments were having some effect, even among Idaho Power employees.

It later occurred to me that the letter with its talking points was also designed to give Power Company employees

---

78   Bernton, Hal. "State regulators raise ban on irrigation-pump hook-ups." *Times-News*, Jan. 26, 1984.

ammunition to use in public relations efforts. At that time, any town of any size in the Company's service area had an Idaho Power office where people could pay their bills and obtain service. Each office had a manager, who was generally a respected member of the community. The managers participated in community projects, were involved in service organizations, and established credibility in their respective communities. These people were good ambassadors for Idaho Power and often engaged in speaking for the Company on a variety of issues at service clubs, schools, and the like. During the Swan Falls fight the presentations not only dealt with the Company's history, how it operated, what electricity did for us, and so on, but also gave Idaho Power's slant on the subordination/water rights issues. It was an effective information network.

Of course, the Power Company had a phalanx of spokesmen in Boise to spread the Company's position to legislators and the public at large. In that regard, I dropped a note to my old friend and supporter, Bill Lanting, who was now chairman of Idaho Water Rights Defense:

> I can guarantee you that it is going to be a difficult battle here in the Legislature. The Idaho Power lobbyists and attorneys have been here in force and have had a significant impact. We do not have the ability to even come close to matching them in the lobbying process. I think that is where your organization can really have its influence felt. If you, Forrest and the others can continue to educate the public, including the farmers and legislators, it is going to be extremely beneficial in getting an appropriate Swan Falls resolution either through the Legislature or through the courts. Your efforts and support are greatly appreciated.

Although Bill's organization, Ray Rigby, Kent Foster, and others devoted their volunteer efforts to educating and lobbying the members of the Legislature, they were clearly outmatched by Logan and his forces. He was extremely effective in the legislative process and a lot of legislators owed him favors. He was a true force to be reckoned with.

The Governor had staff that were assigned to work with the legislators and Pat Kole was working them on behalf of my office, but it was still an uneven match. We desperately needed help from individual water users, be they irrigators, industrial users, domestic users, or municipalities, to even up the odds. The only way to do that was to up the ante from a rhetorical standpoint. The perfect opportunity presented itself on January 27 at a symposium that took place in a facility owned by Funk Irrigation Company near American Falls.

The symposium was the bright idea of Ben Cavaness, an American Falls attorney who had a good understanding of the stakes at issue in the fight. People on all sides of the issue were invited. In my mind, the symposium was a turning point in the public relations war. It seemed to me that the Governor and I continued to pick up steam for our side of the issue from that point forward.

On my way to the meeting, I was aware that many of those in attendance would be Swan Falls II defendants who wanted the Governor to sign the contract so they would not have to worry about Idaho Power's priority claims against their water rights. I remembered comments that Senator Jordan made to me in the early 1970s about the responsibility of public officials to do the right thing. It was my job, as his legislative assistant, to write position papers and constituent letters for his approval on practically every issue except natural resources. That work was done by Ray McGuire, who handled the Senator's Interior Committee work. I asked the Senator how he planned to vote on a bill banning the sale of

Saturday night specials—cheaply-made handguns that were hitting the streets in Washington, New York, and other large cities around the country. I assumed that he would oppose the bill because that would be in keeping with the sentiments expressed in the letters we were receiving from constituents. His comment was that there was no legitimate reason for people to have these firearms, which often were as dangerous to the shooter as to the victim, and that he would be supporting the bill. He said that a public servant has the responsibility to do what he knows is the right thing, rather than to simply do what the letter writers demand. Senator Jordan told me if you do the right thing and it appears your constituents are not with you, it is your responsibility to educate them as to your side of the issue and try to convince them that it is, indeed, the right thing. He said that he voted for the Gun Control Act of 1968 because, while it would not have any effect on legitimate firearm owners in Idaho and was not needed there, it was a different story in Washington and other big cities. Even though he was a conservative Republican, he voted for the Civil Rights Act of 1964, as well as the Voting Rights Act of 1965. There had been some grumbling in Idaho about these votes, but he spoke out to make his case and was reelected in 1966. My thought going into the symposium was that the Governor and I were on the right side and if the issue was explained to those in attendance, particularly the future consequences if the Power Company prevailed, even the Swan Falls II defendants who wanted a quick solution would understand.

Logan was at the symposium and gave a strong presentation in favor of the Power Company's legislation. He said it would release around 5,000 people from jeopardy in Swan Falls II, giving them the relief they needed, while not jeopardizing the position of either party in Swan Falls I. A number of people voiced support for his position.

When I began my presentation, several people inquired as to why they should not support the Idaho Power approach because it would protect their individual water rights against Idaho Power's claims. I explained the deal between Governor Jordan and Idaho Power, the fact that Idaho Power would have a potential veto over future water rights applications above Swan Falls including those their children might file, and that Idaho Power's divide and conquer strategy would gut the State's effort to take back control of the Snake River. Perhaps it was just my imagination, but it seemed I could actually feel a shift of opinion in the audience in favor of subordination either through court action in Swan Falls I or through the Evans-Jones legislation. This was reflected in the tenor of the questions toward the latter part of my talk and also in subsequent presentations. It appeared that people were beginning to realize that there was more at stake than just a fight over the water rights in Swan Falls II. We seemed to be gaining traction with this group and I found that to be the case after the symposium as I continued my speaking schedule around the Snake River Basin from that point on.

However, we still had our work cut out for us. The previous day the House State Affairs Committee had endorsed the Power Company's bill on a 12-9 vote.[79] Representative Patricia McDermott of Pocatello, a Democrat, supported the legislation, saying "water users mired in uncertainly over the Swan Falls water-rights controversy deserve relief."[80] The legislation was also supported by a number of Swan Falls II defendants. Darrell Savage, a farmer who managed a large irrigation project that pumped water directly out of the Snake River near Hammett, spoke in support of the bill, telling committee members "thousands of water users can't be expected to remain in limbo for the years it would take to resolve the entire Swan Falls issue in court." I told the

79   UPI. "Swan Falls water bill wins early skirmish." *Times-News*, *Jan. 27, 1984.*
80   Associated Press. "Bill drops many Swan Falls defendants." *Post-Register, Jan. 27, 1984.*

committee that the legislation was vague, didn't bind Idaho Power adequately, and was sure to be challenged in court. However, it looked like the skids had been well greased in Idaho Power's favor going into the committee meeting.

The day of the symposium, the Times-News published a guest opinion by Larry Taylor that essentially reiterated the talking points Jim Bruce made in his letter to Power Company employees. Also, the Idaho Conservation League and two consumer-advocacy groups—the Idaho Citizens Coalition and Idaho Consumer Affairs—came out against the Evans-Jones bill and in favor of the Idaho Power bill. Pat Ford, director of the Conservation League, claimed that our bill might lead to undesirable development. He called for development of a comprehensive water plan that took quality-of-life considerations into account. Al Fothergill, a nice gentleman who spoke on behalf of the Idaho Citizens Coalition, claimed that electricity rates would jump and water quality would decline if the Evans-Jones bill passed. Governor Evans refuted Fothergill's claims, saying that he did "not anticipate in the near future an increase in utility rates."[81]

On January 30, we got some good help from a credible and respected source. John Corlett, who for years had been one of the most respected political editors in the State and was now an occasional commentator for the Idaho Statesman, published a piece in the Statesman titled, "Few Grasp Importance of Swan Falls Controversy." He hit the nail on the head, particularly with respect to the public in Southwestern Idaho, saying[82]

> The controversy surrounding the Swan Falls Dam water rights issue is so complex, I fear that many legislators do not understand it. Probably the ordinary Ida-

---

81   Associated Press. "Groups oppose Swan Falls legislation." *Idahonian (Moscow). Jan. 28/29, 1984.*
82   Corlett, John. "Few grasp importance of Swan Falls controversy." *Idaho Statesman, Jan. 30, 1984.*

ho citizen does not understand it and as a result cares less.

Still the issue is of utmost interest to all southern Idahoans, and I have been hoping someone would put it in perspective.

As one who has written thousands of words since 1936 about water and water rights, it is difficult for me to understand how we arrived at a situation in which Idaho Power has authority, or is seeking authority, to oppose depletion of water in the Snake River upstream from Swan Falls Dam, its 75-year-old structure.

It is significant that a Republican attorney general and a Democratic governor have joined forces to fight Idaho Power to subordinate its water rights to allow development. Their proposed legislation has been introduced in the House, and it is bitterly opposed by Idaho Power.

The bill had hardly been introduced before the House State Affairs Committee reported out with a do-pass recommendation a measure desired by Idaho Power. And so the battle is on.

A former director of Idaho Power told me recently it was his belief the company must subordinate its water rights to consumptive upstream developments, even if they "reduced the Snake River to a trickle." He was referring to Idaho Power's agreement in its federal license to build the three dams in Hells Canyon to subordinate its water rights to upstream development.
But no one in the company then really expected development to reduce the Snake to a trickle. After World War II, Idaho Power promoted irrigation of arid land by pumping from the aquifer and from the Snake River. By the mid-1970s, more than 1.5 million acres had been developed by pumping, which added revenues

to Idaho Power coffers.

By the late 1970s, Idaho Power began opposing proposed development of arid lands by pumping, realizing it could not withstand continued depletion of the Snake. It had failed to get permission to build a coal-fired plant near Boise in 1976, and ultimately gained additional generation from coal plants in Wyoming, Nevada and Oregon. It conducted an extensive conservation program to reduce use of power.

Certain organizations argued that additional upstream development should be stopped to reduce electric rate increases.

Surprisingly (to water users and others), the Idaho Supreme Court held that the federal license for the Hells Canyon dams did not subordinate Idaho Power's water rights above Swan Falls, and held the firm had a water right of 8,400 cubic feet per second for the dam. It sent the water-rights suit back to district court to determine if water rights granted to individuals and companies above Swan Falls had been forfeited by Idaho Power's failure to contest them in the past years.

Idaho Power then filed suit against about 7,500 water-rights owners and applicants seeking to divest them of those rights, or in the alternative, pay for them.

John's comments about public knowledge and perception of the Swan Falls dispute were right on point. If your livelihood depended on water, you understood the stakes at issue in the dispute. If you had an office job in Boise, the issue sounded fairly complex but generally appeared to boil down to a fight between farmers and people using electricity for their homes. The Power Company's message was resonating in Ada County. That manifested itself in fairly strong support for Idaho Power's position by Boise-area legislators.

It did not help, either, when the Idaho Wildlife Federation came out in opposition to the Evans-Jones bill.[83] The Federation said the matter should be resolved in court, rather than through the Legislature, and that a more constructive move by the Legislature might be to raise the minimum streamflow in the Snake River. Quite frankly, the Governor and I preferred to allow the matter to be resolved in court, as it looked like the Power Company may have a bit of an upper hand in the Legislature. Further, we had no strong opposition to somewhat of an increase in the minimum streamflow above the current 3,300 cfs at the streamflow gauge just downstream from Swan Falls Dam, but that would have to be decided later and not by the Legislature. That was a matter within the jurisdiction of the Idaho Water Resource Board.

With the environmental and consumer groups lining up against our position, the Governor and I were being portrayed as indifferent to those concerns. That was certainly not the case. At the time, I was trying to get the Legislature to provide funding for a consumer protection division in my office, which had been eliminated a couple of years before I took office. Further, both the Governor and I believed that environmental considerations should be taken into account in allocating and managing Idaho water. We felt that the environmental and consumer groups could benefit from a bit of education on the issue.

The Governor and I had a slight victory on the House floor on January 30. Our supporters were able to get the Power Company bill amended to include language I had proposed to require the Company to follow through with its statement that it would release the 5,000 or so defendants from Swan Falls II if the legislation passed.[84] The amendment was a

---

83   Associated Press. "Wildlife Federation Opposes Water Rights by Legislation." *Idaho State Journal*, Jan. 31, 1984.
84   "Jones v. Idaho Power." *Coeur d'Alene Press*, Jan. 31, 1984.

mixed blessing, however, because, while assuring greater protection for the released defendants, it made the bill a bit more palatable overall and somewhat more likely to pass.

In the meantime, the Governor and I were picking up support for our subordination legislation. On January 31, the Idaho Water Resource Board endorsed our bill, which was no big surprise.[85] We also got the support of the Bonneville County-Cities Planning Committee, comprised of Idaho Falls, Ammon, Iona, Ucon, Swan Valley and Erwin, and Bonneville County.[86] Idaho Falls Mayor Tom Campbell said he would contact area legislators about the bill but said Idaho Power had strong lobbying power. He added, "Idaho Power almost dominates the Legislature." The Mayor was not guilty of understatement in that regard.

Recognizing that Idaho Power's bill was likely to pass, the Governor and I revised our strategy a bit. We adopted the position that both bills should pass and that immediate action on the Evans-Jones bill was essential to resolve the entire controversy. One strong factor in our favor in that regard was the fact that the Governor had the ultimate say-so on the legislation with his veto power. If both bills passed, he could sign them both into law. If the Power Company's bill passed and ours somehow got sidetracked, he could haul out the veto stamp. That was a decided advantage for our side.

85   Associated Press. "Water Board Endorses New Irrigation on S.R." *Idaho State Journal*, Feb. 1, 1984.
86   Associated Press. "Cities Make Case for Water Rights." *Idaho State Journal*, Feb. 2, 1984.

A LEAP MONTH TO REMEMBER

1984 was a leap year so there were 29 days of some of the most intense Swan Falls maneuvering and fighting during February. The Evans-Jones proposal was gaining support in the eastern part of the State, but Pocatello was a troubling exception. There, the citizens and their legislators appeared to have mixed opinions. John Dillin, Jr., a staff writer for the Idaho State Journal, described the split in Pocatello with an analysis that applied equally well in Southwest Idaho:[87]

> If any legislative issue has the Southeast Idaho delegation splintered, it's the Swan Falls water rights issue.
>
> Two Swan Falls bills are floating through the legislature. One awaiting a House vote would remove most of the 7,500 water users from an Idaho Power lawsuit over Snake River water rights. The other, awaiting House committee action, places the needs of irrigators and other Snake River water users above the hydroelectric generating needs of Idaho Power.
>
> "It's a complex issue. Many people around here and at home are still grasping to find true and future meaning of the issue," said Rep. Dwight Horsch, D-Aberdeen.
>
> The legislature got snarled in the water issue last session, spawned by a 1982 Idaho Supreme Court decision that Idaho Power has the undisputed right to some 8,400 cubic feet of Snake River water per second during the summer irrigation season. Summer months are when upper Snake River irrigators place the most stress on the river basin.

---

87   Dillin, John. "Swan Falls Problem Splits Area Solons." *Idaho State Journal,* Feb. 2, 1984.

To protect its water rights above Swan Falls dam, located in Southwest Idaho, Idaho Power filed a lawsuit last spring against 7,500 water users who presently are rediverting Snake River water upstream from the dam.

Most lawmakers support an Idaho Power bill to drop the water users from the suit, but some of that support is conditional. Many lawmakers want to see the subordination bill approved at the same time. Backers of Idaho Power, though, want the subordination bill bottled up.

Some legislators are suspicious of the utility bill. "Is it fair that Idaho Power is holding those water users hostage?" asks Rep. Cornell Thomas, R-Pingree.

"The future of agri-base and other growth is at stake. Do we want to stagnate our industries by turning the Snake River over to a utility?" Horsch says.

FMC Corporation, one of Pocatello's important smokestack industries, has dispatched a full-time lobbyist to explain the impact of subordination. The impact is two-fold, said Dirk Kempthorne.

Based on a Public Utilities Commission estimate, a 20 percent rate increase to develop a new Idaho Power thermal plant would increase FMC's annual power costs by $6 million.

Even more important to FMC, who consumes about 15 percent of Idaho Power's electricity, is the potential loss of production during peak load periods. Currently, FMC enjoys uninterrupted service from Idaho Power. These shutdowns could amount to between $1-4 million, depending on the water year.

"The impact is somewhere between $7 million and $11 million a year, but we like to use the conservative figure," Kempthorne said.

Concerns of substantial rate increases bring conditional support to subordinate Idaho Power's water rights.

"Whenever you start speaking of subordination, I have a concern about who will pay the bill. Who will pay for the property right taken away from Idaho Power?" asks Rep. Larry EchoHawk, D-Pocatello. "The decision is still undecided in court, and maybe that's where it should be. But if the state exercises its police power, the state will have to pay, probably through higher rates."

Rep. Patricia McDermott, D-Pocatello, says it would be unfair for residential ratepayers to subsidize any increased costs bore by other water users through subordination. "Those who get the economic benefit from those water rights should pay for it," she says.
Horsch says pitting classes of ratepayers is unfortunate. He says it should be "all ratepayers against Idaho Power."

"It bothers me to see residential ratepayers pitted against the farmer and the developer. That's wrong. Developers and farmers are nothing but very large ratepayers who are just as interested as anybody about the rate base and realize full well the value of hydro power versus the costs of thermal or nuclear power," Horsch said.

As mentioned in the article, Idaho Power was receiving support from industries like FMC that used substantial amounts of electric power and those industries were throwing their lobbyists into the fight. That was particularly helpful in the Legislature but not so much with the public at large.

On the other hand, Idaho Water Rights Defense was stepping up its efforts in support of subordination. On

February 2, it ran an ad in the Post-Register titled "Idaho Should Control Idaho's Water...NOT IDAHO POWER!" The ad contained the names of several hundred of the Swan Falls II defendants and pictured Idaho Power as a wolf in sheep's clothing drinking a bucket of Snake River water while a little waif named "Idaho water right holders" received a few drips of the water in its cup. A review of the ad disclosed that many of the named defendants in Swan Falls II were water right holders located above Milner Dam. Therefore, it was clear that Idaho Power was challenging the long-standing belief among water users that Idaho Power's water rights for its hydropower dams were served solely by inflows into the Snake River below Milner. There was actually nothing of a written nature that would stand up in court to preclude the Power Company from arguing that it had claims to waters above Milner and it looked like the Company was going for broke.

In the meantime, Al Fothergill launched a publicity campaign, sending guest opinions to a number of daily newspapers, claiming that the Governor and I were hoodwinking the public by contending that the issue was control of the Snake River, when in actuality it was a matter of whether to have low or high power rates.[88] Fothergill cited the study paid for by Idaho Power, although he said it was financed by the Legislature. He said that Idaho Power did not make a consumptive use of the water; the water only flowed through its generators to produce low-cost electricity. What he didn't mention is that once the water flowed through the generators at Swan Falls Dam, virtually all of the water flowed out of State and was not available for consumptive uses in Idaho. In anybody's book, that would be a waste of an increasingly valuable natural resource.

On February 3 I wrote a letter to the editor of the

---

88   "Swan Falls plan contains potential for political chicanery." *Times-News*, Feb. 2, 1984.

Times-News, responding to Larry Taylor's January 27 guest opinion. My letter focused on Idaho Power's contention that the subordination of its water rights at the Hells Canyon complex only extended upstream to Swan Falls. I wrote:

> In his guest opinion in the January 27 issue of your paper the public information specialist for Idaho Power Company appears to have overlooked some of the history written by his company. It is admitted that the power company subordinated its water rights for hydropower generation at Hells Canyon to upstream development. However, the implication is that the subordination for upstream growth and development only extended to Swan Falls. History would indicate that Idaho Power originally intended to subordinate its hydropower rights to development all the way up the Snake River.
>
> Senator (then-governor) Len B. Jordan insisted that the power company subordinate its water rights at Hells Canyon to development all the way upstream as a condition for being allowed to build three dams on the Hells Canyon. He knew that water would be needed for growth of our communities in Magic Valley and on up the river, for expanded agricultural development, and for industrial and commercial growth. If the subordination were to extend only up to Swan Falls, it would be practically meaningless since there is little consumptive use between Swan Falls and Hells Canyon. Jordan had vision which allowed him to see into the next century and he would not have agreed to such limited subordination.
>
> Idaho Power Company certainly understood subordination to extend upstream past Swan Falls. R.P. "Pat" Parry, the pioneer Twin Falls water lawyer who

represented Idaho Power in the Hells Canyon matter, appears to have agreed with Jordan. In testimony before Congress on the Hells Canyon legislation in 1952 he said:

> In the case of the private power company and its low-head dams there will be no such conflict (between hydropower and consumptive uses) for the company, probably for selfish reasons, has taken the position that its power water rights shall be subordinate to all upstream irrigation rights both present and future.

Indeed, Thomas E. Roach, former president of Idaho Power Company, testified before the Federal Power Commission in July, 1953, that:

> [O]ur company for a period of 37 years or more has had a very firm and fixed policy of complete coordination of the use of the Snake River waters for the development of hydroelectric power with the needs of that water for irrigation and has followed the policy of always placing the use of that water for irrigation in a prior position to the use of the water for hydroelectric development.

Thus, it seems that all parties were in agreement at the time of the Hells Canyon transaction that upstream development would have priority over hydropower generation in the use of the Snake River waters.

These people knew that Idaho's growth was dependent upon water, as evidenced by the fact that all of the major communities sprung up along the Snake River. They realized that water can be used for many purposes, such as irrigation, running plants, serving communities, and generating hydroelectric power.

Memories grow short, however, and when the Idaho Supreme Court ruled in November of 1982 that the Power Company had an apparent unsubordinated water right at Swan Falls for 8400 cubic feet per second, the Power Company started recalling the deal with Len Jordan in a somewhat different light. Although all parties were surprised with the Supreme Court's decision and although the Snake River had been operated since the 1950s in a fashion which indicated that the Power Company's water rights were subordinate to upstream development, the Power Company began denying that there was ever a subordination deal. The written history, however, indicates otherwise.

Regardless of what happened, the fact is that subordination of hydropower rights is crucial to the future growth and development of the State of Idaho. If we expect to have a growing tax base, adequate water supplies for expanding communities, new jobs and tax base from water-utilizing plants and industry, and other growth that is necessary to provide us with a vigorous economy, there is going to have to be some water available. If the power company is allowed to tie up the main stream of the Snake River so that 8400 CFS can flow through its Swan Falls generators and out to the Columbia River, we will not have fulfilled our responsibility to future generations. But, on the other hand, we cannot and should not allow excessive depletion of flows for hydropower generation and should take into account the effect of new development on hydrogeneration. In other words, there needs to be a balance in the future use of our water resources. We cannot allow the Power Company to lock up our water for the single purpose of hydropower generation, neither can we allow our water resources to be locked up for any other single purpose.

Clive also found a 1968 statement made by Albert Carlsen, who was then the president of Idaho Power, reaffirming the subordinated nature of the Power Company's water rights at its dams on the Snake River. The statement was made to the Technical Advisory Committee of the Idaho Water Resource Board on January 15, 1968. Among other things, Carlsen said, "Any attempt to divert Snake River water to the Southwest will find Idaho Power Company in the front line of defense with all the resources at our command.... These rights of Idaho Power Company have been voluntarily subordinated by the Company to present and future irrigation and other consumptive uses in the Snake River watershed. Therefore, the licensed rights of Idaho Power and their subordination for the benefit of present and future irrigation needs in the Snake River Valley provide the only real legal protection against threats of out-of-state diversion." Carlsen sent a copy of the testimony to Senator Jordan by letter dated January 25, 1968, apparently to assure the Senator that the subordinated status of its water rights would protect the State against attempts to divert Snake River water to California or Colorado.

Concern over diversion of Snake River water became a big issue in Idaho after Parsons Corp. in Pasadena, California, announced a grandiose plan in 1964 to divert water from Alaska down through the Pacific Northwest states to serve growing water needs in California. The North American Water and Power Alliance (NAWAPA) contemplated either an underwater pipeline from Alaska to California or an overland route that would pass through Canada, the Pacific Northwest states, and on down to southern California. On its way, the project would pick up some Snake and Columbia River waters and send them to water crops and fill swimming pools down south. It obviously became a big political issue in Idaho. Senator Jordan's opponent in his 1966 reelection campaign used it as an issue to beat the Senator over the head. This was a little odd because no member of Idaho's congressional delegation was more knowledgeable on water issues nor had done more to advocate for the protection and wise use of Idaho water.

The State reacted to the proposal by doing a number of things. One was to demonstrate that there was no surplus water in the State for export to other areas. Although not a practice that was particularly advertised, the water resources folks became somewhat more generous in recognizing or approving water right claims or permits, not particularly questioning amounts or feasibility. If a person seeking to obtain a water right, either through the permitting process or under the constitutional approach, overstated their need or their ability to put the water to beneficial use, there weren't many questions asked. Thus, a certain amount of inflation made its way into the quantity of water claimed to be put to beneficial use. That lent weight to Idaho's argument that Snake River water was fully appropriated, leaving none to be grabbed and sent elsewhere.

Senator Jordan and Senator Frank Church joined other northwest senators in another protective measure — imposing a moratorium on federal studies of interbasin water transfers to the Colorado River Basin. In 1967 the northwest senators were successful in inserting language into Senate Bill 1004, the Colorado River Project bill, placing a ten-year moratorium on such studies. The House was not particularly pleased with the moratorium but eventually went along and when the bill was signed into law in 1968 it contained the ten-year moratorium. That provides the context for Carlsen's comments.

What Carlsen was saying was that since Snake River water was available for consumptive uses, the State could allocate for such uses to the extent there would be no water available for export. It could only do that because Idaho Power's water rights for its Hells Canyon dams and all those upriver were subordinated and subject to depletion for irrigation and other consumptive uses. If its rights were unsubordinated, practically the full flow of the Snake River would have to pass through or over Swan Falls Dam and on out of the State, making it appear that there was plenty of surplus water for export. If Idaho wasn't going to use it for consumptive uses, California would be more than happy to do so. Carlsen was assuring Senator Jordan that because Idaho Power's water rights were fully subordinated, Idaho water was safe from being exported to the southwest.

The House went forward with action on the Power Company's bill, approving it by a vote of 64-5 on February 3. The Governor and I supported the bill but the Governor made it clear that he would not sign it unless and until he received our subordination bill.[89] Representative Chatburn also came out in favor of the bill but only after he received assurance that our subordination bill would receive a hearing in the House State Affairs Committee, where it had gone after approval by his committee. The State Affairs Committee chairman, Representative Walt Little of New Plymouth, said the Idaho Power bill "takes care of the problem at the present time. For the future, other legislation has been introduced." That did not necessarily mean that he would support our bill and we were concerned about his statement that, "A water right is a property right. If we take those water rights, it will cost the state millions of dollars." This played into Idaho Power's contention that the Company had an absolute right to the 8,400 cfs at Swan Falls and that it would have to be paid just compensation if the State subordinated the right. My office repeatedly said that there would be no right to

---

89   "Swan Falls bill OK'd; second on way." *Times-News*, Feb. 4, 1984.

any just compensation since the Swan Falls water right had been subordinated by the Hells Canyon agreement. On the other hand, based on the Supreme Court's decision, the Power Company had a colorable argument. If the legislation passed and the State was not able to prove up its affirmative defenses in Swan Falls I, there might be a legitimate question on compensation.

The State Affairs Committee held a hearing on the Evans-Jones bill on February 7. I testified that our bill would not constitute a taking of Power Company property, that the Power Company had agreed to subordinate all of its Snake River water rights, that power rates would not skyrocket, and that our bill would take into the account the need for protecting hydropower production. The hearing was lively and well attended. According to a newspaper report, it was "an overflow hearing that filled the capitol's Gold Room to the walls and spilled into the rotunda."[90]

Both Ray Rigby and Ben Cavaness appeared before the Committee to testify in favor of the Evans-Jones bill. The crowd at the hearing was estimated at about 300, most of whom attended to support our bill. About 40 of those were farmers from the American Falls-Aberdeen area.[91] It was important to have that type of groundswell support and to have the benefit of their testimony. Gordon Toevs of Funk Irrigation said that his company had lost half of its business and laid off 11 employees as a result of the Supreme Court's decision and the consequent moratorium on issuance of water permits. Ken Vollmer, an Aberdeen well driller, said he had to let six employees go because no new water permits were being issued. Gary Gehring, a third generation farmer from American Falls, said he wanted his boys, who would inherit the farm, to decide what to do with the farm—not a public utility.

---

90   Stevenson, Mary. Associated Press. "Water rights hearing spawns conflict." *Times-News*, Feb. 8, 1984.
91   Dockstader, Dan. "Area Farmers Support Swan Falls Bill." *Idaho State Journal*, Feb. 8, 1984.

Water Resources Director Ken Dunn testified that the court decision had slowed down agricultural development and that he had 1,200 water rights applications he had not acted on pending a final disposition of the Swan Falls issues.[92] A representative of FMC Corp. testified against our bill, claiming it would cost the company an extra $7 million a year. He contended his company and other producers of elemental phosphorus "are concerned that continuing cost increases for our products will lead to lower cost substitutes for phosphorus which could severely damage the whole industry." This, of course, was based on the study that Idaho Power had funded.

Tom Nelson also appeared before the committee warning that, "If the state, by passing this bill, can subordinate the Swan Falls water right, there's not another water right in this state that is not subject to subordination or abrogation."[93] There was a move to send the bill to the amending order on the House floor, which was essentially the kiss of death. Representative Linden Bateman of Idaho Falls, came to the rescue, contending that the bill should be sent directly to the floor with a do-pass recommendation. Bateman said, "We have this issue of water leaving the state. The idea of water being allowed to go through those generators and leave the state to me is just a nightmare."[94] The Committee did not choose either alternative, voting 12-8 to send the bill to the floor "with no recommendation as to whether it should pass—a break from normal procedure."[95]

Following the hearing, a group of the attendees met with Governor Evans. "What was anticipated as a small gathering in his office turned out to be a crowd of over 200."[96]

92   Stevenson, Mary. Associated Press. "Water rights hearing spawns conflict." *Times-News,* Feb. 8, 1984.

93   Stevenson, Mary. Associated Press. "Bill to subordinate water rights goes to full House." *Idaho Statesman,* Feb. 9, 1984.

94   Stevenson, Mary. Associated Press. "Swan Falls Bill Heads for House." *Idaho State Journal,* Feb. 9, 1984.

95   Stevenson, Mary. Associated Press. "Bill to subordinate water rights goes to full House." *Idaho Statesman,* Feb. 9, 1984.

96   Dockstader, Dan. "Area Farmers Support Swan Falls Bill." *Idaho State Journal,* Feb. 8, 1984.

The Governor urged them to work with their legislators to get both the Power Company and the Evans-Jones bills on his desk at the same time.

In order to keep the heat on the issue and also to respond to the arguments made by Idaho Power's representatives, I put out a statement on February 9 regarding Tom Nelson's legal advice to Jim Bruce that the company was bound by the 1952 agreement with Governor Jordan. The statement said that the Evans-Jones bill was merely seeking to reinstate the deal that the Power Company had made with Len Jordan to get his support for its three-dam Hells Canyon project. The statement continued,

> Governor Jordan insisted that the Power Company subordinate its water rights at Hells Canyon to development all the way up the Snake River as a condition for building the Hells Canyon complex. He knew that water would be needed for growth in our southern Idaho communities, for industrial and commercial expansion, and for additional cultivated acreage. A deal was struck and it was thought that insertion of subordination clauses in the Federal Power Commission licenses and state water licenses for the Hells Canyon complex would cement the deal for future generations.
>
> Unfortunately, the Power Company lawyers began to search for loopholes. In 1977 the Power Company brought suit claiming that the Swan Falls water license was not affected by the Hells Canyon agreement. Unfortunately, they ultimately prevailed on that claim on certain technical grounds.
>
> The Power Company's claim is inconsistent with the deal it struck with Len Jordan. An internal Power Company legal memorandum from a Power Company attorney (Tom Nelson) to the Power company

president (Jim Bruce), dated June 22, 1976, and entitled "Possibility of Using the Swan Falls Water Right
to Stop Upstream Depletion of the Snake River," states
in part:

If IPC (Idaho Power Company) was to attempt to use
its Swan Falls water right to prevent further irrigation depletion above Strike (CJ Strike Dam), any benefit from stopping such depletion would, of course,
redound to the benefit of flows at Strike, and potentially in Hells Canyon. <u>Thus, IPC would be doing
indirectly what it cannot do directly</u>, that is, protect
its Strike and Hells Canyon projects from upstream
depletion. In our judgment, the FPC license and state
water license provisions above referred to would be
construed to make the Swan Falls right subject also
to depletion, since the IPC plants on the Snake are
all co-ordinated for operation, and since the water
license depletion provision in the Strike and some
of the Hells Canyon licenses were inserted at the request of IPC. (emphasis added)

The memorandum went on to conclude that, "The
Idaho Power Company's water rights for its Swan
Falls plant cannot be used to prevent consumptive
uses from depleting the flow of the Snake River above
Swan Falls."

Although the Power Company at that time seemed
to feel that they had no right to claim unsubordinated
water at Swan Falls, they certainly changed their tune
after the Supreme Court surprised us all with its decision. Regardless, the Power Company should observe
the deal it made with Len Jordan in order to secure the
right to build the Hells Canyon complex.

The strategic location of Swan Falls essentially
gives the Power Company a greatly increased mini-

mum streamflow which has little effect at Swan Falls but which has tremendous effect at the subordinated facilities upstream and downstream. As their attorney said in his memorandum, they have been able to use the Swan Falls matter as a means of accomplishing indirectly what they agreed not to accomplish directly because of the deal they made with Len Jordan. The Evans-Jones bill essentially says that the Power Company should live with its agreements like everyone else must.

In the meantime, Idaho Power was keeping up its public relations efforts throughout its service area. The Idaho State Journal reported that one of its division managers, Larry Gunnoe, spoke at a Chamber of Commerce meeting in American Falls, boiling down the issue to "having either high power rates because Snake River water would be diverted above Swan Falls Dam for irrigation purposes; or having low-cost power with the utility maintaining the water rights for generation at Swan Falls."[97] He said:

The loss of water for hydro generation certainly will affect the ratepayers of Idaho Power. That includes the residents and businesses of American Falls. You're going to pay higher electric rates for your homes, businesses, and public offices in order to continue to divert more water. So your decision would be, what is the tradeoff?"

Gunnoe also used the opportunity to reiterate some of the talking points contained in Jim Bruce's letter to Power Company employees.

The Evans-Jones bill passed the House on February

---

97   Dockstader, Dan. "IPC Official Says It's Simple – Lower Rates or Water." *Idaho State Journal*, Feb. 9, 1984.

10 on a 38-31 vote. Most of the Boise area legislators voted against the bill, while most of the legislators from eastern Idaho voted for it. North Idaho Republicans were split about 50-50, while Democrats generally were split about 50-50. Vard Chatburn, who was well regarded among House members for his knowledge on water issues, was able to muster the majority to get the legislation passed. He had strong support from Mel Hammond, a Rexburg Democrat, who argued that "No conglomerate in this country has the right to control the blood of this state. Idaho Power is not the water master of this state. The water belongs to all of us. All we're doing is putting it back where it belongs."[98] Representative Dwight Horsch, a Democrat of Aberdeen, also played a key role. He argued that the dispute was not properly cast as a fight between irrigators and ratepayers because farmers were both.[99] He said failure to subordinate would stagnate the State's biggest industry, agriculture, and stagnate a way of life, which brought applause from the gallery.

With the House vote in our favor, it was not yet time to celebrate. Laird Noh, referring to the defeat of subordination legislation in the 1983 session, said it would be "very difficult" to get the Evans-Jones bill through the Senate. "I'm not saying it's at all impossible," adding that the addition of protection in the bill for consumers would help its chances.[100]

John Dillin interviewed some of the Power County farmers who had been among the 300 irrigators to attend the House State Affairs Committee hearing.[101] He wrote, "Some referred to the trip as a pilgrimage. Others just wanted to dispel some myths." He reported that the group was "upset that Idaho Power, through effective lobbying and influential

98   Fick, Bob. Associated Press. "House ranks power plant rights beneath other water uses." Times-News, Feb. 11, 1984.
99   Etlinger, Charles. "House Oks pro-agricultural Snake bill." *Idaho Statesman*, Feb. 11, 1984.
100   Etlinger, Charles. "House Oks pro-agricultural Snake bill." *Idaho Statesman*, Feb. 11, 1984.
101   Dillin, John. "Why They're so Emotional about Swan Falls Decision." *Idaho State Journal*, Feb. 10, 1984.

public relations, could successfully block for a second straight year the subordination legislation." One of those farmers, Lyle Michaelson of American Falls, expressed frustration that subordination opponents were confusing family farmers with corporate farming giants. Ben Canvass echoed that frustration, attacking the Power Company for painting the image that farmers are water hoarders and could drive up electrical rates because of unsound "speculative" development. He said, "I am afraid that the nefarious megabuck corporate farmer that is alluded to by Idaho Power and its supporters is much like the Olympia (beer) artesians; they receive a lot of publicity but nobody has ever seen one. This character assassination of some of Idaho's finest citizens for political purposes is reprehensible."

In a follow-up piece, Dillin wrote about the intense lobbying on the Evans-Jones bill. "Legislators agreed that the raging debate over (the Evans-Jones bill) was the most intense in many years."[102] Representative Hammond, the House Minority Leader, said "In 16 years, I have never seen as vigorous lobbying as with House Bill 459. The pressure was intense from both sides." Looking forward to the anticipated showdown in the Senate, Senator Jerry Wellard, a Democrat from Blackfoot said, "When that bill hits the floor there will have been blood already spilled into the aisles."

As it turned out, there was no opportunity for any blood to be spilled on the Senate floor. Logan and his forces struck quickly, effectively killing the Evans-Jones bill shortly after it arrived at the Senate. Rod Gramer of the Statesman explained how it happened:[103]

---

102   Dillin, John. "Swan Falls Lobbying Was Intense." *Idaho State Journal,* Feb. 12, 1984.
103   Gramer, Rod. "Senate tables bill on water rights, seeks compromise." *Idaho Statesman,* Feb. 14, 1984.

Soon after the Senate convened Monday (February 13)
Sen. David Little, R-Emmett, moved to table the bill.
His motion was seconded by Assistant Minority Leader, Ron Beitelspacher, a Grangeville Democrat.
The outcome was decided by senators standing to
indicate whether they were for or against tabling the
measure. No official record was made of the vote.
After the vote, Little said he moved to table the bill
to settle the issue. He said it was unnecessary to go
through the rigamarole of a public hearing because the
bill would have failed in the Senate.
Little said he went to Senate President Pro Tem James
Risch, R-Boise, to see if there was any way to stop the
bill. He said Risch suggested that a motion could be
made to table the bill before it was sent to committee.

Supporters of the Evans-Jones bill were unprepared
for the tabling motion, which was approved on an 18-16 vote.
Republicans voted a 10-10 split and Democrats voted 8 for and
6 opposed. According to a press report, Senator Noh "said he
was surprised by the move to table the bill. He said he thought
he had an agreement with the Senate Republican leadership
that the bill would go to his committee and a hearing would
be held."[104] Governor Evans expressed surprise at the action
and disappointment that it was supported by members of
the Democratic leadership.[105] He called the Senate vote a
"drastic parliamentary maneuver" and said "when I was in
leadership, we avoided this kind of maneuver. It indicates
a minority of the Senate did not want to be recorded on a
vote." The Governor also "sharply criticized Idaho Power for
working behind the scenes to block the bill."

Ken Dunn said he was "shocked that the Senate would
not at least give the resources committee an opportunity to

104   Gramer, Rod. "Senate tables bill on water rights, seeks compromise." *Idaho Statesman*, Feb. 14, 1984.
105   UPI. "Swan Falls dispute: Evans blasts fellow Democrats for
killing water rights bill." *Coeur d'Alene Press*, Feb. 14, 1984.

hold a hearing" on the bill.[106] On the other hand, Senator Little claimed the bill would have forced power rate increases. "To me, if you can subordinate the water, I guess you can subordinate the land. To me the Legislature's trying to take something away from somebody. I just can't take that philosophy." Senator Risch said his vote would have been in favor of tabling the subordination bill.

Governor Evans, Ken Dunn, and Laird Noh "accused Idaho Power Company of being behind the action."[107] Governor Evans said, "We will not let Idaho Power Co. or any other utility control the destiny of our state. Any time you use a drastic parliamentary maneuver to table a bill in the legislative process, it takes the issue out of the hands of the people. This is too important of an issue to let it die." He said Idaho Power was "way out of line, out of bounds." Laird said, "I just thought it was a very planned, smooth, parliamentary maneuver by Idaho Power, designed to cut off discussion in the Senate."

Others reported that Idaho Power was lobbying furiously at the time. According to Senator Ann Rydalch, an Idaho Falls Republican, "Of course, the Capitol was swarming with Idaho Power people. I'm sure it was well-orchestrated by them."[108] Rydalch said she "finally knew what was happening when Little moved to table the bill during the reading that would have assigned it to a committee. 'Then I knew they were up to something. I was so mad. I was so mad. I think this bill should at least have had the chance to survive on the floor. Idaho Power had it greased.'" Senate Majority Caucus Chairman Marsden Williams, an Idaho Falls Republican, said, "The boys had the wheels greased as far as I'm concerned. I don't think the boys played fair with us." He said he and Ricks were upset because no one let the Senate leadership

---

106   Associated Press. "Senate kills Swan Falls legislation." *Post-Register,* Feb. 13, 1984.
107   Stevenson, Mary. Associated Press. "Swan Falls Backers Angered by Bill Tabling." *Idaho State Journal,* Feb. 14, 1984.
108   Black, Bob. "Watkins absent for vote." *Post-Register,* Feb. 14, 1984.

know what was about to happen.

A matter that raised some eyebrows was the absence of Senator Dane Watkins, a Republican of Idaho Falls. When the vote was held. Senator Mark Ricks, a Republican from Rexburg and Senate Majority Leader said, "He (Watkins) took a dodge. He took a dodge."[109] Watkins said he was working in his office and was not aware of the vote and that his speaker system that broadcast happenings on the floor was possibly turned off. A Rexburg farmer and water user who was an effective spokesman for subordination, Dell Raybould, said, "Watkins was conveniently absent when his vote counted in the crucial issue affecting the people of the Upper Snake River Valley. All other senators from the Upper Valley voted solidly to support this legislation."[110] Raybould, who was present during the tabling maneuver, said he had "never seen more blatant dirty tricks maneuvered than I witnessed from the gallery on the Senate floor Monday morning." Dell continued to be a good and effective supporter of the subordination effort and was in fact elected as a member of the Idaho House of Representatives in 2000 and still serves in that body as one of the most respected members on water issues.

The unseemly ambush of the Evans-Jones bill was a main topic of conversation in the Senate the next day. Senator Risch denied engineering the tabling of the motion, although some questioned how it could have occurred without the support of leadership. He said, "although if I'd have had the time it wouldn't have bothered me at all to be in the middle of it. If you're the stickee it's a low down political trick, but if you're the stick or, you're just following the rules."[111] He noted that the same issue was debated last session and said he'd seen no need to spend the "tremendous amount of time" it would have taken to work on the bill.

---

109   Black, Bob. "Watkins absent for vote." *Post-Register*, Feb. 14, 1984.
110   Black, Bob. "Watkins absent for vote." *Post-Register*, Feb. 14, 1984.
111   "Will Swan Falls decision make Senate eat crow?" *Post-Register*, Feb. 15, 1984.

Laird said, "I have no problem with being the stickee," but "I don't think it was a good day for the Senate or for the state of Idaho." Senator Ricks said, "I'm sorry it got short-circuited in the manner it did." He said no one had informed him beforehand that a tabling attempt would be made, even though it was planned a day ahead of time.

Logan denied accusations that Idaho Power was behind the tabling motion. He said he had been in Phoenix but didn't doubt that some of his company's representatives had been involved in discussions.

On Valentine's Day, I told a meeting of the Idaho Farm Bureau Women that the bill was bushwhacked by Power Company supporters and that "misleading information and scare tactics are being used as a smokescreen by special interest groups that may have hidden agendas." I mentioned that the Idaho Conservation League was supporting Idaho Power, "using the Swan Falls issue to try to make the Snake River a free-flowing 'wild' river, regardless of the fact that this would waste precious water resources." The now-familiar arguments were also made that electric rates would not skyrocket, that Power Company stockholders would receive a potential windfall if their company was able to consolidate its hold on the Snake River, and that the company was trying to disavow the agreement it made with Governor Jordan to subordinate its Snake River water rights.

At the same time, Clive was busy writing another Swan Falls bill for Vard's committee. The bill was drafted to respond to arguments made in opposition to the earlier Evans-Jones bill. Some legislators had expressed concern that the earlier bill would subordinate hydropower rights at dams throughout the State instead of just the Idaho Power dams on the Snake River. That was true but it was essentially irrelevant. Hydropower-producing dams were scarce in other parts of the State and if the water rights at those dams were not already subordinated, the subordination would have little practical effect based on geography. The first bill was drafted to apply generally so as to avoid any potential assertion that it was special legislation in violation of the State's constitution. However, the new legislation was drafted to apply just to the Snake River Basin dams.

Another criticism was that the provision in the initial bill requiring consideration of the effect on hydropower of a new consumptive water right application was too narrow. While the Water Resources Department could turn down a water right application that had a substantial impact on hydropower production, it was argued by the Power Company and others that although one water right application might not have any discernable effect, many such applications would have a large cumulative effect. The Governor and I intended that the Water Resources Department would take the cumulative effect into account under the initial bill and that regulations would be adopted to that effect, but our new bill made it clear that this would be required.

The new bill also incorporated provisions of the Idaho Power bill so that there would be no need for the Senate to act upon that bill. Our hope was that we could convince the Legislature to use just one piece of legislation to resolve the controversy instead of having to wait for two separate bills to arrive at the Governor's desk at the same time.

A somewhat hopeful sign appeared in the Pocatello paper on Valentine's Day, cloaked in wild animal metaphors. While the Idaho State Journal had done fairly good reporting on the Swan Falls controversy, its editorial stance was firmly in support of Idaho Power. This stance was also reflected by most of the Pocatello legislators. The piece in question was a combination of news and opinion that appeared to reflect a slight shift toward the Evans-Jones position. The headline read, "Idaho Utility May Be In For 'Alligator Wrestling.'"[112] The piece started, "If Idaho Power Company didn't know it in the beginning, they certainly realize that they have a 'tiger by the tail' now in terms of the Idaho farmer." It continued, "A certain public utility better be prepared to do some real 'alligator wrestling' in the coming weeks." The article concluded that claims being made against the Evans-Jones bill didn't "hold water," and that farmers were intent on getting relief under such a proposal.

Also on Valentine's Day, Vard and Representative Horsch announced that the new and improved Evans-Jones bill would come before the House Resources and Conservation Committee on February 15. Representative Horsch, who had been an enthusiastic and effective advocate for the earlier bill, said, "I know this is the fourth time up to bat in two years, but the issue is too important to give up now."[113] Referring to the State Water Plan, which set the streamflow of the Snake River near Swan Falls at 3,300 cfs and assumed subordination of the Power Company Snake River water rights, Horsch said, "The Legislature didn't work so hard in 1977 to come up with a water plan to allow a conglomerate owned by out of state stockholders to control the Snake River." Regarding the new bill, Vard said, "The major change is that it limits the impact to strictly the Snake River and its tributaries." Vard said that the Senate's tabling of the earlier bill "really took me by surprise," and that Senator Risch had promised the bill would go to Laird's committee for a hearing.

Editorial writers at the Boise and Lewiston papers opined that the Evans-Jones bill was bad policy but that it had been killed in an unseemly manner. The Statesman called the bill "a heavy-handed attempt to solve a dilemma that

---

112   Dockstader, Dan. "Idaho Utility May Be In For 'Alligator Wrestling.'" *Idaho State Journal,* Feb. 14, 1984.
113   Dillin, John. "Chatburn Proposes New Swan Falls Bill." *Idaho State Journal,* Feb. 15, 1984.

arose" from the Supreme Court's decision.[114] The Statesman contended that the legislation would have resulted in higher power rates and that our new bill, while better, was still "bad business." The Tribune said, "The way it was done, although legal, was irregular, and the governor is not the only Idahoan angry over the outcome."[115] Nevertheless, the editorial writer rejoiced in the murder of the bill, claiming it would be to the benefit of ratepayers, while the Evans-Jones proposal would have benefitted "a few land developers in the upper Snake River Valley." The same old fat cat argument. Of interest is the fact that throughout the proceedings, none of the editors or others involved in the dispute named any fat cat that had hogged up Snake River water prior to the Supreme Court's decision in November of 1982, when everyone assumed that the Power Company's water rights were fully subordinated.

In keeping with its usual posture, the Pocatello paper also had an editorial saying that the tabling of the first Evans-Jones bill was "worth the kill." The paper opined, "the method may not have been the best, but the Idaho Senate achieved the right result in killing the Swan Falls subordination bill passed only days earlier by the House."[116]

Vard's committee voted on February 15 to approve the new Evans-Jones bill. Sherl Chapman, executive director of the Idaho Water Users Association, explained the bill to the committee, indicating that it had incorporated provisions designed to respond to Idaho Power's criticisms.[117]

That same day, the Senate passed a bill proposed by Senator Peavey which was apparently in response to my contention that the Power Company stockholders would reap the benefit of controlling the Snake River. The bill essentially provided that ratepayers, rather than stockholders, "would receive the financial benefits if the utility's rights to the

---

114   "Bill deserved standing-vote fate." *Idaho Statesman*, Feb. 16, 1984.
115   "A better deal for most of the people." *Lewiston Tribune*, Feb. 16, 1984.
116   "Worth the Kill." *Idaho State Journal*, Feb. 17, 1984.
117   UPI. "Snake River water plans pass." *Coeur d'Alene Press*, Feb. 16, 1984.

Snake River are transferred or sold to other users."[118] Senator
Peavey said his bill "also directs the state Public Utilities
Commission to approve any water transfers between Idaho
Power and other users." The bill passed on a 22-12 vote.
Senator Noh argued against passage, contending the bill
had "far-reaching implications and hadn't been examined
by experts in water law."[119] He said, "This bill illustrates the
rather cavalier fashion in which a relatively small group of
individuals are attempting to pull the props out from under
[Idaho's water transfer] system." He said Senate passage of
the bill would be an "embarrassment to us," as it would open
the door for the Public Utilities Commission to block transfers
of water rights. Senator Ringert added, "We don't need
the PUC administering water law in this state. We have an
agency to do that." Nevertheless, the bill passed. We were not
particularly concerned about Idaho Power outright selling its
water rights. What was more likely is that it would use the
increased Snake River flow to generate excess power, pile up
profits, make costly water calls against upstream water right
holders it accused of infringing on its Swan Falls water rights,
and stymie applicants for new water rights until they paid
appropriate tribute. The Company could create more havoc
and make more money by holding onto the rights, rather than
selling them.

February 15 was also an active day for the Swan Falls II
litigation. Fourth District Judge Ray Durtshi denied motions
by the State and others to dismiss the Swan Falls II suit.
According to the Associated Press, "Durtshi told attorneys
for the state and some of the water rights holders sued by
Idaho Power that they should resubmit the dismissal request
on different legal grounds."[120]

I was in Idaho Falls on that same day to speak to the

118   UPI. "Snake River water plans pass." *Coeur d'Alene Press,* Feb.
16, 1984.
119   Associated Press. "Battle continues over utility water rights."
Idahonian, Feb. 16, 1984.
120   Associated Press. "Battle continues over utility water rights."
Idahonian, Feb. 16, 1984.

Idaho Falls Rotary Club about the Swan Falls battle. I told the Rotarians, "We were doing pretty well with our legislation until Monday, but we kind of got bushwhacked by a very irregular, unusual and somewhat ungentlemanly procedure in the Senate."[121] I explained the new Evans-Jones bill and, according to the newspaper report, "said the bill would give priority to industrial, commercial, agricultural and domestic uses of Snake River Plain water, but also supports low-cost hydropower. All future water rights applications would be assessed for their individual and cumulative effects on hydropower generation."

Apparently in response to the tabling controversy, the media folks looked into the personal interests of those involved in the controversy. Rick Shaughnessy of the Times-News wrote an article focused on Senator Risch, noting that he was "connected to a party that is directly involved in the skirmish over Snake River water."[122] Shaughnessy reported that Risch's law firm "received $11,625 in legal fees for work performed for Idaho Power in 1981 and 1982," and that one of Risch's partners received an additional $8,180 for legal services in 1981. The Senator acknowledged that his firm had done legal work for the utility in other years also and that "in election campaigns, he has been accused by his opponents of being owned by Idaho Power." The article continued, "In organizing opposition to the proposed subordination of the utility's water right at Swan Falls, Risch acted in a manner consistent with the wishes of an intense Idaho Power lobbying effort. But Risch says his motives are in the best interests of the utility's customers, which include a vast number of Idaho residents." The Shaughnessy article also mentioned Senator Ringert, who was named as one of the 7,500 defendants in Swan Falls II. Senator Ringert said, "I don't see that I have a duty to any client that would conflict with my responsibility

---

121   Retallic, Ken. "Senate bushwhacked bill, Jones says." *Post-Register,* Feb. 16, 1984.
122   Shaughnessy, Rick. "Conflicting roles: Lawmakers find more ties to Swan Falls than just their vote." *Times-News,* Feb. 16, 1984.

to analyze these questions for the good of the state."

The Times-News had an article the following day in which Shaughnessy explored the interests of others, including myself.[123] He noted that Representative Horsch, who favored subordination, disclosed during debate that he was a defendant in Swan Falls II. According to Shaughnessy, "before the Aberdeen Democrat launched into his defense of the interests of potential new irrigators, he briefly stated how his personal interests would be affected by the" initial Evans-Jones bill. Horsch noted that the Power Company's bill would protect his water right but that it did not go far enough and would not protect future water rights applicants.

With regard to myself, Shaughnessy reported, "Attorney General Jim Jones, of Jerome County, prepared a list of his family's water uses or applications that have been named in the lawsuit. Jones has testified that his interests would be served by the utility's amnesty plan. But he says he does not favor that plan without subordination—a position at odds with his interests."

The article noted that, "About one-third of the Legislature is affected by the issue through their membership in an organization that is named in the lawsuit 43 times—the Church of Jesus Christ of Latter Day Saints." The church was unaware of its involvement in the suit but a spokesman said that its member-legislators "are encouraged to vote their own conscience on all issues." It is likely that most, if not all, of these water claims were for domestic use at LDS churches. Idaho Power had committed that it would not challenge the water rights of domestic users.

On the public relations/education front, I spoke to the Twin Falls Optimist Club on February 16 and got a nice article in the Times-News.[124] In addition to the themes in the Idaho Falls Rotary Club speech, I told the Optimists that the

---

123   Shaughnessy, Rick. "Lawmakers appear following own interests on Swan Falls." *Times-News,* Feb. 17, 1984.
124   Freund, Bob. "Jones pushing water issues." *Times-News,* Feb. 17, 1984.

State intended to pursue its litigation efforts in both State and Federal proceedings. "If we don't prevail in the state courts, we are going to federal court and have the subordination clause construed by the federal courts." This would be in proceedings regarding the interpretation of the subordination clauses in the federal power licenses for Hells Canyon, as well as the Jordan–Idaho Power agreement. It would also involve administrative proceedings at FERC. I addressed essentially the same themes at the Jerome Chamber of Commerce meeting the next day.

I have to say that even though I invoked the FERC card quite often, we had qualms about what that agency might do in a contested battle between the State and its regulated utility. It is true that FERC put the subordination conditions in the Shoshone Falls and Upper Salmon Project licenses at the request of the Department of Interior, but it also quickly removed them at Idaho Power's request. FERC was generally regarded as somewhat favorable to the industries it regulated. Further, hydropower was just a small part of the work of the agency and it did not display a great deal of expertise in the area, particularly with regard to state water right issues. And, it seemed to move at glacial speed. Our best bet was to get a legislative solution where we had more control over the matter. If the Senate stymied that approach, which it appeared was likely, the second best solution would be through State court, even though that posed uncertainties as evidenced by the Supreme Court's decision.

The Sunday papers on February 19 were full of Swan Falls news articles and commentary. Al Fothergill's guest opinion was published in the Post-Register.[125] An Associated Press article by Mary Stevenson featured Vard Chatburn and Logan Lanham.[126] When asked why the backers of subordination were not giving up, Vard said, "It all resolves

---

125   Fothergill, Al. "Very few benefit if water rights subordinated." *Post-Register*, Feb. 19, 1984.
126   Stevenson, Mary. Associated Press. "Swan Falls Subordination Issue Won't Go Away." *Idaho State Journal*, Feb. 19, 1984.

itself back to whether the state of Idaho is going to be the state rivermaster. We who depend upon irrigation for our livelihood are just so concerned that we need to keep control of the waters of the Snake within the Department of Water Resources that we're going to attempt to subordinate that hydropower right." When asked what he thought about the revised Evans-Jones bill, Logan said "Not much." He said, "The basic issue is using the police powers of the state to take one person's property away from him without payment and giving it to someone else. Where are you going to quit?"

The Statesman had two articles—one by Rod Gramer, speaking of the strange bedfellows in the Swan Falls fight, and the other by Rick Ripley, the editorial page editor, speaking of the adversarial situation between myself and Idaho Power. Gramer said it was hard to image that Senator Peavey and Idaho Power were on the same page in the Swan Falls fight because Peavey had bitterly and successfully opposed Idaho Power's earlier proposal to build a coal-fired plant southeast of Boise. According to Gramer:[127]

> The Peavey-Idaho Power coalition is one of the many strange, unexpected alliances at work in Idaho politics.
>
> On one side, Democratic Gov. John Evans, Republican Attorney General Jim Jones and two leading Republican legislators, Sen. Laird Noh and Rep. Vard Chatburn, want to subordinate Idaho Power's water rights to irrigation and industrial uses.
>
> On the other side, the entire Senate Democratic leadership, the two top Republican leaders in the Legislature — House Speaker Tom Stivers and Senate President Pro Tem James Risch — former Democratic Gov. Cecil Andrus, Idaho Power and the Idaho Con-

---

127   Gramer, Rod. "Democrats join business in odd political alliance." *Idaho Statesman,* Feb. 19, 1984.

servation League (Can you believe this coalition?) say those water rights belong to Idaho Power's ratepayers.

The Ripley article focused on myself and the Power Company. It read:[128]

Idaho Attorney General Jim Jones acknowledges that he feels "a little uncomfortable" in his role as a combatant of Idaho Power Co.

"Idaho Power supported me in the election," Jones says. The utility donated $500 to Jones' campaign, yet he has led the charge to subordinate Idaho Power's water rights at Swan Falls Dam, taking the type of stand that aspiring young Republican politicians generally don't take against a business.

That is not to say the issue is a partisan matter. Gov. John Evans, the state's leading Democrat, has teamed up with Jones. Their legislation to subordinate Idaho Power's rights split House Republicans 25 to 25 and House Democrats 13 to 6. Still, Jones has slammed Idaho Power hard.

Last month Jones accused Idaho Power of operating secretly when it convinced the Federal Energy Regulatory Commission (FERC) to remove subordination clauses from federal power licenses for the utility's Upper Salmon and Shoshone Falls Dams in 1979. In December, he charged that Idaho Power failed to tell the Legislature when it applied to increase its Swan Falls water right while the lawmakers debated subordination last year.

It turns out that Idaho Power, which advertises that it "puts the light in your light bulb," doesn't like to be accused of operating in the dark.

---

128   Ripley, Rick. "Jim Jones, Idaho Power make strange adversaries." *Idaho Statesman*. Feb. 19, 1984.

After Jones made his accusations, Idaho Power's vice president for public affairs, Logan Lanham, visited the attorney general in his office. "I told him in no uncertain terms, as I've been known to do, that he can question my judgment, but he had better never again question my honesty and my integrity," said Lanham, a powerful figure around the Statehouse.

Jones also is seeking subordination in the relicensing of Swan Falls, which FERC currently is considering. That prompts Jim Taney, Idaho Power's director of public relations, to say, "I'm a little concerned about an attorney general of this state who would contend that the federal government has the right to subordinate a state water right."

But Jones says Idaho Power is being "two-faced" in forwarding that argument. The heart of his advocacy for subordination lies in the contention.

Jones' mentor, the late Len Jordan was in the governor's chair when Idaho Power applied for federal power licenses for the Hells Canyon, Brownlee and Oxbow dams. Jordan refused to support the applications unless the company agreed to subordinate its water rights to allow upstream development. Idaho Power did so.

The company concedes that its water rights at the three dams still are subordinated, and Jones says clauses in federal power licenses for the dams and other Idaho Power installations subordinate 85 percent of the utility's hydrologic capacity in the Snake River.

"That's why it's a little bit two-faced for the power company...to make the claim for subordination," Jones says. They've done a 180-degree about-face and said, 'Gee, that's federal meddling.'"

As a practical matter, subordination of the water rights at the three Hells Canyon dams means little currently because most of the water that reaches Swan Falls flows on to the installations.

The Supreme Court affirmed Idaho Power's water rights in a surprising decision in 1982, and Lanham says of Jones, "…what the hell, he's just trying to get around what the court said," He contends Jones is trying to take away the company's property rights without compensation.

"How many times do you compensate them?" Jones says. They've already been compensated by enjoying the privilege of building the dams in Hells Canyon."

Jones sees the issue "as a struggle between the power company and the state as to who is going to control the future parceling out of water rights in the Snake River."

It's evident that his position could prove costly. Asked whether Idaho Power would support Jones in future campaigns, Lanham laughed for several seconds, then said, "You're four years down the road. I don't know. I don't think you make a decision on one issue per se."

He also confided that the political action committee members who doled out Idaho Power's campaign funds in 1982 supported Jones because "he was more up front in answering their questions" than his opponents. That was before the Swan Falls issue came to a head.

Logan's comment regarding his visit to my office to advocate for his integrity was a bit puzzling. I do not recall such a meeting and it would have been unusual because there had been little interplay between the two of us as a result of the on-going hostilities. Had he come to my office to make such a comment, he certainly would not have gotten the last word.

   After Ripley's article appeared in the Statesman, a couple of political supporters invited me to lunch. Larry Mills and Bart Brassey were well-regarded, mainstream members of the Republican establishment in Boise and had supported me from the time I jumped in to run against George Hansen in 1978. During the course of our lunch conversation, they mentioned that there was talk going around that I would be a one-term attorney general because of my fight with the Power Company. They allowed as how things had not worked out so well politically for folks who had fought with Idaho Power in the past. They were right, of course. I didn't regard it as being any kind of threat but, rather, just bringing to my attention some of the scuttlebutt that was going around in the political circles. At that point I wasn't particularly worried about how things would work out politically. My thought was to prevail, which would undoubtedly require continuing escalation of hostilities. It seemed the Governor and I were starting to gain ground and that at some point we would prevail, either in the Legislature or the courts, or possibly force negotiations toward a reasonable settlement.

   Conveniently, the Times-News published an editorial in its Sunday issue on February 19, titled "Jones' Water Bill on the Right Track."[129] The editor wrote, "A new subordination bill drafted by Attorney General Jim Jones is on the right track to solving water priorities created by the Idaho Supreme Court's Swan Fall decision....The updated legislation, to be introduced by the House Resources and Conservation Committee, appears to strike a proper balance in the competing issues of subordination." This was a welcome boost for the new Evans-Jones bill. A letter to the editor in that same paper remarked that the tabling of the bill "could

129   "Jones' water bill on the right track." *Times-News*, Feb. 19, 1984.

be costly."[130] "We run a real risk of losing our water to out-of-state interests should we not utilize our water resources the most effective way. Allowing unused water to flow to the Pacific is not the most effective way. But, what does Idaho Power care, they are mostly owned by out-of-state interests anyway." Public involvement in the Magic Valley area was critical because of a number of the House members from the area were supporting Idaho Power. Tom Stivers, the Speaker of the House, was firmly in the Power Company's corner, as well as Gordon Hollifield, a Jerome Republican who represented my own legislative district, and John Brooks, a Gooding County Republican. Both Brooks and Hollifield were firmly behind Idaho Power and opposed to any effort to subordinate its Swan Falls right.

Randy Stapilus, a reporter for the Idaho State Journal, had a Sunday article in which he wrote, "The debate over the Swan Falls Dam has been a political spectacle unlike any other this state has ever seen or may ever see again. Many years from now, historians may record it as a special event in Idaho's history, unique in its impact both political and substantive.[131] He noted that the Capitol was swamped with lobbyists during the consideration of the subordination bill in the House and that "Idaho Power had called out its heavyweight lobbyist, Vice President Logan Lanham, who hadn't in recent years spent much time around the legislature but put in long days this year." Randy certainly grasped the importance of the Swan Falls issue, as well as the importance of water, generally, to Idaho's future. Following years of newspaper reporting, Randy launched out on his own, establishing an on-line media operation devoted in large part to water issues. He continues that operation to this date and is well known and well regarded in the water community. I always appreciated Randy because he was the first political

---

130   Eckert, Armand. "Aghast at senators' inabilities." *Times-News*, Feb. 19, 1984.
131   Stapilus, Randy. "Why that Swan Falls Legislation Is so Important." *Idaho State Journal*, Feb. 19, 1984.

reporter to interview me in 1978 when I made my debut on Idaho's political scene — my ill-fated challenge against George Hansen.

The Idaho State Journal also had an article by Dan Dockstader about a public forum held on February 16 in Rupert to discuss the Swan Falls controversy. Senator Peavey and Conley Ward, a Commissioner at the Idaho Public Utilities Commission, made presentations about how subordination would increase consumers' electric bills.[132] Our friend, Ben Canvass, made a presentation refuting those claims. The report indicated that about 200 people attended the meeting, many of them farmers from Ben's neighborhood. Of particular interest is the fact that the Idaho Potato Growers Association held a brief meeting afterwards in which they endorsed the new Evans-Jones bill. On behalf of the Association, Ben said that Idaho Power was attempting to "pit established farmers against neighbors and then scare the rest of the state with 14 to 17 percent increases. They want to make us as the villain by being the only few benefitting.... We should let the Snake River be all of the people's and not just a corporation's."

The Post-Register had a Sunday commentary by Ben Plastino, generally recognized as the dean of Idaho political writers, who wrote, "Whatever happens during the 1984 Idaho Legislature, passage of a bill subordinating the water rights of the Idaho Power Co. is imperative."[133] I appreciated having Ben's support because he was a knowledgeable individual and had been an observer of Idaho politics for decades. Every time I went to an interview with Ben during my eight-year tenure as Attorney General, he would pull out his trusty old Royal typewriter from underneath his desk, place it on top of the desk, and pull out some scraps of paper that looked like paper towels to stuff into the typewriter and start typing down your answers to his questions. He was not the speediest

132   Dockstader, Dan. "Water Rights: Both Views Heard." *Idaho State Journal,* Feb. 19, 1984.
133   Plastino, Ben. "Water rights legislation imperative." *Post-Register,* Feb. 19, 1984.

typist in the world, so the interviewee had to employ slow-talking techniques. Toward the end of my tenure, during the late 1980s, everyone at the Post-Register had a desktop computer installed for their use. Nevertheless, when a person came in for an interview, Ben would reach down to grab his beloved Royal to take down the proceedings. He regarded the computer as kind of a desk ornament. In any event, Ben's commentary devoted a couple of columns to the happenings in the Legislature during the preceding week and then gave nice coverage to my talking points about the new Evans-Jones bill in the remaining two columns.

The issue was finally getting the media coverage that it needed and deserved. Not wanting to miss the opportunity for a little more of the same, I responded back to the Pocatello paper's errant February 17 editorial:[134]

> Your editorial misunderstanding of the Swan Falls issue begs a response. Your editorial of February 17 essentially says that Pocatello and Southwest Idaho should not or will not have Snake River water available for future growth and development. You would support locking up the main flow of the Snake River for production of hydro power.
>
> Your editorial fails to take into account the fact that Pocatello and other cities along the Snake River will need to have additional water for domestic purposes to serve growing populations in the future. You ignore the fact that some water should be set aside for future commercial and industrial needs so that we can build plants and thereby create jobs, payrolls, taxes and tax base. There may be alternatives for producing electricity but there are no alternatives to serving domestic and other consumptive needs for water.

---

134   The Journal published the guest opinion on Feb. 28, 1984.

Unless control of the Snake River is returned to the State of Idaho and unless we set aside some water for future growth and development through subordination of Power Company water rights on the river, Southern Idaho will become a no-growth area. That may be why the Idaho Conservation League opposes subordination of hydro power rights to consumptive uses of water. If Idaho Power Company is able to establish a "minimum stream flow" of 8400 cubic feet per second at the Swan Falls Dam (almost three times the present minimum stream flow set by the State Water Resource Board) we will have turned the Snake River into a wild and free-flowing river. This disregards the history of the Snake River as a "working river," as Senator Len Jordan called it. He recognized that it is the primary reason that Southern Idaho bloomed and flourished.

If we allow the Power Company and Conservation League to establish such an increased stream flow at Swan Falls, we will furnish Oregon, Washington and California with a great deal of precious water so that they can grow and prosper at Idaho's expense. Idaho would not need the additional power generated by such an increased stream flow since, without water, we could not support substantial growth. But I am confident that the electricity would be sold to the other states which could grow with our wasted water resources.

The Governor and I have proposed a multiple use concept with regard to Snake River water. We believe that water should be set aside for future growth in Southern Idaho but that we should not unduly deplete the stream flow to the disadvantage of electric consumers. Our legislation calls for a balanced use of water so that we can have water available for development, as well as relatively low power rates. That policy can succeed because we have had it in effect in Southern Idaho since statehood.

Water is a basic essential of life and consumptive uses must have priority over less essential uses such as production of hydro power. This was recognized in 1952 by Idaho Power Company and then-Governor Len Jordan. It was agreed that Idaho Power Company's water rights at Hells Canyon would be forever subordinate to consumptive uses all the way up the Snake River through Southern Idaho. Jordan insisted on subordination and the Power Company agreed to it as a condition of having the privilege of building three dams on the Hells Canyon. That agreement has been partially abrogated by a loop-hole which the Idaho Supreme Court found in 1982 but the damage can be repaired by the subordination legislation. No one is taking Idaho Power Company's water but, rather, we would make them give it back for the future of Southern Idaho—so that communities can have domestic water to grow; so that job-creating industry can be attracted to Idaho; so that some additional water may be available for cost-effective agricultural expansion at some time in the future. We can't lock up the main flow of the Snake River for any one of these purposes. Neither can we waste our precious water resources by using them only for production of hydroelectric power. We can have water for all of these beneficial purposes and will have with the passage of the subordination bill.

Similar guest opinions were sent to the Idaho Statesman and Lewiston Morning Tribune, responding to their February 16 editorials celebrating the untimely death of the Evans-Jones bill.[135]

---

135   The Statesman published the guest opinion on Feb. 29, 1984. The Tribune published the guest opinion also.

On February 21, the Statesman published a letter to the editor from Tom Hovenden, writing on behalf of the Idaho Cattle Association, chastising the paper for its "negative coverage of the Swan Falls water rights issue."[136] Tom's theme was that agriculture, including the cattle industry, had built a "very solid agricultural economy" that benefitted folks in the city and that "selfish Boise-River thinking that now prevails in the Legislature" failed to take into account that water was needed to build and sustain an agricultural economy. He asserted that the "current agricultural price level plus the high cost of pumping water has virtually put an end to further new development." Dedicating the Snake River primarily to the purpose of generating hydropower to serve folks in the city was short sighted and wrong. It was interesting food for thought.

Reverberations from the tabling ambush were still being felt in the Senate a week later. Mark Ricks certainly was justified in criticizing leadership for cleverly springing that surprise upon him and the other supporters of the subordination bill. However, apparently he hurt other Senators' feelings by saying so on the floor. Senator Ricks, who was then in his sixth year in the Senate, said, "I've always tried to operate with everything above-board," and that legislative maneuvering "has been a little hard for me to adjust to."[137] The Senator said he had "learned his lesson" — to not say anything critical of his colleagues.[138] Mark was a true gentleman, but I saw absolutely no need for him to apologize for being the "stickee."

That same day, I sent a memo to Pat and Clive suggesting that we broaden our estoppel claim in Swan Falls I. The focus to date had centered on the analysis Tom Nelson made in his 1976 memorandum to Jim Bruce. Tom

---

136   "Coverage of Swan Falls water-rights issue is not fair to farmers." *Idaho Statesman,* Feb. 21, 1984.
137   Associated Press. "Senator Ricks 'learns his lesson.'" *Post-Register,* Feb. 21, 1984.
138   Etlinger, Charles. "Ricks sparks tussle over Snake rights." *Idaho Statesman,* Feb. 21, 1984.

said estoppel presented a difficult question— "Long and continuous known acquiescence in another's use and enjoyment of a property or a privilege may preclude one from subsequently asserting his own claim." He cited the Bell Rapids project, which Idaho Power encouraged and which drew water directly from the Snake River not too far above Swan Falls. As with other upstream farmers and farm projects, Idaho Power had supported the development with the intent of furnishing electric power for the pumping. Tom opined that the Power Company would probably be estopped from enforcing its Swan Falls right "to the detriment of upstream junior pumpers to whom it furnished power." He said, "If IPC now attempts to enforce the Swan Falls right against Bell Rapids, it is saying, 'We saw you spend the money, we will deliver power for pumping and collect money for it, but don't deplete our Swan Falls flow right.'"

This argument would probably have been persuasive to the district court in the Swan Falls I remand, perhaps even to the Supreme Court. That is likely why the Power Company was willing to release the 5,000 defendants in Swan Falls II who had developed or made substantial investment toward developing their projects. However, this estoppel defense, just like the Idaho Power legislation, would give no relief for future water right applicants.

In thinking about the issue, it seemed that we also needed to look at a more global claim—one that would apply both to past and future water rights. In that regard, the memo said, "The defense would be that Idaho Power is estopped from claiming a superior right to the Snake River water as a result of the Hells Canyon deal. Jordan would not have supported the 3-dam Idaho Power plan had the Power Company not agreed to subordinate, as evidenced by their statements at the time. Based on their assurances, Jordan changed his position and agreed to support the Power Company proposal. The doctrine of estoppel applies, precluding the Power Company from now coming in to say that it has a superior right over the parties who received water licenses from the State." The two estoppel arguments were not inconsistent and both seemed to be legally viable.

On February 22, I announced that the Federal Energy Regulatory Commission handed a small victory to the State in the FERC relicensing proceeding for the Power Company's dam at Twin Falls.[139] That license, which contained a subordination clause, had expired in November of 1983. The State moved to intervene in the proceeding for the purpose of retaining the subordination provision, but Idaho Power opposed that motion. FERC rejected the Power Company's arguments, stating in its order, "It appears to be in the public interest to allow (the State of Idaho) to appear in this proceeding." I mentioned that the State was also seeking to intervene with respect to the Swan Falls hydroelectric project but that FERC had not yet ruled on that motion for intervention.

The following day, the Post-Register published a guest opinion written by Ken Robison, a Boise consumer and wildlife advocate.[140] Robison argued that subordination would drastically increase electric rates, while harming fish habitat in the river. He cited the study funded by Idaho Power and the claim that electric rates would rise by $52 million a year. He said the only thing farmers would get from subordination would be higher power rates and possibly lower prices. The publication of this type of article in the Idaho Falls area was not too worrisome because public opinion in that area was solidifying in favor of subordination. The legislators from the area, including Senator Watkins who had missed out on the tabling vote, were solidly in support of the Evans-Jones bill.

The influential Committee of Nine, the advisory group

---

139   Associated Press. "Move boosts state hopes in fight over water rights." *Post-Register,* Feb. 22, 1984.
140   "Swan Falls controversy no benefit for farmers." *Post-Register,* Feb. 23, 1984.

to Water District No. 1 located in Idaho Falls, announced that it revoked its support for Idaho Power's bill and asked Governor Evans to veto the bill if it passed the Senate.[141] This was significant because the Committee voted earlier to support the Idaho Power legislation. Water District 1 is Idaho's largest water district, extending upstream from Milner Dam and including most of the upper Snake River Basin. Typically, Committee of Nine members are experienced and knowledgeable on water issues and regarded as such by the water using community. At that time, Reed Oldham of Rexburg was the chairman of the Committee. Both he and the Water District watermaster, Ron Carlson, played a substantial role in supporting the subordination effort throughout the Swan Falls battle.

The new position of the Committee of Nine was contained in a resolution which noted that Upper Snake water users "have consistently supported a reaffirmation of the subordinated position of hydropower water rights that existed prior to the 1982 Supreme Court Swan Falls decision.... Upper Snake water users have also supported and encouraged legislation that would offer power companies protection from the PUC considering protection of hydropower rights in rate setting actions." The resolution acknowledged earlier water user support for both the Idaho Power and the initial Evans-Jones bills but stated "the Idaho State Senate tabled (the Evans-Jones bill) through a parliamentary action demonstrating contempt for both the Idaho House of Representatives and those residents of Idaho supporting (the subordination bill).... This demonstration of bad faith has caused water users to reconsider support for (the Idaho Power bill)."[142] Therefore, the Committee of Nine urged a gubernatorial veto of the Idaho Power bill. Essentially, the Committee was supporting the position that Governor Evans and I had taken — that approval

---

141   "Water users seek veto." *Post-Register,* Feb. 23, 1984.
142   "Water users seek veto." *Post-Register,* Feb. 23, 1984.

of the Idaho Power bill should be contingent upon approval of our bill.

On February 24, I notified the Boise media that I would be addressing the Ada County Republican Women at a luncheon meeting on February 27 to give "a definitive outline of the Swan Falls issue, including historical background, the status of and plans for federal and state litigation, the effect and prospects of the legislative proposals and the implications of the issue for Idaho's future." The media were invited to attend "if for no other purpose than to dispel the myth that subordination does not have popular appeal in the Boise area." The presentation was well received by the Republican women but the Boise print media apparently was not impressed enough to waste any ink on the speech.

Senator Noh raised another potential problem related to Idaho Power's apparent strategy in the Swan Falls fight—that it may attempt to remove subordination conditions from the power licenses for its three Hells Canyon dams when they came up for relicensing in 2005.[143] Laird noted that although the current power license for the dams contained subordination language, the Power Company's state water rights did not include subordination language. This was clearly an oversight and probably a result of the State figuring it didn't need to put that language in the state water rights since it was included in the federal power licenses. And, when the deal was struck in 1952 between Governor Jordan and Idaho Power, a gentlemen's agreement was regarded as all that was necessary to seal a deal.

Laird's thesis was that the Power Company had been successful in removing subordination conditions from the Shoshone Falls and Upper Salmon licenses by telling FERC that it should defer to the State, which had not placed subordination language in the State water licenses, and

143   Shaughnessy, Rick. "Senator says water-right battle spreads to western Idaho." *Times-News,* Feb. 24, 1984.

would likely use that same argument with FERC when the Hells Canyon license came up for renewal. Thus, he contended that water users below Swan Falls and above the Hells Canyon complex could be in jeopardy in the future. Ken Dunn, the Water Resources chief, lent some support for this thesis, indicating he knew of one party that was investigating the purchase of unappropriated storage water in Cascade Reservoir with the intent of exchanging that water with Idaho Power to compensate for water the party was withdrawing from the river near Glenns Ferry, above Swan Falls. Ken said, "The first guy that does it will breed the rest of them," and that the "end result could easily be that vacation homes on the reservoir would no longer have a body of water in their front yards."[144] The solution, of course, to the potential jeopardy that southwest Idaho water users might face in the future was passage of subordination legislation.

Greg Panter, speaking on behalf of Idaho Power, said that Laird's concerns were "a scare tactic to convince people downstream of Swan Falls to believe they're going to be adversely affected" if subordination legislation is not approved by the Legislature.[145] Whether Laird's comments were a scare tactic or a wake-up call, they were designed to show water users below Swan Falls that perhaps they had best not just sit on the sidelines.

Bill Loughmiller, a Twin Falls farmer, used the Senate tabling maneuver as the theme of a bumper sticker. The bumper ornament read, "Pay your power bill—buy a senator."[146] Loughmiller said the sticker was created as "an expression of our disgust in the Senate. They didn't even give us a hearing. They didn't even give us a discussion. We felt we were being run over by a railroad train."

An old family friend, Representative Noy Brackett, a

---

144   Shaughnessy, Rick. "Senator says water-right battle spreads to western Idaho." *Times-News,* Feb. 24, 1984.

145   Shaughnessy, Rick. "Senator says water-right battle spreads to western Idaho." *Times-News,* Feb. 24, 1984.

146   Associated Press. "Bumper stickers jab senators on Swan Falls issue." *Times-News,* Feb. 26, 1984.

Twin Falls Republican, displayed one of the stickers around the House floor, but said he was advised by House Speaker Tom Stivers that he shouldn't do so. Stivers responded, "I didn't advise him of anything. Noy's a big kid — he's over 21. I just don't think a state representative should be showing that kind of thing around the floor."[147] Noy was a respected rancher from the Three Creek area, who came from pioneer stock. His word was his bond and he had a good, down-home sense of humor. Apparently, some did not appreciate it.

One of Idaho Power's main talking points was that the 8,400 cfs water right the Idaho Supreme Court apparently granted the company at Swan Falls was property that could not be taken without just compensation and that subordination of the right constituted a taking. My stock response was that the State was only trying to take back what belonged to it in the first place. However, the Power Company argument resonated with subordination opponents. In response, we prepared a position paper titled, "Does Subordination Constitute a Taking of Power Company Property?" The paper outlined the 1952 agreement between Governor Jordan and the Power Company, set out the statements made by Pat Parry, Thomas Roach, and Tom Nelson, and concluded: "There is no taking of power company property because the power company agreed to give up whatever priority they may have had over upstream consumptive uses in order to obtain the right to build their three Hells Canyon dams. That agreement has now been repudiated and they are now claiming they have a right to be compensated for what they voluntarily gave up at the insistence of Len Jordan. The same battle that was fought 32 years ago is now being essentially re-played."

Nevertheless, on February 22, Representative Walt Little, a subordination opponent, requested an opinion from

---

147   Associated Press. "Bumper stickers jab senators on Swan Falls issue." *Times-News*, Feb. 26, 1984.

my office as to (1) the statutory authority that would permit the Legislature to take a court-confirmed water right under the State's police power, (2) what legal authority would permit the State Water Resource Board to condemn a 1,000 cfs water right at Swan Falls Dam, and (3) if the 1,000 cfs water right could be condemned, could it be placed in the State water bank for subsequent distribution for upstream consumptive uses.

Pat Kole responded on February 27, concluding the State's police power was "probably broad enough to regulate and in effect, take a court confirmed water right," that the Idaho Constitution "would permit the state water resource board to condemn a 1,000 cfs water right at Swan Falls," but that the 1,000 cfs water right condemned by the Board "probably could not be placed in the state water bank for subsequent distribution to other upstream consumptive uses absent a statutory change." The office was not asked about, and did not opine upon, the question of payment of just compensation. The only value of the legal advice was to confirm that the Water Resource Board could condemn Idaho Power's Swan Falls water right, which was something that the Board had been considering for months. However, it did not have much effect on the debate over subordination because any effort to condemn part of the water right would have been premature since it still was not clear whether Idaho Power had a compensable property right at Swan Falls.

The next thing I knew, Idaho Power was attacking me in a news release for taking "diametrically opposed legal positions on state water rights."[148] Apparently, this had to do with an amicus brief I joined onto in a case pending before the U.S. Supreme Court. The amicus brief was prepared by the Wyoming Attorney General in support of an appeal by the Los Angeles Department of Water and Power, claiming

---

148   "Jones Takes Opposing Views on Water Rights, Utility Says." *Idaho State Journal*, Feb. 28, 1984.

that one of its water rights was annulled without payment of just compensation. The brief said that "vested appropriative water rights are constitutionally protected property interests," and that the taking of the utility's "vested property rights is contrary to the interests of sound public policy." Logan said the Power Company was "confused to say the least....On the one hand, Attorney General Jones is telling the Idaho Legislature that it's all right for the state to seize Idaho Power's water right (at Swan Falls dam). But at the same time, he's telling the U.S. Supreme Court that sort of action is illegal under the Constitution. We think his argument to the Court is exactly on target, and we just wish he would read his brief again."

My wish was as it had been since I got involved in the fight—that Idaho Power would simply acknowledge the agreement struck with Len Jordan and admit it had no property interest in any of its water rights above the Hells Canyon complex.

Idaho Power's other main argument was that power rates would skyrocket with subordination. The Company repeatedly referred to the study it funded for the interim committee claiming that rates would increase by $52 million per year if its rights were subordinated. My office found a good economist to review the study. Brian McGrath, an assistant professor of economics at Boise State University did an excellent job of debunking the study in a written commentary he provided us on February 26. He pointed out the speculative nature of the Idaho Power study, the questionable nature of the assumptions upon which its conclusions were based, and the fact that a number of economic principles were overlooked in the study. We were able to put it to good use from that point forward in responding to the rate increase scare tactic.

The Committee of Nine weighed in again with a new slide presentation that was shown to the Greater Idaho Falls Chamber of Commerce on February 28. The slide show titled, "Snake River Water for All," was developed to present the Committee's side of the Swan Falls water rights issue, according to Ron Carlson.[149] Ron said the Swan Falls decision left a cloud over all future water uses in his area and provided a potential windfall for Idaho Power's stockholders. He indicated he was holding more than 550 water right applications because of the moratorium imposed by the court decision, more than half of which were for properties of less than 40 acres, many of them in the 5 to 10 acre range. The slide show would be presented to interested groups around the area.

The House State Affairs Committee voted 11-10 on February 29 to send the new Evans-Jones bill to the full House without a recommendation for passage. Ben Cavaness and Forrest Hymas both appeared before the Committee to argue in favor of the bill. The Committee's vote on the first Evans-Jones bill had been 12-8, so we lost a bit of our margin on the new proposal. But, could anyone expect good news on leap day?

Just a few hours after the committee vote, I was speaking to a group in Payette about the Swan Falls controversy. I told the group that those downstream from Swan Falls could also suffer adverse effects if Idaho Power was not required to honor the agreement it made in 1952 with Len Jordan. According to the report in the Argus Observer, I said the "Evans-Jones proposal seeks 'balanced use of Idaho's limited water resources' and revives the theme of Len B. Jordan during the 1950s, 1960s, and 1970s while Jordan was Idaho's governor and a U.S. Senator. Jordan cautioned Idahoans to 'use it or lose it' when he called the Snake a 'working river.' He strongly favored multiple use of the water, benefitting agricultural, industrial and domestic users in addition to hydroelectric generation. In his final Senate years, Jordan said

149   Retallic, Ken. "Committee of Nine views river as something for use by everyone." *Post-Register*. Feb. 29, 1984.

Idaho's people had first priority to use the water but no right to waste it depriving other Pacific Northwest states' people of its benefits."[150] Those in attendance, most of whom were water users themselves, seemed to be receptive to the message. I hoped they would convey that to their area legislators.

---

150   Crosby, Ann. "Jones addresses Swan Falls issue for Payette group." *Argus Observer (Ontario, Ore.),* March 1, 1984.

MARCH COMES, AND LEAVES, LIKE A LION

The Committee of Nine met on March 1 to select officers, consider the up-coming water year, and learn of developments in the Legislature.[151] Bob Reichert of Twin Falls was elected as chairman to succeed Reed Oldham. Dale Rockwood of Iona was chosen as vice-chair and Reed Murdoch of Blackfoot was elected secretary-treasurer. Ron Carlson was reelected to a seventh term as District 1 watermaster. Clyde Storer of Ririe, Clyde Beck of Roberts, and Paul Berggren of Idaho Falls became new members. The other three members were Les Saunders of Hazelton, Dave Rydalch of St. Anthony, and Leonard Scheer of Rupert. I mention these people because they were all very helpful in the subordination effort. During the course of the dispute, I had most of them on my mailing list to receive letters, press releases and the like. They played a big part in solidifying the support of legislators in their respective areas for the Evans-Jones bills. Ron Carlson told the Committee that because of setbacks in the Legislature water users were going to have to be more involved in legislative matters. "They are going to have to recognize threats that exist from other interests and to take some decisive action to head off any other attempts to gain control of Snake River water supplies."[152]

Meeting the following day, the Idaho Irrigation Pumpers Association, another water user group, voted to support both the new Evans-Jones bill and the Idaho Power bill. There were two dissenting votes on our bill, reflecting concern that subordination would raise pumping costs for existing irrigators while supporting competition for the

---

151   Marker, Joe. "Water supply, Swan Falls concern water users." *Post-Register*, March 2, 1984.
152   Marker, Joe. "Water supply, Swan Falls concern water users." *Post-Register*, March 2, 1984.

products they raise.[153] I appeared before the group to give my talking points in support of our legislation, but was apparently not able to convince the two that subordination posed no risk of higher power rates.

I took my talking points to a luncheon meeting in Pocatello on March 3, outlined the history of the Swan Falls dispute and boiled it down to whether the Power Company was going to honor the deal it made with Len Jordan.[154] I said the Power Company was well compensated for the agreement to subordinate all of its water rights above Hells Canyon by virtue of being allowed to build the three-dam complex. Therefore, no compensation would be owed if the company was made to honor its agreement. "We want to repair the damage done by the Idaho Supreme Court when they didn't realize just compensation had been given to the utility."

Back at the Legislature, the House passed the new Evans-Jones bill on March 5 by a 37-33 vote.[155] We lost ground because the vote on the first bill had been 38-31. Representative Haagenson sought to send the bill to the amending order, which may have caused the bill's demise, but that effort failed on a 30-39 vote.[156] Vard argued that the bill struck a balance between the use of water for hydropower and consumptive purposes. "This is the first time the ratepayers will have a direct influence on consumptive water uses. All future diversions will be evaluated for their impact on water uses." Idaho Power's lobbying effort was intense and accounted for the change in the vote. My perception was that we were gaining ground in public opinion but losing a bit among legislators because of Logan's efforts. Once again, Gordon Hollifield and John Brooks supported Idaho Power by voting

---

153   Zellar, Ron. "Irrigators back proposed laws on Swan Falls." *Idaho Statesman,* March 3, 1984.

154   Cook, Ed. "Jones Contends Idaho Power 'Bargained Away' Water Right." *Idaho State Journal,* March 4, 1984.

155   "House takes second shot at water bill." *Times-News, March 6, 1984.*

156   UPI. "Compromise Snake subordination bill clears House hurdle." *Idaho Press-Tribune,* March 6, 1984.

against our bill.

That same day, Laird's committee considered and approved Idaho Power's bill. Laird was the only committee member voting against approval.[157] During discussion of the bill, Laird pursued the issue of whether Idaho Power considered its Hells Canyon complex "subordinated into perpetuity." Tom Nelson, speaking on behalf of the Company said, "by oversight, subordination language was not inserted on most of the state licenses on the complex," but that he never asked the Company if it would seek to have subordination clauses removed from the federal licenses on those facilities when the present licenses expired. Laird pursued the issue, asking if he would agree to have subordination clauses inserted into the state water licenses for the three dams. Tom answered, "I have no problem with that," but indicated "he would have to check with Idaho Power 'policy-makers' to obtain approval."

On March 7, the House State Affairs Committee approved John Peavey's bill that would require the Public Utilities Commission to approve any sale of a hydropower water right. Conley Ward argued in favor of the bill during the hearing, saying, "With water being such a critical aspect of the utilities' operations, something that important to a utility's costs, the PUC should have a role in determining whether they can sell it or not." This is the bill that also required proceeds from such a sale to benefit ratepayers.[158] I was not losing any sleep over this bill, as it was unlikely that it would have any practical effect. It appeared to be designed for the most part to deflate our argument that the Power Company stockholders would benefit if the Supreme

157   "House takes second shot at water bill." *Times-News*, March 6, 1984.
158   Stevenson, Mary. Associated Press. "Swan Falls Bills Move Toward Resolution." *Idaho State Journal*, March 8, 1984.

Court's decision stood. However, we never thought it likely that the Power Company would sell any of its Swan Falls water rights, especially if the Peavey legislation was enacted. What would be more likely is that the Power Company would protest every new water right application above Swan Falls and try to extract payment from the applicant in exchange for dropping the protest. Or, if it did not receive its full allocation, it might well make a water call and obtain tribute from junior upstream water users for excusing the call. In the meantime, it would be able to generate surplus energy for out-of-state sales at prices much higher than it was allowed to charge in Idaho. It would not make much sense to sell its Swan Falls rights.

That same day, Laird's committee took up consideration of the Evans-Jones bill with an overflow crowd of 140 people.[159] After six hours of testimony and discussion, Laird postponed action on the bill. Senator Peavey said that he planned to offer several amendments to the new bill, including a requirement that the amount to be paid to Idaho Power as compensation for its water rights be stipulated in the legislation. Sherl Chapman argued on behalf of the Idaho Water Users Association that the Evans-Jones bill was needed to prevent Idaho Power from becoming the water broker for the Snake River. He said, "It seems to us to make more sense to have the state decide how much of the remaining water should be used for hydro and how much for consumptive uses." He opposed Senator Peavey's proposal to set any amount for compensation, saying that should be decided by the courts. He was supported in that argument by Robert Lee of Rexburg, a former director of the Idaho Water Resource Board, who noted that the Swan Falls facility produces "an infinitesimal amount of power" and that any compensation should be limited to hydropower losses at that dam.

---

159   "Panel considers bill to give state control of river." *Idaho States-man*, March 8, 1984.

The Senate acted quickly on the Idaho Power bill, voting on March 8 to approve it by a 21-13 vote. The bill headed to the Governor. Laird urged Senators to vote against the bill, saying, "I felt for a period of time that this particular suit is more bluff than it is legal substance."[160] He said attorneys disagree about how much protection the defendants in the suit will get if the bill becomes law. Noting that new information indicated another 1,500 defendants might be subject to the lawsuit, he said, "We still have a whale of a mess, I'm afraid."[161] Senator Risch argued the proposal was "valid, fair and equitable. It takes care of the people who have spent the money" to develop their land.[162] He added that "the chief executive will probably veto this anyway." Later, the Governor confirmed the Senator's comments. He said, "I think it's very important that the people of Idaho have passage of a subordination bill."

Two articles of interest appeared in the March 11 issue of the Statesman. Reporter Ron Zeller wrote that Senator Noh was delaying consideration of the new Evans-Jones bill to give the committee a few days to think things over and that he hoped a compromise could be reached. Noh said, "The bottom line to me is that we not do anything that indicates Idaho Power has a water right before the court has a chance to rule on that."[163] Senator Peavey indicated "he would propose compensation for water losses at the older, unsubordinated dams in the Idaho Power system.... Swan Falls, Bliss, Shoshone Falls, and Upper Salmon." Of course, two of those dams had previously contained subordination conditions, which the Power Company caused to be removed. It is not clear why compensation was owed for those dams.

The other article of interest in the March 11 Statesman

---

160   Stevenson, Mary. Associated Press. "Bill frees defendants in Swan Falls suit." *Idaho Statesman,* Mar. 9, 1984.

161   Associated Press. "Senate passes water bill." *Post-Register,* March 8, 1984.

162   Shaughnessy, Rick. "Senate clears Swan Falls bill." *Times-News,* March 9, 1984.

163   Zellar, Ron. "Swan Falls compromise?" *Idaho Statesman,* Mar. 11, 1984.

indicated that the U.S. Bureau of Reclamation was "studying several proposals by farmers to buy unallocated space in Cascade Reservoir and trade it to Idaho Power Co. for rights to pump water from the Snake River near Mountain Home."[164] Sherl Chapman indicated that such a swap would "allow Idaho Power to release water in the summer months to generate electricity, replacing power that is lost because water is pumped from the Snake River." This article followed up on Laird's contention that folks below Swan Falls could well be impacted by failure to subordinate Idaho Power's water right. Citizens concerned about the effect on Cascade Reservoir had contacted Senators Beitelspacher and Dave Little, both of whom were supporting Idaho Power's position.

On March 11 the Lewiston Tribune published a letter written by Representative Carl Braun, a Democrat from Orofino who supported subordination. Representative Braun was responding to the Tribune's February 16 editorial supporting the tabling of the first Evans-Jones bill. He said, "I wish the issue was as simple as you make it. The issue is not whether those wishing to develop new farmland will have water available, but whether or not any consumptive water user—which includes industry, municipalities and irrigated agriculture—will be able to continue to develop and expand our economy." He went on to say that the Evans-Jones bill "would have provided a mechanism by which our state water resource agency would have been able to intelligently apportion the water in the Snake River drainage between consumptive water users and hydropower generation. By killing the bill, opponents have insured that unless new legislation passes, the economy in the Snake River drainage basin above Swan Falls will stagnant and our economic base cannot expand." Representative Braun was regarded as a clear-thinker and straight-shooter, which gave credibility

---

164   "Swan Falls case may affect Cascade Reservoir." *Idaho Statesman,* Mar. 11, 1984.

to the Evans-Jones position in an area where we needed the support.

True to his word, Governor Evans vetoed the Power Company bill on March 12.[165] In his veto message he said:

> I know that a large class of people are facing litigation without the enactment of this legislation and I am sympathetic to their plight. I feel, however, that it is imperative that these people not only be afforded the protection offered in this legislation, but that in addition, the state subordinate hydroelectric rights to upstream beneficial uses. It is essential for both the class of people facing litigation and the state that we address both of these issues in unison, as they are inextricably intertwined.

The Governor said the best solution to the problem was the Evans-Jones bill currently pending before Laird's committee.

Shortly before the Governor vetoed the Power Company bill, the House rejected Senator Peavey's bill requiring Public Utility Commission approval of any sale of hydropower rights by a utility.[166] The vote was more than 2-1 against the bill. The majority was against giving the PUC any role in the water rights arena.

The day after the Governor's veto, the House sustained an attempt to override the veto with a 38-31 vote against override.[167] Vard led the charge against the override, arguing that House members should sustain the veto to force action on "those water matters that are the concern of most all of us sitting in the chamber." On the other hand, House Speaker Tom Stivers called the veto a "gross injustice" to the 5,000

---

165   UPI. "Swan Falls, speeding bills vetoed." *Press-Tribune,* March 13, 1984.
166   Associated Press. "Evans Vetoes Bill to End Swan Falls Suits." *Idaho State Journal,* March 13, 1984.
167   Associated Press. "House backs veto of water-rights bill." *Idaho Statesman,* March 14, 1984.

water right holders who would have been released in Swan Falls II.[168] Stivers said, "That probably was not (the Governor's) most brilliant move of the session," and that subordinating Idaho Power's water rights could "in effect lead to subsidized water for future farm development."

Governor Evans' job of corralling skittish Democrat legislators was not made any easier when his predecessor and successor, Cecil Andrus, expressed support for Idaho Power's position at a state-wide gathering of Democrats in Boise. Andrus characterized the subordination effort as an attempt to "change a hundred years of law that has held us in good stead. It troubles me to think that we would subordinate any person's legitimate water rights in the State of Idaho."[169]

The Idaho State Journal published an article on March 16 about another difficulty resulting from the Swan Falls fight.[170] According to the article, "Idaho's Swan Falls water rights controversy is stalling expansion of a Bannock County fairgrounds irrigation well that could provide more than enough water for the Pocatello facility and reduce the county's expensive water bill there." The gist of the article was that the expansion of the well had been placed on hold because of the moratorium on issuance of new water rights resulting from the Supreme Court's decision. The article brought home the fact that more than agricultural interests were affected by the Swan Falls decision.

The controversy was starting to generate some published commentaries by the general public. A letter from Ethel Farnsworth of Boise to the editor of the Statesman caught my eye because it made the point that the sky had not fallen and power rates had not skyrocketed during the previous decades when everyone, including Idaho Power, believed all of its Snake River water rights were fully subordinated to

---

168   Associated Press. "Stivers Rips Swan Falls Evans Veto." *Idaho State Journal,* March 16, 1984.
169   Associated Press. "Andrus Questions Subordination Effort on Water Rights." *Idaho State Journal,* March 15, 1984.
170   Cook, Ed. "Water Rights Controversy Stalls Well Expansion." *Idaho State Journal,* March 16, 1984.

consumptive uses. She said, in part,[171]

> Everyone in Ada County is not in favor of having Idaho Power Co. control the water in this state. People who have studied the problem thoroughly realize that to promote industry and all economic development, the state of Idaho should control its own water. Development brings prosperity to the state. Before the Supreme Court ruling, the state of Idaho was in charge of the water with no great disaster. The system served us well. It was not broken. The Supreme Court ruling did that.

On the other hand, another Boise writer, Marjorie Geddes Hayes of Idaho Consumer Affairs, sent guest opinions to a number of papers arguing against subordination.[172] She argued that Idaho was blessed with cheap hydroelectric power, that the study financed by Idaho Power indicated subordination would cause power rates to increase, and that consumers would be adversely impacted by subordination.

Ray Orle of Twin Falls responded to the Hayes guest opinion, saying that she got "the yearly award for not knowing your state, the Swan Falls issue or your own consumer affairs interests."[173] Orle said he did not support more farm development but that was not the point. "The issue is Idaho Power wanting control of the Snake River and Idaho as we know it today. The key question is who owns Idaho water. Believe me, subordination is a priority of ownership and the alternate uses of Idaho's greatness."

Apparently the news articles regarding the potential effect of subordination on Cascade Reservoir caught the attention of some because a letter to the editor published in the

---

171   "More substitutes for power than water." *Idaho Statesman,* March 14, 1984.
172   "Don't subordinate Snake River water." *Times-News,* March 14, 1984.
173   "Water ownership is question." *Times-News,* March 18, 1984.

Statesman expressed concern about "what a colossal disaster larger fluctuations in water levels would be for fishing in Cascade Reservoir."[174]

Ted Roth of American Falls, vice president of the Idaho State Wheat Growers Association, wrote to the Idaho State Journal to criticize the Pocatello Chamber of Commerce for opposing the Evans-Jones legislation.[175] He said, "When your chamber directs your legislators to vote against a bill that affects irrigation and the expansion of land development by being able to apply water, then I think you are not considering all the facts." He indicated that the talk about skyrocketing power rates was simply a scare tactic and that power rates would go up regardless of whether or not the Power Company's water rights were subordinated. He also pointed out that the city folk needed to understand that their livelihoods depended in large part on the farm economy and the future availability of water to support it.

Laird's committee met on March 21 to take up the Evans-Jones bill again. The meeting produced some fireworks but no concrete action. Three sets of amendments were proposed during the session — one by Senators Peavey and Little, another by Senator Ringert and a third by Ben Cavaness. The Peavey-Little amendments dealt with compensating Idaho Power for the "taking" of its water right. The Cavaness amendments were designed to clean up language in the bill and tighten the compensation provisions. Senator Ringert's amendments, which he did not get to explain, dealt with priority dates of water rights.[176] Senator Beitelspacher sparked the fireworks when he moved to get the bill sent to the Senate's amending order before the committee was able to consider the three sets of amendments. Laird adjourned the committee, saying "I'm not about to have this committee get into that kind of nonsense." Laird said he objected to Beitelspacher's timing and

---

174   Skelton, Glenn. "Disaster for fishing." *Idaho Statesman*, March 17, 1984.

175   "'All the Facts.'" *Idaho State Journal*, March 19, 1984.

176   Stevenson, Mary. Associated Press. "Arguments heat up Senate debate on Swan Falls." *Post-Register*, March 22, 1984.

that he regarded the motion as an effort to kill any attempts to get a subordination bill through. "I think it's patently unfair, without even having the chance of the committee hearing the amendments, to want to move the bill out on the 14th order. I wasn't about to be stampeded into it there with two minutes past the time the meeting was supposed to adjourn."[177] Laird called the Peavey-Little amendment "absurd," saying, "It's a public-relations effort to say it's subordination. It's not subordination; it's compensation."[178]

Chances for Senate passage of the Evans-Jones bill looked quite dismal at this point. This was the second time Laird's committee was unable to get the bill reported to the Senate floor intact and it was not clear that there would ever be favorable action.

On another front, Ken Dunn and I were preparing to go to Washington to pursue a Federal strategy. We hoped to get the Department of Interior involved in supporting the subordination effort. The Department had historically supported the inclusion of subordination conditions in federal licenses for hydropower projects. Indeed, the subordination provisions in the Shoshone Falls and Upper Salmon Project licenses were inserted at the request of the Department's Bureau of Reclamation. We thought that by visiting the person in charge of reclamation operations, we could get some much-needed help in the pending FERC proceedings. It was obvious we needed to proceed with the utmost secrecy so as not to tip our hand to Idaho Power and its supporters. It was agreed that the approach to the Department would remain hush-hush.

My staff contacted Senator McClure's office to find out who at the Department we needed to speak with and to get an appointment set up. We were advised that Hal Furman, the Deputy Assistant Secretary for Water and Science, was

---

177   Stevenson, Mary. Associated Press. "Arguments heat up Senate debate on Swan Falls." *Post-Register*, March 22, 1984.
178   Shaughnessy, Rick. "Attempt to alter Swan Falls bill ends in heated exchange." *Times-News*, March 22, 1984.

the person to contact. We asked the Senator's office to set up an appointment at the earliest possible date and were told this would be done. However, the wheels must have turned fairly slowly because it seemed like it took quite a while to get the appointment. After about three weeks of waiting, we got word that Furman would see us on March 28.

In order to give Furman background on the purpose of our meeting, I sent him a letter[179] on March 23:

> As you may be aware, the state of Idaho is embroiled in a legal controversy with the Idaho Power Company over the use of the waters of the Snake River. Specifically, the issue is whether the company has subordinated its hydropower water rights to upstream consumptive uses. Since the genesis of this controversy was an intense and often bitter fight between the Department of Interior and the Idaho Power Company, I thought it would be beneficial to explore with you the past and current role of the department in the development of the Snake River. Before detailing the questions I intend to raise at our meeting on Wednesday, March 28, 1984 at 10:30 a.m., however, a brief review of the history of the hydropower controversy might be helpful.
>
> Early on, the Department of Interior developed an extensive plan for reclaiming the desert lands in southern Idaho. The plan centered around the construction of multiple-use dams. The dams were to be constructed principally for irrigation and secondarily for power. Thus, the department adopted a policy of insisting that all hydroelectric projects be operated in a manner that would not conflict with future upstream consumptive uses. The earliest statement of this policy appears in the Twin Falls Federal Power Commission license. The

---

179   Clive drafted this letter. In an act of mercy for readers, I have not included the attachments referenced in the letter, but have left in those references to indicate that we had solid support for the assertions made in the letter.

department insisted on the inclusion of Article 14, a subordination clause, as B. E. Stoutemyer, District Counsel, states in a letter to R.W. Faris, State Commissioner of Reclamation, in a letter dated June 21, 1937, "for the protection of the present and future irrigators of the Snake River Valley. (Attachment A)

During the late forties and early fifties, the department sought authority to construct a high dam in the Hells Canyon reach of the Snake River. In an often bitter fight with the Idaho Power Company that progressed through the congress, the FPC, and the media, the issue of subordination was the focal point. Idaho Power Company, among other allegations, charged that a federal project would undermine present and future state water rights. (Attachment B) In order to blunt this criticism, the various bills proposed by the department specifically provided for subordination of all hydropower water rights to all upstream consumptive uses. (Attachment C) Though for political reasons the department ultimately dropped out of the battle over Hells Canyon, the insistence of the department and state officials resulted in the inclusion of Article 41 in the Federal Power Commission license.

Article 41. The project shall be operated in such manner as will not conflict with the future depletion in flow of the waters of Snake River and its tributaries, or prevent or interfere with the future upstream diversion and use of such water above the backwater created by the project, for the irrigation of lands and other beneficial consumptive uses in the Snake River watershed.

After the subordination clause was inserted into

the Hells Canyon license, the department followed a routine policy of requesting this clause in all other FPC licenses. The department was successful in its request for inclusion of a subordination clause in the Upper Salmon and Shoshone Falls licenses; however, it was unsuccessful in the Bliss licensing.

As a consequence of state and federal efforts, approximately 90% of Idaho Power's hydroelectric water rights were subordinated by either express provisions in the state water licenses or by the Federal Power Commission licenses. The remaining 10% was thought to have been subordinated by an agreement between the state and Idaho Power Company during the Hells Canyon licensing process. (Attachment D) Much to everyone's surprise, the Idaho Supreme Court held that the remaining 10% might not be subordinated to upstream consumptive uses. This issue remains to be resolved by the courts.

During the course of litigation it came to our attention that Idaho Power Company had successfully petitioned to have the subordination clauses your agency had requested in the Upper Salmon and Shoshone Falls licenses removed. (Attachment E) This action will potentially unsubordinate another 10% of Idaho Power Company's hydroelectric water rights. Clearly, this will have a devasting impact on Idaho's growth unless it is reversed.

In light of this controversy, it is critical for my state to have a clear statement regarding the Department of Interior's position on several issues.

1.   Does the department still adhere to the policy that all hydroelectric projects shall be operated in a manner that will not conflict with future upstream consumptive uses? (Attachment F)

2.   Has the department followed a similar subordination policy on rivers other than the Snake? If so, which ones?

3.   Does the department intend to take any action to reverse the FPC order removing the subordination clauses in the Upper Salmon and Shoshone Falls licenses? I believe there may be substantial grounds for such action because John C. Chaffin of your office has indicated that the department did not receive notice of Idaho Power Company's petition. (Attachment G)

4.   Does the department intend to intervene in future FERC relicensing to insure that subordination clauses will be maintained?

If you would be prepared to discuss these matters at our meeting, I would be most grateful.

Ken and I arrived at Mr. Furman's office in the Department of Interior on March 28 at the appointed hour. Mr. Furman seemed to be an affable gentleman, but he stopped Ken and I dead in our tracks during the exchange of preliminary pleasantries. Mentioning that we were from Idaho, he said that he enjoyed playing golf with a fine citizen of our state just the previous week—a great guy named Logan Lanham. I was practically floored. How could Logan have learned about our plans and beat us to the punch? We had not told anyone about the visit. Nevertheless, Ken and I dutifully gave our spiel, following up on my letter, while Mr. Furman listened quietly, not giving any indication as to what he thought about the issue. The whole time I was thinking that our secret meeting plan had somehow sprung a leak. We left with another exchange of pleasantries. The minute we stepped out of Furman's office, I told Ken, "We're screwed." And, we were, but more about that later.

Laird's committee took up the Evans-Jones bill a third time on March 23. This time it was reported out to the amending order on a 7-2 vote. Obviously, we would have preferred that the bill go to the Senate floor with a "do pass" recommendation, since the amending order essentially subjected the legislation to a feeding frenzy of killing amendments. During the committee proceedings, Senator Ringert had an opportunity to explain his amendments. Ringert's amendments would permit subordination of any hydropower right acquired after 1928, the year the Idaho Constitution was amended to give the State the power to regulate and limit the use of water for power purposes.[180] Laird observed that the water rights at Swan Falls Dam and several other Idaho Power dams go back further than that and would be exempt from the bill if the amendment were adopted. The Ringert amendments would subordinate Idaho Power's water rights at the Bliss Dam in the Hagerman Valley, allowing storage of water for irrigation and other purposes. Laird said the Ringert amendments represented a "compromise position" and he could "reluctantly" support them.

The Peavey-Little amendments would set a cap of 500 cfs of water that could be subordinated and would allow a maximum of 20,000 new acres of land to be put under irrigation every two years. It also required a water right to be condemned in order to be subordinated, with the right going into the State water bank and payment being required by the person who acquired the condemned right.[181]

When the Evans-Jones bill came up for consideration on the Senate floor on March 26, the Senate adopted the Peavey-Little amendments that Senator Peavey characterized as "subordination with compensation."[182] He said, "This

---

180   Stevenson, Mary. "Swan Falls Bill Goes to Senate." *Idaho State Journal,* March 25, 1984.
181   Stevenson, Mary. "Swan Falls Bill Goes to Senate." *Idaho State Journal,* March 25, 1984.
182   Shaughnessy, Rick. "Vote Kills Swan Falls subordination." *Times-News,* March 27, 1984.

does not use the police powers of the state to take anybody's property away from them. If the Supreme Court decides it (the Swan Falls water right) is not a valid water right, then the provisions of the bill are meaningless." Peavey was the only Magic Valley-area Senator to support the proposal. Laird called it "sham subordination—a rather desperate attempt to convince people it is subordination, when in fact it is condemnation." He predicted the bill, as amended, would be vetoed. Senator Ringert's amendments were defeated on an 18-15 vote.[183] On the House side, Representative Walt Little introduced another version of the Idaho Power bill so there were now two bills favoring Idaho Power pending in the Legislature.

The following day Governor Evans declared the amended version of the Evans-Jones bill unacceptable and said a legislative solution to the dispute was improbable. "I would suggest maybe the whole Swan Falls issue is dead for this session."[184] He continued, "The state of Idaho should have control of distribution of those water rights. It should not be a private utility. I'm going to pursue that issue in the courts because we can't get a resolution in the Legislature. Maybe it's just too complicated for the Legislature to handle." The Governor said he had not yet made a decision on the new Idaho Power bill proposed by Representative Little. The Governor noted, "the water rights dispute had been further complicated by the fact that he and former Democratic Governor Cecil Andrus are on opposite sides of the debate."

The House voted to approve the new Idaho Power bill on March 28 on a 62-7 vote. Vard tried to amend the bill to include a subordination provision but lost on a 35-34 vote. Representative Ernest Hale, a Republican from Burley, urged support of the amendment, saying "The life blood of Idaho is at stake here. It boggles the mind to allow a private utility

---

183   Zellar, Ron. "Senate Oks water-permit bill." *Idaho Statesman,* March 27, 1984.
184   Associated Press. "Evans: Solons Won't Settle Swan Falls." *Idaho State Journal,* March 28, 1984.

to tell us what we can do and can't do."[185] On the other side of the issue, Representative Hollifield said, "We're holding these 5,000 people hostage. You're going to have to let these people have their water rights." He argued that Idaho Power will not be running the State if it prevails "because the people won't stand for it." Representatives Hollifield and Brooks both voted against Vard's subordination amendment.

The following day, the Senate approved the amended Evans-Jones bill on an 18-17 vote. Pat Kole expressed concern about the bill, saying it would "cut our feet out from under us" if it became law. "The bill as written indicates to the court that the state loses. Its inherent assumption is that the power company has a legally protected water right for which it's entitled to compensation."[186]

The 1984 legislative session came to a thankful end on March 31, just before April Fool's Day. The House failed to act upon the Senate-approved amended version of the Evans-Jones bill. However, the Senate voted 20-13 to approve the new Idaho Power bill, sending it to the Governor's desk. Senator Kermit Kiebert, a Democrat from Hope, said, "I thought it was quite appropriate that the last bill we acted on was a water bill. We started with a water bill, and we ended with a water bill."[187] Now it was up to Governor Evans.

---

185   Kenyon, Quane. Associated Press. "Swan Falls bill reincarnated." *Times-News,* March 29, 1984.
186   Black, Bob. "Senate passes pro-IPC water bill." *Post-Register,* March 30, 1984.
187   Associated Press. "Diluted water-rights bill clears Senate." *Times-News,* April 1, 1984.

OFF TO THE (POLITICAL) RACES

The Governor and I met on April 3 to discuss the fate of the new Idaho Power bill. Going into the meeting, both of us were committed to the legislation's demise. The discussion was centered around how the veto should be explained. It was a bit ticklish because there was still some sentiment among the defendants in Swan Falls II that the Governor should sign the legislation. They wanted immediate protection and contended that the State could still move forward with efforts to subordinate the Power Company's Swan Falls water right. However, the Governor and I both thought that signing the legislation would substantially impede the subordination effort. We agreed that a veto was necessary and the Governor indicated he would do so in a couple of days.

On April 6 Governor Evans pulled out his red veto stamp and firmly affixed it on the Idaho Power bill. He told the press that the legislation could have hampered the State's effort to regain control of the Snake River and that "it is vital to Idaho's continued growth and prosperity for the State to remain in control of the allocation of our precious water resources.[188] He said all of those who need irrigation water for their farms have a stake in the resolution of the issue of control over future uses of Snake River water.

Quane Kenyon of the Associated Press reported that "Idaho Power Co. responded angrily Friday to Evans' action. The veto showed 'a complete disregard for the economic interests and desires of the majority of Idaho,' Idaho Power Vice President Logan Lanham said in a news release."[189]

Just because the Legislature had adjourned did not mean that issues regarding that body were over with for the year. We had gotten wind in late February that Logan was

188   Associated Press. "Governor vetoes Swan Falls bill." *Post-Regis-ter,* April 6, 1984.
189   Kenyon, Quane. Associated Press. "Evans vetoes bill to toughen initiative law." *Idaho Statesman,* April 7, 1984.

trying to line up primary election challengers to some of the legislators who supported subordination and at the same time support those who voted for Idaho Power's legislation. It was known that Gordon Hollifield and John Brooks would have trouble convincing Magic Valley voters that they deserved reelection because of their opposition to subordination in face of the then-prevailing support for subordination in their districts. Although it was somewhat of a tricky matter for the Attorney General to become involved in primary election politics, it looked as if that was somewhat of a necessity. I let it be known to some of our supportive legislators that I would be available to speak on their behalf, if they deemed it helpful. Early in March I began looking for potential candidates to run against Brooks and Hollifield. The filing deadline for the May 22 primary was April 13, so it had to be done before then.

With regard to John Brooks, I heard that a former client in my law practice in Jerome, Gary Robbins of Dietrich, was considering a run against Brooks. I got in touch with Gary and gave him all of the encouragement I could muster. He indicated he was getting support from many others and eventually filed to run against Brooks.

While there was a good deal of dissatisfaction with Gordon Hollifield in my home legislative district in Jerome County, I had not heard of anyone who planned on challenging him. It looked like I was going to have to find a candidate. I first approached a lady who I had worked with when I was chairman of the Jerome County Republican Central Committee, Maxine Bell. She was a go-getter, had a good head on her shoulders, and was well spoken. She and her husband, Jack, had been active members of the Farm Bureau and were well respected in the community. She would have been an ideal candidate. Maxine said that the timing was not good for her and that she did not think she had what it took to do the job. While I expressed strong disagreement with that point, it looked like she was not going to be in the running. I like to think, however, that I planted a seed that eventually grew very nicely. Maxine ran for and won that legislative seat in 1988 and has since become a highly-regarded member of the Legislature, serving as chair of the House Appropriations Committee and co-chair of the Joint Appropriations and Finance Committee. I knew Maxine would be a fine legislator and she has certainly proven to be.

Next on the list was a second cousin, Waldo Martens, a thoroughly decent, mostly-retired farmer, who lived south of Jerome. When I approached Waldo about running, he said he had never thought about it and wasn't sure he was cut out for political office. I told Waldo that he was the kind of level-headed person Jerome County needed in the Legislature and that I thought he would enjoy the experience. After giving it some thought, Waldo agreed to run against Hollifield.

The legislative session brought forward a number of people who stepped up to support the subordination legislation. One who stood out was Bruce Newcomb of Burley. Bruce was a farmer, whose father and uncle had been pioneers in using sprinkler irrigation in their farming operations. Bruce was smart, well-spoken and knowledgeable on water issues. All of those qualities were effectively employed during the session and it appeared that Bruce had the knowledge and gumption to be of help as the Swan Falls fight proceeded. Bruce did have a certain amount of interest in politics, having previously run for office as a Democrat, but he allowed as how he was not particularly wedded to that party. Quite frankly, it didn't make any difference to me as there were good subordination supporters on both sides of the fence. In any event, we had regular contact leading up to the primary election and beyond. As we know, Bruce went on to run for and win a House seat when Vard retired in 1986, became recognized as an expert on water issues just like Vard, and was a highly regarded Speaker of the House.

During the subordination fight in the Legislature, I had been able to rely upon a group of knowledgeable water lawyers to provide support, advice and assistance. It was good to run ideas by them and to get the benefit of their thinking. Regular members of the group were Ray Rigby, Roger Ling of Rupert, Kent Foster, and Ben Cavaness. We also maintained fairly frequent contact with Senator Ringert, who probably had the most experience on water law in the Legislature, a good deal of his legal practice being devoted to the issue. Of course, I had my in-house attorneys—Pat Kole and Clive Strong. Pat had been our spokesman during the legislative session and continued to be the front man on the Swan Falls issue thereafter. Clive was the technical guy and it didn't take long to learn that he was always on top of issues and always provided solid legal analysis. I got to the point where, if there was any question on the legal aspect of any issue, I placed full faith and credit in Clive's opinion. When Clive gave an opinion on an issue, you could bet that he was right on target.

With the adjournment of the Legislature, media coverage of the Swan Falls issue fell off a bit but there was still some lingering interest. Ken Retallic wrote a good six-part series on the issue for the Post-Register. The first article was published on April Fool's Day, titled "Water rights kettle close to boiling over."[190] In that article, Ken described the history of the dispute to that date, concluding that the debate boiled down to five critical questions:

- Will letting the water flow through an unsubordinated Swan Falls dam effectively halt future upstream development? Or would the state be better served by instream benefits of cheap hydropower and wildlife and recreation?

---

190   *Post-Register,* April 1, 1984.

- If Swan Falls is subordinated will there be a rush to irrigate more land, causing a sharp rise in electric rates?
- Would subordination of Swan Falls be a taking of property? If so, who should be compensated, the stockholders or the rate payers?
- Who will decide the issue, the Legislature or the courts?
- Will there be fundamental changes in state water policy and laws, once the Swan Falls issue is settled?

Ken's statement of the issues was not too far off, although there was a third alternative for possible resolution of the issue besides the Legislature or the courts — a settlement between the State's executive branch and Idaho Power. In fairness, this had not really been discussed, other than in the context of the proposed contract to release the 5,000 or so defendants in Swan Falls II. With the heated debate between the State and Idaho Power it did not appear possible that a global settlement could be reached. It was my impression that the Company felt it held the upper hand and believed it had no reason to talk settlement.

The second of the series was titled "Is future development in dire danger?"[191] In that article, Kent Foster characterized the issue as "a dispute over basic water policy in this state about the use of water. Is it more important for Idaho that remaining available water resources be diverted from the sources of supply and applied to beneficial uses such as agriculture, municipal and industrial, or is it more important that it be left in the underground aquifers and streams for instream uses such as power production?"

Ken's third article was titled "Will subordination kick

---

191   *Post-Register*, April 2, 1984.

electric rates sky high?"[192] The article focused on the study funded by Idaho Power that claimed electric rates would climb by about $52 million per year and the study done for my office by Brian McGrath concluding that continuation of the State's long-standing policy of subordination of hydropower rates would have a negligible effect on power rates. Ken concluded that the truth lay somewhere in between. Actually, there may have been some truth in both points of view. It all depended on what assumptions one made as a basis for conducting the study. If one assumed that the State would hand out water rights to every Tom, Dick, and Harry who filed to use water out the Snake River below Milner and that the handing out would be done without regard to the effect on hydropower and other in-stream uses, the study favored by Idaho Power would probably be more correct. However, if one assumed that the State would consider the effect of water right applications upon instream uses, as the Governor and I proposed, the McGrath study result would be more correct. It was not so much a matter of scientific calculation but, rather, the direction of State water policy.

The fourth article asked, "Is subordination a 'theft' of property?"[193] The article essentially laid out my talking points, as well as Idaho Power's, on the subordination issue. It was helpful in that it laid out Judge Walters' rationale for determining that Idaho Power had subordinated all of its water rights above Hells Canyon in the 1952 agreement with Len Jordan. Before this, there was little or no media coverage of Judge Walters' holding, which had been reversed by the Supreme Court. Two of the comments in the article about his district court decision were:

- the effect of the subordination language in Article 41 of the Hells Canyon license had

---

192   *Post-Register*, April 3, 1984.
193   *Post-Register*, April 4, 1984.

subordinated all of Idaho Power's water rights used in hydropower production at all of its facilities on the entire Snake River watershed.... The court reasoned that since the entire river is one hydropower system, with Idaho Power operating its dams in a coordinated manner, such system could not be subordinated in bits and pieces.

- As to Idaho Power's demand for compensation for loss of its Swan Falls water rights, the district court held that Idaho Power had waived whatever right it had to demand such compensation in accepting licenses with subordination provisions. The court reasoned that Idaho Power was barred from seeking damages since, although it had the right to compensation for its Swan Falls water rights, they had been bargained away in exchange for the (Federal Power Commission) license.

Judge Walters understood that the subordination agreement encompassed more than just the bare language of the Hells Canyon license.

The fifth article in the series titled "Water rights dispute returns to court," dealt with issues to be resolved in Swan Falls I and Swan Falls II.[194] The article noted that my office received authorization from the Legislature to hire two new attorneys to work on the case starting July 1. Kent Foster said he expected the Supreme Court's decision in Swan Falls I "to be modified or totally reversed." He noted that in Swan Falls II, the list of 5,000 defendants who were at jeopardy was substantially inflated and that when non-consumptive and domestic users were eliminated and duplication of defendants

---

194   *Post-Register,* April 5, 1984.

was accounted for, there were only 3,800 defendants who would benefit from being released by Idaho Power.

The final article in the Post-Register series was titled "Swan Falls solution could force major Idaho water law changes."[195] This article was quite helpful because it outlined some needed changes in Idaho water policy. Ron Carlson cited to recommendations of the Governor's Swan Falls Task Force—management of surface and groundwater in a coordinated fashion and adjudication of the Snake River Basin—saying they were necessary elements of a new water policy. "We've got to define what our water rights are for everyone's protection. Unless the water rights are determined through a general adjudication, Idaho water law does not provide a mechanism by which water uses can actually be administered." Another one of our good supporters, Reed Hansen, an Osgood farmer who planned to run for a legislative seat, told Ken, "We need an accurate status of the aquifer, and the Idaho Department of Water Resources is not being funded enough to monitor the aquifer. Any compromise on the Swan Falls issue requires a commitment to study the entire Snake River Basin so that its waters will not be over appropriated." Reed said that continued development could lead to a drop in the Snake River Plains Aquifer level and its discharges at Thousand Springs. This, of course, would affect the flow at Swan Falls.

Overall, the Post-Register series was helpful in raising the profile of the Swan Falls issue and gave the public the benefit of both sides. It would have been helpful for such a series of articles to have been published in the western Idaho newspapers.

For its part, the Times-News did a postmortem on the legislative fight, focusing on the split between Magic Valley legislators.[196] In the article, Rick Shaughnessy said that the

---

195   *Post-Register*, April 6, 1984.
196   Shaughnessy, Rick. "Swan Falls: watershed for area delegation." *Times-News*, April 3, 1984.

conflict had been highly emotional "pitting irrigators against irrigators, Democrats against Democrats, and Republicans against Republicans in a battle for the remaining water in the Snake River." He noted how Senators Noh and Peavey had been on opposite sides of the issue and that four House members, including Hollifield and Brooks, supported Idaho Power.

Ron Zellar of the Statesman wrote about the new focus on the two Swan Falls suits in the absence of a legislative solution.[197] He wrote, "Idaho Attorney General Jim Jones and as many as 50 private attorneys are preparing for court dates in a suit by Idaho Power Co. after the Legislature failed to agree on a solution to the water-rights dispute." He quoted Pat Kole as saying, "I'm not sure where they're going to find a room big enough." If nothing else, Swan Falls II was sure to be a boon to private attorneys.

And, with the adjournment of the Legislature, the legislators and combatants turned their attention to the up-coming primary election. John Campagna of Hailey took the opportunity to send a letter to the editor of the Statesman, claiming that a "large smoke screen is being built around Swan Falls."[198] Mr. Campagna noted that he was one of the people in Blaine County named as a defendant in Swan Falls II and that other defendants from his area included Sun Valley Company, the Elkhorn Resort, the Bellevue Cemetery Board, several homeowner groups, and 14 southern Idaho municipalities. He pooh-poohed Senator Peavey's concern about skyrocketing power rates, saying, "Keep in mind that Swan Falls generates less than 1 percent of Idaho Power's total output." The claimed $50 million per year rate increase would be "some rate jump for a facility with so small an output. Why is Idaho Power making a grab for all of the water upstream from Swan Falls when this facility is one of the smallest

197   Zellar, Ron. "Lawyers prepare for Swan Falls case." *Idaho States-man,* April 4, 1984.
198   "A large smoke screen is being built around Swan Falls dispute." *Idaho Statesman,* April 7, 1984.

they have and wouldn't be missed if it stopped functioning tomorrow, and why is Sen. Peavey helping them?" He correctly concluded, "There are alternatives to generating power but there are none to no water."

The Idaho Supreme Court created turmoil in the primary election by striking down a legislative reapportionment plan and ordering the use of a plan devised by a district court judge that called for floterial and multi-member legislative districts. The Supreme Court's order was issued on April 9 and the primary election was scheduled for May 22 so candidates, including incumbents, were scrambling to decide which seat to file for. My office sought relief from the U.S. Supreme Court, including a delay of the May 22 primary, but we were not successful in that effort.

Despite the turmoil, candidates came forward and it was clear that many were motivated at least in part by the Swan Falls issue. Reed Hansen announced his candidacy for an open seat in the House of Representatives. Reed had been involved in the Swan Falls fight as a member of the Idaho Water Resource Board and was quite well-versed on water issues. In his announcement, Reed said that the water rights controversy was just part of his reason for running but said, "I would, of course, support, as a legislator, the subordination of the Swan Falls hydro water right. And I would trust the planning process to the state water board and the state water plan to protect the public interest."[199]

Cousin Waldo announced his candidacy on April 9, "blasting (Rep.) Hollifield's stance supporting Idaho Power in the Swan Falls water rights controversy."[200] He said, "If we let the power company run that water over their generators and run it out of the state, it's lost to the people of Idaho. We should use all the water available in the Magic Valley for it to prosper and grow and to do that, we have to subordinate Idaho

199   "Reed Hansen announces bid for seat in Idaho Legislature." *Post-Register,* March 30, 1984.
200   Freund, Bob. "Martens to oppose Hollifield." *Times-News,* April 10, 1984.

Power's water rights at Swan Falls." Gary Robbins filed his
candidacy against Representative Brooks, saying he was "on
the side of those interested in subordinating the Idaho Power
water right at Swan Falls."[201] John Brooks filed for reelection,
focusing his announcement on everything but water issues.[202]
Lynn Tominaga of Paul filed for a Senate seat because "his
concern over availability of water from the Snake River and its
aquifer—resulting from two years of legislative debate on the
Swan Falls issue—convinced him that his experience in water
issues is needed in the Statehouse now."[203] Keith Huettig, a
Hazelton farmer and a long-time friend of mine, also filed for
the same seat, citing his support for subordination.

In the Upper Valley area, a number of individuals filed
for legislative seats, based in large part on the subordination
issue. Cyril Burt from St. Anthony filed for a House seat
saying, "We've got to protect the (water) rights of agriculture.
Agriculture is the backbone of our state's salaries."[204] Roger
Hoopes, a Rexburg attorney, filed as a Democrat for a House
seat, saying "Idaho's water resources should not be controlled
by large, profit-motivated companies."[205] Golden Linford of
Rexburg filed for a House seat saying, "We must not allow
control over our water, which is so vital to our economy, to
be lost to downstream users."[206] Two Ada County incumbent
legislators, Gene Winchester of Kuna, and Jerry Deckard of
Eagle, filed for the same House seat. Deckard had supported
Idaho Power in the legislative session, while Winchester had
supported subordination.

201   Shaughnessy, Rick. "Dairyman takes moderate stand." *Times-News*, April 26, 1984.
202   Shaughnessy, Rick. "Gooding farmer pursues re-election on spending stand." *Times-News*, May 6, 1984.
203   Shaughnessy, Rick. "Swan Falls dispute makes Tominaga run." *Times-News*, April 24, 1984.
204   "Burt seeks protection for irrigators." *Post-Register*, April 13, 1984.
205   "Water importance stressed." *Post-Register*, May 2, 1984.
206   "Candidate laments loss of influence." *Post-Register*, May 3, 1984.

The principal Swan Falls combatants also postured for the election. On April 11, Jim Bruce wrote to Governor Evans to express concern about his vetoes of the two Idaho Power bills:

It was with a great deal of regret that I noted your vetoes of House Bill No. 408 and House Bill No. 734. The problems addressed by those bills remain to be resolved.

The press has reported speculation by some proponents of subordination that Idaho Power Company was "bluffing" in filing (Swan Falls II). As of now, approximately 1,500 defendant have been served. In order to protect the Company's rights, I have instructed the Company's lawyers to commence serving those defendants who would have been protected by the provisions of the bills you vetoed. No bluff was intended, at the start or now.

As you noted in your veto message, the basic legal questions need to be settled in court. However, you failed to state why thousands of users have to face needless expense, or why future industrial, commercial and municipal uses have to face the risks attendant on the outcome of the litigation.

The Company has previously communicated its willingness to sign the contract agreed on with your staff and the Attorney General's office in the fall of 1983, pursuant to Senate Bill No. 1180 (the Power Company's 1983 contract legislation). Your stated reason for not signing the contract was the filing of a lawsuit in Bingham County challenging the constitutionality of Senate Bill No. 1180. However, as I also told you, the Company is willing to dismiss those users protected by Senate Bill No. 1180 <u>with prejudice.</u> The risk of the unconstitutionality of Senate Bill No. 1180 would thus fall solely on the Company.

Governor, you have it entirely within your power to eliminate the costs and risks of the litigation for thousands of users, present and future. I urge you to reconsider your position and sign the contract. We would appreciate your early response.

Copies of the letter made their way to the media, appearing in the April 15 issue of the Post-Register and the April 16 issue of the Idaho State Journal. The Journal contacted Pat Costello for the Governor's position and Pat indicated that any change in the Governor's position would be based on evaluation of an opinion on the pending lawsuit from my office.[207] The Journal contacted me and reported that I said "it is 'out of the question' that the state would revive negotiations on the proposed contract as it is currently worded. 'There is no compelling reason to risk signing an unconstitutional document.'" I did say that my office wanted to continue negotiations with Idaho Power with hopes of narrowing the many complex issues surrounding the water rights case, but any new contract "will have to include some mention of subordination of Idaho Power's water rights."

The Idaho Wildlife Federation held its state convention in Sun Valley on April 14. Herman McDevitt, a Pocatello attorney who had "been a conservation activist for 30 years," warned the members against subordination of Idaho Power's Swan Falls water right.[208] McDermott argued, "We can't subordinate Idaho Power's Swan Falls water rights. There are some smart people in Phoenix and L.A. and the minute they hear that's been done, they'll rush to the courts and maintain we've admitted we have an excess of water and they'll want basin transferral. We owe Washington and Oregon that water

207   "Idaho Power Asks Evans To Reconsider Contract." *Idaho State Journal,* April 16, 1984.
208   Hovey, Larry. "Warning on Swan Falls' subordination delivered." *Times-News,* April 15, 1984.

and it should be left in the river for them." This contention is diametrically opposed to that of former Idaho Power President Albert Carlson, who had assured Senator Jordan that subordination would protect Idaho from a possible out-of-basin transfer of Snake and Columbia River waters. And, it appeared that McDermott was not bothered by the idea of having the full flow of the Snake River below Milner Dam running virtually unused through Idaho Power's dams and out of State for the use of our downstream neighbors.

The April 19 issue of the Times-News published a letter from Senator Noh, responding to Herman McDevitt's comments to the Wildlife Federation. Among other things, Laird wrote:

The sports page of the Sunday edition carried a report by Larry Hovey of a speech by Herman McDevitt to the Idaho Wildlife Federation on the subject of subordination of Idaho Power's water rights on the Snake River. Mr. McDevitt is always a provocative speaker, and he has long been interested in natural resource management.

He also represents one of some 14 Idaho law firms, most of which are politically active, that shared $214,000 of Idaho Power business in 1982. Federal Energy Regulatory Commission form No. 1 lists his firm as having received some $18,000 for 1982, the most recent year for which I have access.

In my opinion, outdoor and environmental interests should be wary of adopting Mr. McDevitt's general argument that Idaho Power will somehow protect their interests if the water is placed under its control.

Unfortunately, the perception of many is that the important conflict in the Swan Falls case is only between irrigators and electrical ratepayers. The more critical question is who shall shape water use and policy in the coming years of scarcity; the executives and attorneys of Idaho Power Co. behind closed doors or the elected representatives of the people with public hearings and open meetings?

My office received information that some defendants in Swan Falls II thought the State would be defending them in that suit. We thought it advisable to let them know that this was not the case. I sent out a press release on April 17 warning "water right holders being sued by Idaho Power Company to defend themselves in court or risk losing their water right." The press release noted that Idaho Power had begun serving its complaint upon defendants in the suit and that people who received a summons would have to file a written answer or defense within 20 days in order to prevent being defaulted. I said, "My office will be vigorously defending against the Power Company in the lawsuit and I expect we will shoulder the major burden of the case. However, we cannot represent individuals with respect to their individual water rights. It is absolutely essential that the individual defendants come forward to represent and protect their own interests." The press release got good coverage.[209]

Putting some additional heat on the Governor and the defendants in Swan Falls II, Logan sent the Governor a letter on April 23, urging him to sign the 1180 Contract. He said that all four copies had been signed by the Power Company. Needless to say, Governor Evans did not take the bait. It was clear though that Logan's move was focused on the election, which was just 30 days away.

In fact, things were heating up in the electoral arena. The Governor, myself, and subordination supporters were working to rally the troops to support candidates on our side of the issue. Likewise, the Power Company was twisting arms

---

209   *Post-Register,* April 18, 1984; *Idaho State Journal,* April 18, 1984; *Press-Tribune,* April 19, 1984; *Times-News,* April 19, 1984; *Idaho Statesman,* April 22, 1984.

and making contributions to candidates who had, or would, support its side.

I did not realize the extent and depth of the opposition effort until my six-year-old daughter, Kathy, came home from school, upset with what happened in her first grade class at Washington School that day. Kathy explained that somebody from the electric company had come to talk to Mrs. Kaylor's class about electricity. During his talk, the electric company representative said that Jim Jones, the Attorney General of the State, was trying to take the Power Company's water away from it and that moms and dads would have to pay a lot more for electricity and it would hurt the fish. She said that a couple of times during that part of his talk, she raised her hand to say something but Mrs. Kaylor would not call on her. She thought Mrs. Kaylor understood that she wanted to say that the Attorney General was her dad and he wasn't a bad person. I thought, that's hitting a little bit below the belt. I had no problem with someone coming to the class to explain what electricity was and how it was made but interjecting politics into the presentation was a bit far afield for a primary school talk.

On our side of the issue, Reed Hansen was busy on the speaking circuit. In speaking to the St. Anthony Chamber of Commerce on April 23, he told the members that "agricultural development in the Upper Valley would be halted and related businesses would be hurt if Swan Falls water rights aren't subordinated. If we are stopped here, we will see towns like Rigby, St. Anthony and Ashton wither away."[210] He told the Chamber that subordination of the Swan Falls right would not greatly increase power rates because that facility was "such a small part of the company's hydropower system that it would have little effect on power generation."

Several days later, the Post-Register editor expressed

---

210   Koon, Cathy. "St. Anthony's future at stake?" *Post-Register,* April 24, 1984.

skepticism that the towns mentioned by Reed would wither away without subordination but agreed that the Swan Falls dispute had to be resolved. The editorial concluded that "there has to be a settlement. Idaho cannot be placed on 'hold' in the absence of a Swan Falls solution, that hopefully, assures Idaho's farming future. There is time to settle. There is time to measure available water and the underground recharging mechanism. There is time to reinforce and update the Idaho Water Plan to not only meet future farming needs, but minimum flows for the sake of a larger society."[211]

Toward the end of April, Governor Evans received a letter from the Idaho Irrigation Pumpers Association urging that he sign the contract with Idaho Power.[212] It appeared that the Power Company's efforts to stir up concern among the Swan Falls II defendants was having some success. The letter said that the signing of the contract would be in the "best interest of all Idaho," and that "nearly all of our members are present water users who have everything to lose and nothing to gain by the continued litigation of this controversy."

Following up on its efforts to stampede the Swan Falls II defendants, Idaho Power sent them an "important notice" beseeching them to call or write to the Governor and urge him to sign the contract. According to the letter, "If signed by the Governor, the contract will remove your water rights listed in the summons from the costs and risks associated with this litigation. Pursuant to the contract, Idaho Power Company's voluntary dismissal of legal action against you would constitute a voluntary subordination of its water rights to those users, such as yourself, who hold rights which qualify for protection by the contract." Of interest is the fact that the letter, written to defendants in a lawsuit filed by the Company and being pursued against them, did not mention that it might be a nice idea if they checked with their own

---

211   "Comments from candidates, commissioner worth review." *Post-Register*, April 29, 1984.
212   UPI. "Water rights." *Idaho Press-Tribune*, April 30, 1984.

legal counsel as to how their property interests might be affected by the suggested course of action. I brought this to public attention with a press release accusing Idaho Power of giving irrigators "bum legal advice."[213] I mentioned that the "notice being served by the power company is a heavy-handed attempt to secure negotiating gains and concessions from the state. It amounts to a polite form of blackmail which ought not to be tolerated."

In the meantime, the U.S. House of Representatives was engaged in action that could have a spill-over effect on the subordination fight. Legislation to establish a National Board on Water Policy was under consideration in the House Committee on Interior and Insular Affairs. Initially, the legislation contained a provision extending the moratorium on interbasin transfers that Senators Church and Jordan had written into law. However, during committee consideration of the legislation, that moratorium provision was deleted at the behest of a California congressman, Robert Lagomarsino.[214]

Based on the removal of the moratorium language, I wrote Idaho's congressional delegation to warn that this created a potential threat to Idaho water and that action needed to be taken to ensure that the moratorium language was reinstated, if the bill was to move forward. In a press release issued on May 3, I informed the delegation, "That the State's Swan Falls water rights dispute with Idaho Power Company poses a threat to Idaho water. 'If the Power Company prevails, the downstream states, and possibly California, would have a much larger volume of Idaho water to pursue and appropriate to the detriment to Idaho growth and development.'" I told the Senators and Congressmen that, "The State Water Plan which calls for a minimum streamflow of 3,300 cfs at Swan Falls was thrown into complete turmoil by the 1982 Idaho Supreme Court Swan Falls decision. If we are

---

213   Associated Press. "Jones: Irrigators given bad advice." *Post-Register,* May 4, 1984.
214   Associated Press. "Bill allowing Columbia diversion study opposed." *Lewiston Tribune,* April 26, 1984.

required to provide Idaho Power Company with 8,400 cfs of water at Swan Falls, almost triple the present minimum flow, we will essentially be wasting a tremendous amount of water downstream, making it subject to appropriation by Oregon, Washington, and, possibly, California. Once they gain a hold on that volume of water, we will lose it forever and Idaho's future will be severely damaged." Senators McClure and Symms got legislation passed in 1986 making the moratorium permanent.

Bruce Newcomb announced on May 3 that he and other concerned water users had formed a political action committee to support legislative candidates who favored subordination of Idaho Power's water rights.[215] Bruce told a gathering in Burley that the new PAC was formed in response to another PAC, United for Idaho, which he said "is dominated by Idaho Power and commands a great amount of legislative power — enough to have effectively thwarted subordination efforts in the last two legislative sessions." He continued, "We're nonpartisan. If you're for subordination, we're for you. If you're against subordination, we're against you." Forrest Hymas, a member of the PAC's steering committee, told the group that "subordination means yielding to another right. It means Idaho Power can use the water but must yield it to another use."

Governor Evans responded to Jim Bruce's overtures regarding the Power Company's contract proposal on May 9. The Governor's thoughtful letter provided an outline of how the Swan Falls fight might be resolved:

> I appreciate your offer to enter into a contract for the dismissal of certain defendants in (Swan Falls II). I share your desire to limit the necessity for and extent of litigation over Snake River water rights. I, too,

---

215   Shaughnessy, Rick. "Water users band together to sway election." *Times-News,* May 5, 1984.

would favor a negotiated settlement of this dispute. However, rather than the partial settlement contemplated by the contract you have offered, I propose that we enter into serious discussions of a complete settlement agreement. To that end, I offer the following observations.

I firmly believe that the issue of Snake River water rights allocation is the major resource policy issue which will face Idaho for the balance of this century. The resolution of this issue will greatly affect economic development and economic opportunity for all of Southern Idaho for generations to come. Such a fundamental public policy question ought to be resolved by the most careful and thorough public processes, and not necessarily in the context of litigation.

Thus far, the debate over Swan Falls water rights has focused on the question of whether irrigated agriculture or hydropower generation offers the greatest economic benefit to our state. In my view, that is not the issue. I agree with you and your company that it is in the interests of both current ratepayers and our future economic growth to maintain a strong hydro-power base. I agree that in future allocations of water resources we cannot afford to ignore the implications such allocations have on hydro-power generation. However, I fundamentally disagree with the Idaho Power Company position that the best way to assure adequate water for hydro-power generation is by recognizing the utility's power to veto future consumptive uses in the Snake River Basin. Such decision-making clearly should be a governmental responsibility, bounded only by broad public interest considerations, and not the prerogative of a private corporation.

I would propose that we utilize the minimum

stream flow concept as the primary means of protecting hydro-power generation. In exchange for an assignment of Idaho Power Company's water rights on
the Snake River to the State of Idaho, the State could
establish a new higher minimum stream flow at a level
mutually agreeable to the State and the power company. I would further suggest that the state establish
a process by which future allocations of water on the
Snake River could be reviewed against a set of criteria which reflect a balance of all the competing public
and private interests: water requirements for all new
industry and agriculture, wildlife and conservation
concerns, as well as preservation of our hydro-power
base.

As you are keenly aware, the Idaho Power Company has a direct stake in the prosperity of all sectors of
our Idaho economy. I would hope that you and I can
now approach this challenge as partners in the pursuit
of a common objective, and not as adversaries in a law
suit in which there will be no winners.

That same day, the Northside News, Jerome County's
weekly paper, published a guest opinion by Gordon
Hollifield, explaining his opposition to the Evans-Jones bills.
This provided a nice opportunity to launch a public attack
against Gordon, which I did by way of a May 10 response.

The guest column written by Gordon Hollifield in
your May 9 issue deserves a response. Gordon is dead
wrong when he claims that subordination would increase the threat of exportation of Idaho water to California. The fact is that subordination would protect
our water against claims on it by other states. If Idaho
Power Company wins the subordination battle, Ore-

gon, Washington, and possibly California, would have 8400 second feet of precious Idaho water to utilize for their growth and development at Idaho's expense. That is one of the main reasons why we must have subordination — so that southern Idaho can grow and develop and provide opportunities for future generations.

Southern Idaho grew on a subordination policy. That policy has provided us some of the lowest electric rates in the country, together with productive farms and healthy communities. Idaho Power Company agreed with that policy and particularly agreed that its hydropower rights on the Snake River would be subordinated to upstream consumptive uses for agriculture, industry and domestic consumption. The power company found and exploited a loophole in the subordination agreement and by virtue of a 1982 supreme court decision was able to tentatively tie up 8400 second feet of water at the Swan Falls Dam — one of their least productive power facilities. Subordination would merely repair the damage by reinstating the subordination policy and making the power company live with its previous agreements.

If we do not have subordination, there will be a flow of 8400 second feet of water past Swan Falls and that flow will leave the State to be grabbed by Washington, Oregon, or California. They will receive the consumptive benefit of that water to serve their drinking needs, to grow crops which will compete against Idaho products, and to supply industries which will be denied to Idaho for lack of water. We will have allowed 8400 second feet of single purpose water (used only for hydropower production) to be "wasted" downstream. If Idaho is foolish enough to allow such a large volume of this most precious resource to go to other states, we are going to have to do a lot of explaining to future generations.

The State Water Plan which was adopted on the premise that the greatest amount of Idaho water should be retained in the State to serve consumptive uses, called for a minimum streamflow at Swan Falls of 3300 cfs. It was recognized that this flow of water would leave the State and be subject to appropriation by downstream states. The streamflow was set in order to provide a minimum flow for generation of hydro-power and for protection of aquatic life. Idaho Power Company would have us almost triple that minimum streamflow which would, in effect, triple the amount of water leaving the State. Once we lose it, we will never get it back.

Subordination is the key to protecting Idaho water for Idaho's future. It calls for a balanced use concept for our scarce water resources — a concept that has served us well for almost 100 years. We must have the policy reinstated if we hope or expect Jerome and other southern Idaho towns and communities to have any future growth and development.

May 10 signaled the start of what would become a massive multi-media advertising campaign by Idaho Power on the subordination issue, which was obviously intended to affect the primary election contests on May 22. The campaign started out with radio advertising and then grew to include print media — half and full page ads in the daily newspapers in Idaho Power's service area, as well as some weekly newspapers — and slick television advertisements.

Recognizing what was likely in store, I issued a press release on May 11 blasting Idaho Power for "electioneering in the final days of the primary election with money extracted from electrical ratepayers." Idaho Power bought advertising space on radio stations in Twin Falls, Hailey, Jerome, and Pocatello to run an anti-subordination campaign from May 10 to May 30. The press release stated:

> The (Idaho Power) ad is misleading because it implies that subordination would dramatically increase electrical rates and benefit big developers. Quite to the contrary, subordination would reinstitute the long-standing policy which gave us a productive agricultural economy with some of the lowest electric rates in the country. Subordination would insure jobs for workmen, business opportunities for our sons and daughters, and adequate drinking water supplies for growing communities throughout southern Idaho. It would benefit people such as Merle Stoddard, a sixty-four year old widow from Twin Falls, who indicates that she is being sued by the power company over a well which serves an acre of property she owns in Melon Valley. Jones was referring to a letter received from Mrs. Stoddard, outlining her distress of being sued by Idaho Power Company to terminate her use of a community well — the use allegedly being in conflict with Idaho Power Company's water right at Swan Falls.
>
> Jones questioned the power company "scare tactics" regarding the effect of subordination on electric power rates. "Just a few days ago power company officials appeared before the Public Utilities Commission to project a long-term surplus of electrical power to serve the needs of Idahoans. At that time the power company officials were contending that additional small hydroprojects should not be authorized at current contract rates, based upon their projections of an approximate fifteen-year surplus of energy. If there is

to be a long-term energy surplus, a person wonders why the power company should want to double or triple the minimum amount of water available for hydropower production on the Snake River. The answer is power company profits—the more water the power company can tie up, the more energy it can produce, and the more profits it can make. Since there is a projected surplus of power in Idaho, it only makes sense that the excess power will be sold out of state. The power company will generate enhanced profits using Idaho's most precious resource, our water, with no resulting benefit to Idaho. The electricity sold out of state will help underwrite competitive growth in our neighboring states. Subordination, on the other hand, would allow that excess water to be utilized for growth and development which would benefit Idaho industry, agriculture and all citizens who have acquired a habit of drinking water.

Idaho Power Company is spending hundreds and possibly thousands of dollars in funds collected from electric ratepayers in an obvious attempt to influence the outcome of the primary election races. There appears to be a pattern of running the advertisement in areas where some of the power company's friends and supporters are facing primary election challenges. This certainly appears to be a heavy handed attempt to bolster the utility's profit picture through the legislative process.

The press release included the May 4 letter I received from Mrs. Stoddard who said, "I am furious that this company can harass people and can legally take away their water right. If I had the money I would sue them for harassment. I don't, but I am willing to help anyone who is for the rights of the people and not a Maine owned company to be elected to the legislature so we can have some decent laws to protect people from large companies."

I organized a press conference at the old Holiday Inn in Twin Falls for the following day, May 12, to follow up on these themes. Senator Noh and Mrs. Stoddard joined me at the press conference. It must have been a popular event, because Logan Lanham and two other power company representatives drove down from Boise to attend. They sat in the front row with two tape recorders shared amongst the three of them. I assume that was to take down every word I said and to be in a position to act as a truth squad, so to speak. In any event, I used the occasion to blast away at Idaho Power and told the press that "the presence of three Idaho Power officials at the press conference was evidence I had 'blown the whistle where it needs to be blown.'"[216]

Following my remarks, Logan took the floor to deny that the ads were produced specifically for the primary elections. He said that the ads were "part of a larger effort to explain to ratepayers how the company believes the proposed subordination of its water rights at Swan Falls Dam will cause electricity rates to rise dramatically."

On May 16, seven Magic Valley legislative candidates held their own press conference to attack the Idaho Power advertising campaign. The candidates included Gary Robbins, Waldo Martens, Representative Noy Brackett, Lynn Tominaga of Paul, Keith Huettig of Hazelton, Michael Dahmer of Jerome, and John Robirts of Buhl. Gary called the ads "an unfair use of the media and the ratepayers' money." The candidates' joint press release stated that, "The ad campaign is contributing unfairly to the election prospects of (Idaho Power's) candidates. Idaho Power may call these ads a public education program, but we call it electioneering, nothing

---

216   Moffat, Dave. "Jones lashes at utility ads." *Times-News*, May 13, 1984.

less than an outrageous attempt to tamper with Idaho's primary election."[217] Contacted by telephone following the press conference, Larry Taylor said, "this company doesn't have any candidates." He said the ads were not political in nature and were just a continuation of the company's efforts to educate its customers.

Gordon Hollifield was apparently feeling some heat on the subordination issue because the same day of his opponent's press conference, he said he was "not totally opposed to subordination."[218] In response to criticism from Waldo, Hollifield said he consistently favored subordinating that part of the company's water right that was in use by irrigators or that would be put to use by developers who had significant investment in the physical assets of their proposed developments. What he meant was that he supported the Power Company's bills. Rick Shaughnessy wrote, "the issue is an emotional one in the Magic Valley and is being used as a major campaign issue in several primary races—especially the Hollifield-Martens race. It has given birth to a political action committee specifically endorsing subordination of Swan Falls. Martens was identified as one of the candidates whom the PAC intended to aid financially."

On May 17 I wrote to Governor Evans regarding his May 9 letter to Jim Bruce, commending his suggestions for a proposed settlement. The letter[219] stated:

> The comments and suggestions contained in your letter of May 9 to Idaho Power Company President James Bruce are certainly appropriate. I whole-heartedly agree that discussions should be commenced with Idaho Power Company for the purpose of settling all issues involved in the Snake River water rights controversy. Idaho must have water available for addition-

---

217   Shaughnessy, Rick. "Utility's advertisements blasted by legislative candidates." *Times-News*, May 17, 1984.
218   Shaughnessy, Rick. "Candidate says he's not totally opposed to subordination." *Times-News*, May 17, 1984.
219   Clive provided much input for this letter.

al consumptive uses, together with low-cost energy, in order to provide jobs and opportunities for future generations. A piecemeal approach toward settling the Snake River water rights dispute does not hold out the promise of laying the necessary ground work to insure Idaho's future.

The suggestion that hydropower water rights be assigned to the State and that future hydropower usages be protected through minimum streamflows is well worth exploring. This would allow the Snake River to be handled in a coordinated fashion, as it was prior to the 1982 Supreme Court decision, as well as giving Idaho's electric consumers some additional protection against having our low-cost hydropower being forever transported out of state.

In February, 1982, the United States Supreme Court rendered a decision which causes me concern under the present conditions which exist in Idaho. The Court decided in New England Power Company v. New Hampshire, 455 U.S. 331, that a state could not prohibit the exportation of low-cost hydropower generated within its boundaries through the regulatory process. Therefore, if Idaho Power Company is able to hold on to the expanded water right at Swan Falls, the hydropower produced there and at all other power company facilities on the Snake River could be sold out of state regardless of Idaho's objections. Other cases indicate that the state might have a better chance of retaining hydropower generated in Idaho for the purpose of serving Idaho needs if the state's interest is more of a proprietary nature, as opposed to strictly a regulatory nature. Subordination of hydropower rights to consumptive uses, together with a wise policy for handling those consumptive uses, could give the State a better chance of retaining the hydropower benefits for Idaho citizens in the future. Assignment of hydropower rights to the State could do the same.

Of real concern is the recent power company projection of a long-term surplus of energy for service of Idaho needs. As you may recall, the Idaho Power Company recently appeared before the Public Utilities Commission to object to additional small hydro projects, stating that it would produce surplus energy until around the end of the century. It is apparent that the surplus energy would be sold out of state. If the power company is able to obtain additional excess water through its Swan Falls water right, it will generate additional excess energy to be sold out of state. The company certainly has a powerful incentive to do so because of the additional excess profits which will be generated with the increased flows. Once that energy leaves the state and out-of-state businesses and consumers become dependent upon it, Idaho will have difficulty in retaining or recovering the benefit of this low-cost electrical energy unless we have more control over Snake River water, either through subordination or assignment. We could well end up as a private energy reserve for states such as California, allowing our water to be used to subsidize competitive growth in our neighboring states. Idaho could suffer in two ways — having its growth potential stymied and being subjected to increased energy costs for replacement of the lost hydropower.

The point is that the state must be returned to the pre-1982 position of having more say-so over usage of the Snake River, whether through subordination or a negotiated assignment. Otherwise, we will risk our ability to grow and may well lose our low energy rates at the same time. Hopefully, the power company will recognize the duty it owes to the people of Idaho to sit down and enter into meaningful settlement talks. I certainly stand ready to assist in any way possible.

The Idaho Power publicity campaign was getting into full swing in mid-May. Its newspaper ad showed the posterior of a man wearing a pair of Levis. He was pulling his wallet out of the right rear pocket. The ad read:

SUBORDINATION
It'll hit you
right where it hurts the most.

The text under the fellow's derriere said that "if Idaho Power's water rights on the Snake River are totally subordinated—as some land developers would like—the company's electric rates could rise by $54 million a year. An average of over $200 per year per customer." It said that irrigators would be hit especially hard and that their rates might go up by more than 50%, "which could threaten some family farms."[220] A video version of this ad was running on television stations along the course of the Snake River. As previously noted, the advertising campaign commenced on May 10. We determined later that "the campaign gradually increased in intensity until it reached a peak on May 22, election day, and then subsided."[221] The Power Company's advertising schedule for television ads on KMTV in Twin Falls was typical. Three ads ran on May 15, the first day of the KMTV ad buy, with an additional eight ads from May 15 to May 20. Three ads ran each day on May 21, and May 22. Starting on May 23, an ad ran once a day, except for the 25th and 29th, until

---

220   *South Idaho Press, May 15, 1984; Idaho State Journal,* May 20, 1984.
221   January 14, 1985, letter from myself to Rep. Gary Robbins and Rep. Waldo Martens.

the end of the month. The Times-News indicated that the Power Company's initial order called for five-column by 12 inch advertisements to be run on May 13, 15, 17, 20, 21 and 22. The initial buy for the Statesman was the same. Furthermore, a good deal of the advertising occurred in the service area of Utah Power & Light in eastern Idaho. While the Pocatello, Blackfoot, Idaho Falls, and Rexburg media reached a certain amount of Idaho Power customers on their western edges, the majority of power customers along the eastern edge of the State were not Idaho Power ratepayers. But, the legislative candidates from those areas were still seeking office.

I asked Dave High, one of my division chiefs, to see if any campaign finance disclosures had been made under the Sunshine Law with respect to the advertising campaign. The reporting period under the Sunshine Law — the seven day pre-primary report — covered the period from January 1 to May 15. No expenditures had been reported to the Secretary of State. Dave reported that the expenditures would be required under the law if it could be shown that they were, indeed, designed to support or oppose any given candidate or candidates. He indicated that this might not be an easy task, and that it would take some investigation and discovery to possibly make a case. I directed my investigative unit to look into the issue to see how the advertising campaign was fashioned and whether we could identify any particular pattern to support or oppose individual legislative candidates.

As the May 22 primary approached, the southern Idaho newspapers were filled with articles, advertisements, guest opinions, and letters to the editor, dealing with the subordination issue. A May 5 article by Rick Shaughnessy in the Times-News bore the title "Desire for water-rights solution alters legislative races."[222]

A Valley High School classmate and friend, Del Kohtz

---

222   *Times-News*, May 6, 1984.

of Eden, wrote to say that Gordon Hollifield had lost touch with the people of the Magic Valley on the water issue.[223] Merle Stoddard told the Times-News that Idaho Power was harassing her and others with the Swan Falls II suit.[224] My father, Henry Jones of Eden, who wasn't much for writing letters to the editor, told the Times-News and the South Idaho Press that he endorsed Waldo Martens, "an honest, hard-working man" who "understands the water issue and has come out in favor of subordination legislation."[225] My old friend, Bill Lanting of Hollister, wrote to support several candidates — Gary Robbins, Waldo Martens, Noy Brackett and John Robirts of Buhl — all of whom favored subordination.[226] Gary Robbins received support from Blanche and Lindell Cooper of Dietrich, who appreciated his stance on the subordination issue.[227] Neal Bowcut of Burley blasted Idaho Power for its scare tactics on electric rates and for trying to take over the Snake River.[228] Bruce Newcomb contested Idaho Power's claim about skyrocketing electric rates in a letter to the Times-News editor.[229] Slim Miracle of Twin Falls castigated Tom Stivers for opposing the subordination legislation, wondering what it felt like "to be cuddled under an electric blanket with Idaho Power."[230] Alvin Strong of Wendell wrote the Times-News to say that John Brooks did not deserve to represent the people of his district.[231] John Tucker, a legislative candidate from Blackfoot, wrote the Morning News to say, "Water is one of Idaho's invaluable resources and belongs to the people. Subordination is necessary."[232] Gordon Prairie of Jerome wrote the Times-News to ask, "How can the people sit idly by and allow Idaho Power Co. to spend our money

---

223   "Hollifield lost touch." *Times-News*, May 10, 1984.
224   "Vote water concerns." *Times-News*, May 11, 1984.
225   *South Idaho Press, May 15, 1984; Times-News*, May 15, 1984.
226   *Times-News*, May 16, 1984.
227   *Times-News*, May 17, 1984.
228   *Times-News*, May 17, 1984.
229   *Times-News*, May 17, 1984.
230   *Times-News*, May 17, 1984.
231   *Times-News*, May 17, 1984.
232   *The Morning News*, May 18, 1984.

to actually campaign on an issue like this in their attempt to get their supporters re-elected and take over the control of the Snake River...which is Idaho's."[233] Joe Serrine of Jerome told the Times-News he strongly objected to Idaho Power using rate-payer money to run political ads.[234] Randall Brewer, a friend from Three Creek, wrote the Press-Tribune, urging voters to oppose Representative Strasser, who voted against subordination legislation.[235] Lyn Allred of Ketchum expressed support for Swan Falls subordination and opposition to the Power Company's advertising campaign.[236] Jo Vincelette of Ketchum voiced the same message.[237] These were just a few of the letters published in the print media.

Bruce Newcomb got the last word on the issue with a letter to the Statesman, which was published on the day of the election. He wrote:[238]

Idaho Power Co. is speaking with a forked tongue in its efforts to maintain its monopoly on production of hydropower while maintaining a near monopoly on Snake River water rights. Arguing against small hydroprojects, which would be a source of competition for the power company, power-company officials predict a power surplus in Idaho that will last until at least 1997. If there is going to be a power surplus, why should the power company argue so vigorously against subordination of its Snake River water rights? There seems to be a large inconsistency here.

Why should Idaho Power begrudge additional community growth upstream from Swan Falls since it

---

233   *Times-News,* May 18, 1984.
234   *Times-News,* May 18, 1984.
235   *Idaho Press-Tribune,* May 18, 1984.
236   *Times-News,* May 19, 1984.
237   *Times-News,* May 19, 1984.
238   *Idaho Statesman,* May 22, 1984.

is predicting a fairly long-term surplus of power that would be available to serve that growth? The power company certainly does not need to tie up a substantially increased flow of water on the Snake River to produce additional energy since they are blessed with a glut of power at the present time. If they plan to use the additional water to sell power to California on their new transmission line, however, thereby enhancing their revenues, it all may make sense.

In order to maintain its monopoly on production of hydropower within Idaho, Idaho Power argues that there is a surplus and that the small hydroproducers should not be allowed to proceed with their plans. In order to maintain a firm hold over the water of the Snake River, the utility predicts power shortages with drastically increasing rates. The utility must assume a low level of intelligence amongst the citizens of Idaho. Isn't it time we showed them otherwise?

Shortly before the election, the editor of the Idaho State Journal criticized me for criticizing Idaho Power for running its ad campaign.[239] But, I didn't expect anything less from the editor of that paper.

Two days before the election, the Post-Register published an article outlining the views of eight Idaho Falls area candidates in four contested races. All eight favored subordination.[240] One of those candidates, Michael K. Simpson of Blackfoot said:

I do favor legislation to subordinate Idaho Power water rights at Swan Falls to upstream users, primarily because the state of Idaho must be able to control water policy within the state. Whether the Legislature can

---

239   "The Real Story." *Idaho State Journal,* May 18, 1984.
240   Black, Bob. "Primary candidates outline views." *Post-Register,* *May 20, 1984.*

simply subordinate that water right or if compensation must be paid to Idaho Power for that water right is a question that will probably be settled by the courts. The point which seems to be overlooked by the opponents of subordination is that there are alternative means to produce electricity, although more expensive; however, for those purposes for which we need water, there is no substitute. We simply can not allow Swan Falls to halt growth in the upper Snake River Valley.

Reed Hansen had a guest opinion in the Post-Register the same day, responding to that paper's April 29 editorial. The theme of the guest opinion was summarized in its title "Small cities would suffer if water rights are not subordinate."[241] The Morning News in Blackfoot gave me a final opportunity to criticize the Power Company's advertising campaign.[242] I said, "It smacks of nothing less than electioneering, especially in the final days before a primary election." I told Dan Myers, the reporter, that "People are mad. They're convinced the power company is trying to buy a political office for their buddies." The article noted that the advertisements, "carried on radio, television and in newspapers, warn of higher rates if the utility's water rights are subordinated because of the Swan Falls water fight." Idaho Power's spokesman Larry Taylor told Myers, "This campaign has been planned for nearly two years. There's really no relationship between the Swan Falls issue and Tuesday's primary." In response to my assertion that "the more water Idaho Power can tie up, the more energy it can produce and the more money it can make." Taylor said, "That's almost too incredible to justify a comment." For his part, Logan was reported to have spent the day before the election campaigning with Gordon Hollifield in Jerome County.

---

241   *Post-Register,* May 20, 1984.
242   Myers, Dan. "Attorney general blasts Idaho Power." *The Morning News,* May 21, 1984.

On election day, the Times-News editor opined that Idaho Power "should drop its subordination ads."[243] Sounding a lot like the paper's Managing Editor, Stephen Hartgen, the paper said, "In fact, the anti-subordination campaign smells so bad even the largest feedlot operator is holding his nose!" This appeared to be referring to my father, Henry Jones, and his letter to the editor published on May 15. The editorial continued, "Judging from the indignation in the letters-to-the-editor column, the campaign is backfiring on Idaho Power. Even the slickest ad campaigns can't overcome such deep-seated resentments, and can even fuel more animosity." The editor noted that "Local legislative races this week reflect this situation: not one candidate has taken a public, firm anti-subordination position. Conversely, almost every one has prominently advocated subordination." It is no wonder that this clear-thinking editor, Steve Hartgen, was elected to the Legislature in 2008.

The election results were encouraging. Waldo Martens beat Gordon Hollifield and Gary Robbins beat John Brooks. Tom Stivers, who supported Idaho Power, won his election but came close to getting swamped by Douglas Bashaw, a political newcomer. The vote was 2,364–2,007. Gene Winchester prevailed over Jerry Deckard, which was favorable for the subordination position. The publicity generated from the two Magic Valley races was fairly powerful. The South Idaho Press headline read, "Water rights issue defeats veteran legislators."[244] The article said, "Both Hollifield and Brooks voted against subordinating Idaho Power Co.'s water rights to upstream farm use. Their challengers, both area farmer-ranchers, campaigned hard on that issue." The Times-News headline said, "Water issues sink veteran legislators in Magic Valley."[245] The Idahonian headline read, "Water rights issue pulls down veteran Republicans."[246] In an analysis of the

243   "IPC should drop its subordination ads." *Times-News,* May 22, 1984.
244   *South Idaho Press,* May 23, 1984.
245   *Times-News,* May 23, 1984.
246   *Idahonian,* May 23, 1984.

election results, Randy Stapilus of the Pocatello paper noted that Hollifield and Brooks "probably would have won a sixth term but for their votes and floor debate on the Swan Falls case: both opposed subordination of Idaho Power Co.'s water rights at the dam. The Magic Valley is heavily dependent on irrigation and a big majority of the people there favored subordination. Other area anti-subordination Republican legislators — including House Speaker Tom Stivers, Twin Falls — who have never faced serious primary challenges before were severely tested this time. (Stivers, a five-termer and the House leader, was held to a paltry 54 percent in the primary.)"[247]

---

[247]   Stapilus, Randy. "Idaho Legislative Primary Election Yields Surfeit of Lessons." *Idaho State Journal*, May 27, 1984.

A TURNING POINT?

While the victory of the subordination forces was
not significant with regard to numbers, it was a substantial
psychological victory over the Power Company. I took it as a
sign that we were continuing to pick up support for our side
of the issue and suspected that the Power Company viewed it
in a similar fashion. Looking back, it was a turning point—a
principal factor that focused attention on the advisability of
trying to work out a settlement of the dispute.

Indeed, the very day the election results were known,
Jim Bruce wrote to Governor Evans, saying the Power
Company would welcome a chance to discuss settlement as
opposed to litigation. He wrote:

> Thank you for your letter of May 9, 1984. The Compa-
> ny would welcome a chance to discuss settlement, as
> opposed to litigation. We urgently request your recon-
> sideration of signing the contract so that existing users
> will be relieved of expense and uncertainty while we
> attempt to resolve the Swan Falls issues.
>
> In our view, the Company's decision to protect its wa-
> ter rights should not be considered as a "veto" of other
> development, because Idaho's constitution provides
> for acquisition of the Company's water for future de-
> velopment by the utilization of eminent domain pro-
> ceedings.
>
> In your letter, you mention an assignment as a vehi-
> cle for settlement. A better subject of discussion, in the
> Company's view, would be the approach embodied in
> HB 574, as amended. A copy is enclosed for ease of
> review by you. This allows protection of the ratepayer

and preservation of the hydro base as a resource, while permitting viable development to proceed.

In any event, the Company's willingness to discuss resolution of the controversy is not conditioned on the discussion of any particular proposal. We hope you likewise will be receptive to the exploration of any reasonable approach. Company representatives will be available to meet with you at your convenience.

Nevertheless, the Idaho Power advertising campaign continued. A new print ad appeared after the election in which the rear of the man's Levis disappeared and the man's quizzical-looking face asks, "Idaho Power favors subordination?" The text underneath answers, "To existing water users, yes!" The ad then goes on to say that Governor Evans had a contract in his office that could be signed to release existing water users from claims by the Power Company.[248] Later, another ad appeared in which a lady with a quizzical look on her face asks, "Subordination. What the heck is it?" The text of the ad explained that subordination was a policy that would "take away Idaho Power's water rights on the Snake River." It did not explain that the Company's water rights at the Hells Canyon complex, where 85% of its hydropower was generated, were fully subordinated. The ad continued,[249]

> We believe that total subordination—the taking of all of Idaho Power's lawfully acquired water rights on the Snake River—is outrageously unfair to our customers. Why should you be singled out to forfeit just compensation for the crippling of your hydroelectric system? Especially when you would be saddled with a substantial and totally unnecessary financial burden. A burden many supporters of subordination demand

248   *The Morning News,* May 26, 1984.
249   *North Side News,* July 25, 1984.

you bear alone even though much of the water taken would be used—and therefore the benefit it produces occur—outside our service area.

The ad concludes, "To learn more about subordination, contact your local Idaho Power office."

The Public Utilities Commission announced on May 25 that Idaho Power would not be permitted to charge ratepayers for the Company's television ads. A PUC spokesman told the Times-News that the Commission "has a firm policy of excluding from customer rates all expenses related to a utility's political and corporate image advertising, lobbying and charities."[250] Larry Taylor assured the reporter "that the primary election 'was not a prime consideration' in the timing of the campaign. 'Obviously we were aware that this was a political issue, but it was not our intent to do it (the ad campaign) simply to influence the elections.'" Another Company spokesman, Jim Taney, said that the Power Company would continue the advertisements during the summer. "We are fully aware of some people reacting negatively to our advertising, particularly in the Magic Valley rural areas where there seems to be a lot of misunderstanding about who would benefit from subordination and who would get hurt."[251]

Jack Streeter of Mountain Home, a stalwart supporter of subordination, was not satisfied. In a letter to the editor of the Idaho Statesman, he said "The confusing, misleading and largely untrue advertising by an out-of-state corporation, referred to as Idaho Power, is a fragrant [sic] valuation of the sacred trust that is bestowed to a public utility monopoly by the people, to be admitted and regulated wisely by the Public Utility Commission."[252] Jack is a good friend who penned his letter before the invention of spell-check. Albert

250   Bernton, Hal. "PUC won't permit Idaho Power to charge rate-payers for TV ads." *Times-News,* May 26, 1984.
251   "Idaho Power plans to continue criticized water rights ads." *Lewiston Tribune,* May 28, 1984.
252   *Idaho Statesman,* May 30, 1984.

Young of Mountain Home agreed, telling the Times-News editor, "I don't believe what I am hearing on the radio lately about subordination of Idaho Power's so-called water rights. I certainly hope the people aren't fooled by Idaho Power's many recent ads in both the paper and on the air. Most of these ads are misquoted, contradictory, or simply aren't true."[253]

With the Legislature adjourned and the primary election behind it, the media returned to the conflict of interest issue. Rick Shaughnessy of the Times-News was apparently responsible for bringing the issue back, writing an article titled "Idaho Power benefits Risch's firm."[254] He wrote:

> In 1983, after James Risch's rise to the top position in the Idaho Senate, his law firm — Risch, Goss, Insinger and Salladay — performed $43,538.73 in legal services for the Idaho Power Co., according to a federal document.
>
> Those contracted legal services represented a nearly 500 percent increase over the $7,615.90 his firm billed Idaho Power in 1982. The legal work came during the first year of the highly-emotional battle over Snake River water rights that has tied up the Legislature during its past two regular sessions.
>
> Risch, a Boise Republican, has been a staunch supporter of Idaho Power on the Swan Falls water rights issue. In 1984, he led at least one effort — tabling of a "subordination" bill — that aided the company in its efforts to keep the waters of the Snake River in the stream channel where they can be used for power purposes.
>
> Proponents of subordination want the company's water right at the Swan Falls hydroelectric site south of Boise to be made secondary to depletions for other purposes, most notably for irrigated agriculture.

---

253   *Times-News,* June 1, 1984.
254   Shaughnessy, Rick. "Idaho Power benefits Risch's firm." *Times-News,* June 5, 1984.

Risch says the increase in legal services — as reported by Idaho Power in disclosure reports filed with the Federal Energy Regulatory Commission — are not in any way the result of his election to the position of president pro-tempore of the Idaho Senate or of the emergence of Swan Falls as a major legislative issue.

The increase in billings, he says, is the result of increases in claims against the utility for personal injuries — an area of law that his firm practices extensively. He says that it is his partner, Lance Salladay, whose father formerly worked for Idaho Power, who performs most of the Idaho Power work for the firm.

Risch adds that his firm's relationship with Idaho Power does not constitute a conflict of interest. "Every single client I have — and I have hundreds — have an interest in the laws passed by the state of Idaho," he said. He said his own personal interests are tied even more closely to the tax issues considered by the Legislature than by the Swan Falls issue, which is of prime importance to Idaho Power.

Risch's firm has been performing contract legal services for the utility since 1976 and earned $30,011 from Idaho Power in 1978, its previous high year. The firm has averaged less than $10,000 a year in services during that period, according to the federal reports.

Larry Taylor, an Idaho Power spokesman, said the utility tries to locate the best outside legal representation available, keeping in-house counsel to a manageable size and keeping costs to a minimum.

"It's not our intent to try to influence any legislator or piece of legislation through (awarding) businesses," Taylor added.

But Risch's firm wasn't the highest paid of those law firms used by the utility. The Twin Falls firm of

Nelson, Rosholt, Robertson, Walker, Tolman and Tucker billed Idaho Power for $326,183.02 in legal services for 1982, according to the report.

That's nearly 5 times both the $66,578.39 that firm earned from Idaho Power in 1982 and the $64,853 the firm earned in 1981.

Tom Nelson, of the firm, is the principal legal counsel for Idaho Power on the Swan Falls issue.

Meanwhile, the Swan Falls debate continued in the media. Senator Mark Ricks weighed in on the continuing Idaho Power ad campaign calling the ads "misleading" and designed to divide Idaho's water users.[255] Logan told the Jerome Chamber of Commerce on June 16 that Governor Evans can solve the Swan Falls dispute "with the flick of a pen."[256] According to the newspaper account, "He said the power company has no intention of blocking any non-consumptive water use on the Snake River, adding agricultural irrigation is not a consuming water use. Other non-consuming uses include individual culinary wells or those serving municipalities. 'We are only (bringing suit) to stop new development or industrial operation that would take water out of the river and consume it.'" Previously, the Power Company said it was not opposed to municipal, domestic, and industrial uses of water above Swan Falls. Logan now indicated that agricultural irrigation was not a consumptive use, so it is not clear who the scoundrels were that were going to take and consume the water. He was, however, correct in a certain regard. A great deal of any water that is applied to a consumptive use, whether agricultural, industrial, municipal, or domestic, makes its way back into the river or aquifer. It does not simply disappear. Logan also said that should the flow of the river at Swan Falls be depleted to 3,300 second feet, the State's minimum flow, "it

---

255   "Ricks calls Idaho Power ads misleading." *Post-Register,* June 5, 1984.
256   Jones, Bonnie Baird. "'Flick of pen' could solve Swan Falls." *Times-News,* June 17, 1984.

would force the power company to provide some other source of power generation." He did not address the fact that the Power Company was trying to squash the small hydropower producers by claiming that there was going to be a surplus of power in the region until 1997, at the earliest.

That same day the Times-News published a letter from Larry Taylor responding to many previous letters to the editor that were critical of Idaho Power, including that of Bruce Newcomb. Taylor sought to reconcile the Power Company's claims that it would have a surplus of power into the 1990s, with its claims that subordination would require dramatic rate increases.[257] It was a valiant attempt, but a hard sell.

I had written Hal Furman at the Department of Interior on March 23 and met with him on March 28 to find out whether the Department would continue its long-standing policy of supporting subordination provisions in federal power licenses and was assured that we would be hearing from him soon on the issue. Two and a half months later we had received no word from him. Clive discussed the matter with lower-ranking officials in the Department and received no indication that the Department was considering a change in its policy. In order to move things along, Clive sent a letter to John Chaffin, an attorney in the Department's Office of Solicitor, saying in part:

> I recently met again with Bill Burpee and discussed in more detail the Department of Interior's involvement in subordination of hydropower rights. He stated in addition to the department's general mandate to encourage reclamation, there was an implied mandate for the department to subordinate hydropower generated at government projects. Briefly, his analysis is as follows:

---

257   "Idaho Power responds on water rights issues." *Times-News,* June 17, 1984.

The Flood Control Act of 1944…provided that the use of all projects authorized by the Act for navigational purposes would be subordinate to upstream consumptive uses….

This policy of subordinating navigation to upstream consumptive uses was made applicable to the Department of Interior…as well as the Army Corps of Engineers…Thus, navigational use is subordinate to all other consumptive uses at every federal project authorized since 1944 in the western United States….

[T]here are in excess of 50 projects authorized for the Columbia River Basin, many of which are on the Snake River. If the legislative mandate for these projects is to be carried out, then hydropower water rights for private utilities must be subordinated. Otherwise, the private utilities will have a first call on waters in the Columbia River Basin, which will impair future agricultural and industrial development.

In addition to my discussion with Bill, I found the following…letter to Senator Jordan from Kenneth Holm, former Assistant Secretary of Interior. The Assistant Secretary states:

Subordination in favor of upstream water uses has been settled federal policy in connection with the Snake River authorizations for a considerable period of time…we see no reason to conclude that this will not continue to be the policy….

This statement seems to be a clear confirmation of Bill's analysis….

Historically, there is an indisputable department policy of seeking subordination of hydropower rights on the Snake River. The citizens of this state, as previously noted, have relied heavily upon this policy; therefore, the F.E.R.C. should not be allowed to lightly set it aside. Further, the department should not abandon a policy that it has encouraged for the protection of the citizens of Idaho. Thus, I believe it is imperative that the Department of Interior join with the state in securing a review of the F.E.R.C.'s decision to delete the subordination clauses from licenses for the Upper Salmon and Shoshone Falls projects. We would hope you concur in this analysis.

We hoped this letter would back the Department into somewhat of a corner and prompt a response.

A good friend in Pocatello, L. Charles Johnson, a practicing attorney and fellow graduate of Northwestern Law School, sent me his copy of Idaho Power's quarterly "Bulletin" to its shareholders and employees. Charles must have owned some Idaho Power Company stock. The Bulletin contained an article titled, "Company Seeks End To Water Dispute." The article indicated that Jim Bruce and Governor Evans had met in June to discuss the possibility of reaching a negotiated settlement but no decisions had been reached. The article denounced me for asking "the U.S. Secretary of the Interior to subordinate water rights at the Shoshone Falls, Upper Salmon, and Swan Falls hydro plants. If successful, the request would lead to uncompensated seizure of the company's water rights." Jim Bruce said, "We believe Mr. Jones is setting a dangerous and ill-advised precedent by asking for federal intervention in a state water rights issue. Such an action clearly would not be in the best interests of the citizens of Idaho."

As I recall, both Governor Len Jordan and the top brass of Idaho Power Company specifically requested the federal government, acting through the Federal Power Commission, to subordinate Idaho Power's water rights on the Snake River in exchange for the company getting the benefit of building three dams in Hells Canyon. It seemed to me that this agreement set the precedent to be followed.

Another thing that bothered me about this article was the reference to my contacts with the Department of Interior. How did Idaho Power know about that? While publicly I said that the State would be seeking to intervene in various FERC proceedings, we tried to maintain confidentiality about our approach to the Department of Interior. The March 23 letter to Hal Furman and the visit to his office on March 28 had not been disclosed by my office because we certainly did not want to tip our hand to Idaho Power. It could be that Furman and Logan bonded during their golf game prior to the March 28 meeting and had remained in contact since that time, but it was a surprise to me that everybody at Idaho Power seemed to know about our overtures to the Department of Interior, as evidenced by the Bulletin article.

The Bulletin also mentioned that Idaho Power was conducting a survey of its customers in Idaho to determine the level of support for its "no subordination without compensation" stance. At press time, the results of the survey were not available.

The Bulletin proudly announced that the Company expanded its sales of surplus power to other western utilities. "From January through June this year, Idaho Power sold 2,164,600 megawatt-hours to other western utilities, producing about $21 million in revenues. In 1983, the company sold 2,211,123 megawatt-hours in surplus during those months, but received just under $17 million."

An Idaho State Journal article on July 2 reported that during all of 1983, Idaho Power sold $54 million in surplus power."[258] It is uncanny that this amount received from the sale of surplus power is exactly equal to one of the figures that Idaho Power was claiming would be required as an annual

---

258   "Idaho Power Sells Surplus Energy." *Idaho State Journal,* July 2, 1984.

rate increase for its Idaho customers, if its Snake River water rights were subordinated.

My office was working on the Swan Falls issue on several fronts. On June 25, I sent a memo to Rick Le'Gall, one of my investigators, asking him to do some additional checking on the pre-primary advertising campaign by the Power Company. I told Rick I was particularly interested in the Company's advertising schedule for the period leading up to the primary election date, as well as the time period immediately following that date. The newspaper advertisements reached a peak on May 20, 21, and 22, when they would do the most good if they were indeed directed toward the primary election. It was not likely we would pursue charges against the Company, but I was contemplating legislation to clarify the Sunshine Law reporting requirements for issue-oriented ad campaigns.

On the litigation front, I sent out a press release on June 27, announcing that Idaho Power had taken action to release a number of defendants from the Swan Falls II lawsuit. The press release read:

> Attorney General Jim Jones has declared a "small, but significant" victory in the Swan Falls water fight between the State of Idaho and Idaho Power Company. "We have shamed Idaho Power Company into taking action to dismiss many of the small water users which they initially filed suit against in the spring of 1983," Jones said.
>
> On June 13 Idaho Power Company attorneys filed a court document in Fourth District Court seeking the dismissal of a number of the defendants in the so-called "7500" or "Swan Falls II" lawsuit. The suit was filed in April of 1983 against thousands of Snake River water users. Idaho Power Company contended that it

was suing upwards of 7500 water users and applicants for water permits for infringing on Idaho Power's water rights at its Swan Falls Dam. The State of Idaho was included as a defendant in the suit.

"I have contended all along that the power company included many small water users who should never have been brought into the suit," Jones said. "Power company officials contend that they included many defendants who should not have been sued because of poor records secured by the power company from the Idaho Department of Water Resources. That is pure baloney. The power company deliberately inflated the number of defendants in the lawsuit in order to strengthen support for their Swan Falls legislation in the 1983 and 1984 legislative sessions. The power company contends that there are 7500 defendants in the suit but the actual count of individuals and corporations being sued is closer to 3600—half of the amount claimed by the power company."

"Many of the individuals who were actually sued by the power company are small domestic users who could not possibly be infringing on any rights Idaho Power may have at Swan Falls or elsewhere. Defendants included people such as Martin Kniep of Filer who shared a community well at Magic Reservoir with six other persons, using the water only for domestic purposes at a vacation cabin. Other defendants include the Extension Service of the University of Idaho, the Boy Scouts of America, numerous churches, and units of city and county government. Many of these defendants were the so-called 'hostages' which the power company created and which it claimed it wanted to protect by passage of its Swan Falls legislation in 1983 and 1984. Apparently, due to the publicity generated about the unfairness of the suit, the power company determined that it was necessary from a public relations standpoint to voluntarily release some of the 'hostages' from the suit even though Idaho Power has not yet been successful in its efforts to receive the protection which its legislation would have given the company from ratepayers." Jones was referring to a provision of the legislation which would remove Public Utilities Commission jurisdiction from an action seeking to penalize Idaho Power Company for failing to protect its claimed water rights on the Snake River. The ratepayers' claim against the power company could amount to millions of dollars."

Not knowing that Hal Furman mailed a letter to me on the July 2, I wrote the Secretary of Interior on July 3. My letter to Secretary William Clark reiterated all of the points we raised previously with Hal Furman. I pointed out that the Interior Department had supported the insertion of subordination conditions in power licenses for Idaho Power dams on the Snake River in ten out of the last eleven proceedings before the Federal Power Commission and, later, FERC. The letter emphasized that the Department's long-standing subordination policy served the interests of both the Federal Government and the State and urged that the Department become involved in the three pending FERC matters — Upper Salmon, Shoshone Falls, and Swan Falls — to support continuation of that policy.

Hal Furman's letter arrived a couple of days later. The first two paragraphs of the letter were greatly appreciated, but the third paragraph was confusing and disappointing. The letter read:

To answer your letter of March 23, 1984, we have reviewed many aspects of the subordination issue in

the Snake River and the State of Idaho. The water policies and the State Water Plan of Idaho have focused on
the enhancement of the State's agricultural economy.
These policies have been accommodated by subordinating hydroelectric developments to upstream depletions where future beneficial use of the water is of
concern. It is our policy to comply with the water right
laws and State objectives, except where they are in conflict with Federal law. Subordination on the Snake River appears to be consistent with these objectives, and
we have suggested inclusion of subordination clauses
in the licensing of hydroelectric projects where such
development appears to be in conflict with upstream
beneficial consumptive uses of water.

Our primary concerns in supporting subordination
of hydroelectric developments on the Snake River are
as follows:

Protection of water rights for existing Reclama-
tion-sponsored projects;

Provision for an affordable supply for water developments planned for the basins; and

Provisions for affordable water supplies for the future
development of water resources projects in the basin.

Hopefully, subordination would allow these ex-
pansions of beneficial water use without tribute to
power rights.

The Bureau of Reclamation recognizes the competing demands for water in the Snake River Basin. We
encourage you and endorse the need to find a solution
to the subordination/power rights issue under State
procedures and law to ensure firm water supplies for
existing and future developments.

If we can be of further assistance in your deliberations, please let us know.

In essence, Furman was saying that the Department was still committed to subordination of hydropower to consumptive uses and that the policy applied to the Snake River dams, but that the Department wouldn't lift a finger to implement the policy on the Snake River. Basically, "Idaho you're on your own, good luck." I pegged Furman as a typical political hack and I wasn't disappointed. This was a major shift in Department policy. As documented in the letter I sent to Secretary Clark, the Department had consistently requested that subordination clauses be included in the federal licenses for Idaho Power's dams on the Snake River, even without the State's urging or knowledge. Now, it was apparently putting a halt to that long-established policy. Something was up. The policy did not change just because Logan took Furman out for a game of golf. We suspected some Congressional involvement, but had no means of finding out what happened or who might be involved.

In an effort to get to the bottom of what happened, Clive wrote the Department of Interior on August 6, 1984, requesting the following documents under the Freedom of Information Act (FOIA):

1. All documents regarding the Department of Interior's policy of subordinating water rights as a precondition to or subsequent to the licensing of hydropower projects.
2. All documents regarding the Department of Interior's policy of subordinating water rights as a precondition to or subsequent to the licensing of hydropower projects on the Snake River or its tributaries.
3. All letters, correspondence, notes or recording of oral communication, memoranda of communication or other documents sent to,

received from, or regarding Idaho Power Company's water rights or hydroelectric facilities in the State of Idaho.

The Bureau of Reclamation responded to the FOIA request on September 18, 1984, sending 12 documents pertaining to items 2 and 3 but refusing to disclose 4 "faxograms" from the Bureau's Regional Director in Boise to the Commissioner of Reclamation. Those withheld faxograms were dated June 1, June 8, July 18, and August 21, all in 1984. My office appealed the denial and asserted that an inadequate search for other documents had been made. Clive followed up with the Bureau, pointing out that we had copies of pertinent Bureau documents that had not been furnished in response to the FOIA request.

The Department of Interior notified us of its decision on the FOIA appeal by letter dated March 4, 1985. The four faxograms in question were sent along with the decision, but the recommendations contained in the faxograms were redacted, purportedly because release of that information "would inhibit the candid and open expression of opinions, views, and recommendations, cause confusion regarding this agency's position on the matter by disclosing unadopted recommendations, and have a general detrimental effect on the decision-making process in this agency." The Department did not send any information regarding contacts with persons outside of the agency. The four faxograms dealt largely with the State Water Plan, the Bureau's past actions with regard to Snake River dams, the Idaho Supreme Court decision, the subsequent Swan Falls fight, and the potential adverse effects of the court decision upon two Bureau projects—the Salmon Falls and Minidoka projects. The June 8 faxogram read, "the State Supreme Court ruling of November 1982 found that the Swan Falls hydropower plant water rights were not subordinated to upstream depletions—contrary to the presumptions of practically all water managers and planners concerned."[259] The August 21 faxogram observed, "If Idaho Power Company water rights at Swan Falls are not subordinated, additional development of irrigation in the Snake River Basin is unlikely."[260] None of these documents or any other documents provided in response to the FOIA request indicated that the Bureau's regional office recommended a change in the long-standing practice of promoting the subordination of hydropower water rights on the Snake River, although since the portions of the faxograms containing the recommendations were redacted, one cannot say with certainty that this is the case. However, where the Bureau had asked recently for subordination provisions in the Shoshone Falls and Upper Salmon FERC licenses, it appeared unlikely that a prompt turnabout would occur without some explanation. It seemed the change in policy had to come from the top, but it didn't look as if we were going to get to the bottom of that. The simple fact was that going forward we were not going to be able to rely on help from the Department of Interior.

It was somewhat of a surprise when Idaho Power stoked up its advertising campaign in early July. Because of the overtures between the parties regarding negotiations, it was my understanding that the public debate would be toned down so as not to further inflame the situation. With the renewed publicity campaign, I dropped Jim Bruce a note on July 5, saying:

I am really pleased with Idaho Power Company's willingness to enter into negotiations in an effort to settle the Snake River water rights issues. I was particularly pleased, and somewhat surprised, with the items con-

259   Faxogram, dated June 8, 1984.
260   Faxogram, dated Aug. 21, 1984.

tained on the tentative negotiation agenda worked out by our designated representatives. If it can be assumed that all parties are operating in good faith, the water rights controversy may be susceptible to a negotiated settlement in the foreseeable future. The stakes are of such magnitude for all Idahoans that we must certainly do our best to work toward that end.

In my estimation, delicate negotiations of this nature must take place in the proper atmosphere. That is why I proposed two weeks ago, through our designated representatives, that both sides of the controversy refrain from propagandizing efforts while serious negotiations are underway. This was a good faith effort to try to lower the profile of the public debate so that the parties could negotiate in a less highly-charged atmosphere. As an additional gesture of good faith, I considerably revised a speech which I delivered to the Pocatello Rotary Club on July 5. I had intended to portray to the Rotarians a different motivation than Idaho Power Company has been stating for its effort to secure a substantially increased share of Snake River water. That is, that Idaho Power may be more interested in the fortunes of the company than in the plight of the ratepayers. I had intended to get into the proper role of a regulated monopoly in the governmental process. However, it did not seem to be appropriate to do so, even though I think those are proper subjects of public discussion, in light of the on-going negotiations.

I had understood from information received last week that Idaho Power Company agreed that a moratorium on potentially inflammatory public discussion would be well advised. Based on that understanding, I cancelled plans for a rather extensive round of public appearances to discuss Idaho Power's past positions on subordination, the company's motivations, the power outlook for Idaho, etc. I assumed that Idaho Power Company officials would do likewise and that the company's public relations program would be held in abeyance.

I was quite surprised and disappointed that a new advertising campaign has been initiated within the last few days. It appears that the public is going to be subjected to another massive advertising effort, an effort which appears to me to be highly misleading judging from the contents of the radio ad which I have heard. Perhaps the information which I received last week regarding Idaho Power Company's position with respect to my moratorium proposal was incorrect. If Idaho Power Company does not intend to honor a moratorium for the purpose of facilitating good faith negotiations, I think it is extremely unfortunate for all concerned. I certainly cannot stand idly by while monies which I and many other Idaho Power customers have paid on our power bills are used in a massive and misleading advertising campaign during the middle of our negotiating sessions. If there is going to be continued escalation on the part of Idaho Power, I intend to respond by telling the public the other side of the story.

Hopefully, the new advertising campaign was initiated through mistake or inadvertence and it will cease immediately so that it does not haunt nor frustrate the negotiation sessions. Hopefully, also, Idaho Power Company officials will refrain from engaging in propagandizing on the public speaking circuit and in the reported one-on-one meetings taking place between district managers and customers. If that can be done, I think we can have an atmosphere conducive to serious good faith negotiations. Otherwise, I think that such negotiations might be difficult to conduct. As we had conveyed to your representative, any proposed moratorium would not hinder either party's efforts in the courts, through administrative processes, or in trial preparation proceedings. The only restraint would apply to emotionally charged public relations efforts, such as the current advertising campaign. Please let me know immediately whether there is a chance that we can lower the profile of the public discussion so that good faith negotiations can proceed or whether it is going to be necessary to respond to the current advertising campaign by showing that Idaho Power Company's professed concern for the plight of the ratepayers may not be all that it seems on the surface.

Despite the fact that Idaho Power was already well aware of our effort to enlist the Department of Interior in our subordination campaign — just by continuing its historic practice — and despite the unhelpful July 2 letter from Hal Furman, I decided to go public with that effort in hopes that my letter to Secretary Clark might bear fruit by going over Furman's head. I sent out a press release on July 9, revealing the July 3 letter to Clark and the July 2 letter from Furman. I said Furman's letter "reaffirmed" the Department's support for a subordination policy on the Snake River and said, "Hopefully the Department will join with the State in seeking to get subordination clauses inserted in the remaining Snake River projects of Idaho Power Company so that State water policy can move forward." I did not mention the mealy-mouthed third paragraph of Furman's letter and the implication that the Department would vigorously cheer the State on, but just from the sidelines.

Rick Le'Gall began contacting media outlets to follow

up on my June 25 memo, which apparently caught the attention of Rick Shaughnessy at the Times-News. On July 19, he wrote:[261]

> The Idaho attorney general's office has asked Idaho newspapers and broadcasting stations for information about a controversial Idaho Power Co. advertising campaign last spring, but it appears the investigation will meet resistance from both.
>
> The advertising campaign opposed subordination of the utility's hydropower water right at the Swan Falls Dam. It coincided with the primary election campaign of candidates for the Idaho legislature, and was criticized by subordination supporters as unfairly aiding candidates on the other side.
>
> In letters to about 20 newspapers and stations which carried the ads, Richard Le'Gall, a criminal investigator for the attorney general, states: "To allow us to complete our inquiry, it is necessary that you provide us with the following information."
>
> Among the information sought is the cost of the ads to Idaho Power, the scheduling of the ads, the name of the person purchasing the ads, the dates the ads were purchased and any changes that were made to the ads during the period of inquiry — May and June, 1984.
>
> Representatives for some of those companies say they will be less than cooperative with the attorney general's inquiry.
>
> "Some of the information they've requested is confidential and will not be released until it is either subpoenaed or we receive written authorization from Idaho Power to release it," Bill Blake, advertising manager of the Times-News said Wednesday.

---

261   Shaughnessy, Rick. "State seeks facts about ad series." *Times-News*, July 19, 1984.

Logan Lanham, Idaho Power vice president of public affairs, said "I'm not going to authorize" that release. Lanham, Idaho Power's point man on Swan Falls, says the issue is "economic and philosophical," but is not political.

He adds that the company's intention to pay for the ads from retained stockholder earnings instead of passing the costs on to ratepayers should further remove the issue from the attorney general's scrutiny.

But while Lanham was steadfastly opposed to releasing the information, another reportedly authorized KMVT-TV of Twin Falls to provide it. "The information they asked for, we treat as confidential client's information," said Lee Wagner, station manager.

Wagner said he called Idaho Power and received authorization from Jim Taney, public relations director, to release the information. "It could be overridden tomorrow morning," he said of the authorization, adding "I'm sure it (the investigation) caught them (the power company) off guard."

Idaho Attorney General Jim Jones told the Associated Press no paper would be pressured for the requested information. He said the reason for the inquiry is to determine whether the ads are campaign-oriented and required to be disclosed under Idaho's sunshine law.

However, Le'Gall said he was unaware of any law the company might have broken by conducting the ad campaign. He said the investigation was intended to "intelligently address the concerns of people who voiced concerns to this office." He said the office may use the information in an effort to promote new legislation.

However, Allen Derr, an attorney representing the

Idaho Newspaper Association, said use of a criminal investigator to make the inquiries "seemed a little out of line...That shouldn't be used unless a criminal investigation is underway."

Subordination of the utility's Swan Falls water right would make water available to other uses — most notably irrigated agriculture — without compensating the utility or its customers for lost power generation capability.

Proponents of subordination say the utility agreed to subordinate the water right and has already been compensated for doing so. The issue is an emotional one which bitterly divided the Legislature during its last two regular sessions and which caused the oustings of two veteran Magic Valley lawmakers in the May 22 primary election.

When we realized that the Power Company was likely planning to continue its advertising campaign until the November election, Bruce Newcomb and I got together to figure out how to respond. We had no access to funding to run our own advertising campaign. I thought we might be able to get some publicity with a David versus Goliath strategy. That is, announcing a responsive ad campaign that would highlight the overwhelming funding advantage Idaho Power had. Taking a page from Bill Loughmiller's book, we decided bumper stickers were the answer. Bruce would put in an order for bumper stickers, we would have a press conference, and we would hopefully get some good publicity before the general election.

Bruce was going to do a bumper sticker based on a hostage theme. Throughout the legislative session, both sides referred to the defendants in Swan Falls II as hostages. Our side said that the 5,000 or so defendants were being held hostage by Idaho Power. The Power Company said that the Governor and I were keeping the defendants hostage. Four years earlier, the whole country had been gripped by the Iranian hostage crisis where Ayatollah Khomeini's followers had held 52 Americans hostage. So, Bruce's bumper sticker read:

IDAHO POWER Ayatollah
Release the Hostages Power

My bumper sticker was based on the contention that Idaho Power wanted to control the full flow of the Snake River between Milner Dam and the Oregon border so it could make many millions of dollars from selling excess power out of state, particularly to California. Since it was projected that there would be a surplus of power in Idaho for a number of years, where could the power go except out of state? Thus, my bumper sticker read:

SUPPORT IDAHO POWER
Send a Kilowatt to California

I wanted to put Idaho Power's branding character, Reddy Kilowatt, on the bumper sticker but it didn't work out. Reddy was a cute stick figure whose body and limbs were made of stylized lightning bolts and whose round head had a lightning bulb for a nose and wall outlets for ears. Reddy was used on all Idaho Power's promotional materials and the Company apparently used it under a licensing agreement. Reddy would have added a little character to the bumper sticker.

On July 20, Pat Kole sent a confidential memorandum to Pat Costello, the Governor's attorney, regarding the "moratorium on potentially inflammatory public discussion" that I thought the warring parties had agreed to earlier in the month. Pat Costello had been out of town for a while so, to fill him in, Pat Kole wrote:

> In your absence, the Swan Falls issue has heated up. This is my understanding of what has happened.
>
> At our meeting of July 3, 1984, we agreed to have the staff try and piece together a framework for settlement. The staff agreed to meet on July 9, 1984. At the staff meeting, Tom Nelson suggested a moratorium on press comments, advertisements, etc. to lower the inflammatory nature on the controversy. We agreed to get back to each other on the framework and moratorium by Tuesday, July 10, 1984. You and I discussed the fact that the framework and moratorium was agreeable to our principals about 11:45 a.m. on July 10. You also indicated that you had talked to Tom Nelson and that the only problem area concerned IPC's insistence on bringing up the contract issue again. I agreed to call Nelson to head off that problem.
>
> I contacted Tom Nelson about 1:30-2:00 p.m. Tom indicated the framework was acceptable and that the only issue IPC wanted to discuss concerning the contract was timing, no pressure would be put upon the Governor at the meeting. Tom, somewhat to my surprise, said the moratorium required Board of Director approval, but that the campaign scheduled to commence on July 10, had been held up. The IPC board would meet on July 12, and he would have an answer on the moratorium on July 13.
>
> I contacted Tom on July 13 and he did not know

what determination had been made. I contacted him
again at approximately 10:15 a.m. on Monday, July 16,
and he still had no word from IPC. At 2:00 p.m., on July
16, while driving to Twin Falls I heard IPC's new ad.
I contacted Tom and he indicated that IPC would not
have any part of a moratorium. He blamed the attitude
change upon (1) a July 9 press release from our office;
and (2) Logan Lanham's survey apparently shows that
the ad campaign is paying off. To clarify the issues and
lower the profile of the controversy, Attorney General
Jones wrote a letter to Jim Bruce, copy attached. The
letter basically proposes to restrict public speaking and
advertising to let the negotiation have a chance to proceed.

To add fuel to the fire, Senator Reed Budge launched
a highly personal attack upon Attorney General Jones
during the afternoon of Wednesday, July 18. The attack accuses Jones of a conflict of interest by taking action on the Swan Falls issue to personally benefit his
family. Several months ago this entire issue was raised,
and after an investigation, we concluded that signing
the contract would benefit members of the Jones family. By advising the Governor to not sign the contract,
the Attorney General was putting his own family into
jeopardy.

I wanted you to have this information because, as
we have discussed before, it is clear that certain individuals have a vested interest in thwarting these negotiations. Our information indicates that an internal
power struggle at IPC may be underway and we have
to work hard if the negotiations are going to succeed.

The survey Pat was referring to in his memorandum
was a customer opinion survey performed by Idaho Power
during June 20–29 regarding its advertising campaign, the

subordination issue, hydropower versus agricultural usage of water, and the like. Idaho Power claimed that the survey results strongly supported its positions on the issues. In my view, the survey questions were skewed in the Company's favor. For instance, question number 22 asked, "If a large amount of water is removed from the Snake River for irrigation or other purposes...Do you think that cost should be paid by the new irrigation developers, or paid by a general rate increase to all Idaho Power customers?" It is not particularly surprising that the Power Company customers would place 74% of the financial responsibility on new irrigation developers and only 12% would place responsibility on themselves. A better question might have been, "Who do you think should control the flow of the Snake River, the State of Idaho or Idaho Power Company?" I certainly was not going to put a great deal of faith in the survey results. It seemed to me that legislators had generally reflected the views of their constituents and the legislators split on about a 50–50 basis during the just-concluded session. Since then, we picked up two supporters, Robbins and Martens, and they lost three, Brooks, Hollifield and Deckard.

The other issue that Pat referenced in his memorandum was Senator Budge's accusation that I had a conflict of interest in the Swan Falls fight. On July 19–20, while I was on a business trip to Washington, D.C., Budge told the media that my brother, Calvin, had a water right that could be affected beneficially by my position on the subordination issue. He claimed that I had an undisclosed conflict of interest. On July 23, I responded with a press release calling his charges "uninformed and totally false." I added that "my brother stands to gain more by Idaho Power's position in the Swan Falls controversy than by mine." The press release continued:

These worn out conflict of interest allegations be-

gan to surface during the legislative session through
Logan Lanham, the power company's chief lobbyist,
and other power company supporters. Early on, I prepared a list of water permits and licenses in which I or
my family might have an interest, including the one
which Mr. Budge referred to last week. The list was
prepared and made available to news people in anticipation of a potential smear effort. The Times News requested and received a copy of the list during the legislative session and utilized the information from the
list in a newspaper article.[262] The permits and licenses
on the list, including my brother's, would have been
protected by passage and approval of the legislation
which was so vigorously advanced by Idaho Power
Company during the last session.

Years earlier, Senator Budge wrote an article that
was published in the January 6, 1972 issue of the Caribou
County Sun, regarding water issues facing the Legislature.
In that article he said the most important issue of the day
was whether the State was going to "hand (its) water over to
private power companies to make billons on, or keep control
of it for Idaho and its citizens." He said that the Idaho Water
Resource Board had violated the law by "giving Hells Canyon
to a consortium of power companies; the Snake River from
Thousands Springs to Hells Canyon to Idaho Power; and Bear
River to Utah (Power & Light)." He continued, "The profits
to this consortium will run into billions of dollars over the
length of the licensing period. Ninety percent of this high
value power is to be exported from Idaho, while from the
eastern end of the State, high cost coal generated power is to
be imported."
Of course, I attached a copy of the article to my press

---

262   This article was published in the *Times-News* on February 17,
1984.

release. I also noted that Senator Budge said in a publication he sent to the Federal Power Commission on June 9, 1971, that "the economic potential of the Snake River in power revenues, particularly through peaking, is one of the magnitude of Teapot dome." I allowed as how I found myself in agreement with his earlier statements, before he did a complete about-face to support the Power Company.

Quite frankly, I was perplexed as to why Senator Budge made such a complete reversal on the issue and why he launched a personal attack on me. When I threw my hat in the ring for Attorney General, he was a strong supporter and gave me a good deal of campaign help. He invited me to attend a barbecue at Fish Haven to meet and greet local Republicans and introduced me to Barbara Panter, who also was a good supporter during that election campaign. I suspected that Logan or Greg Panter prompted his attack.

Reed was undoubtedly upset with my response to his charges but every dog has his day. The following year he was able to extract a little revenge. I wanted to get legislation through that would allow me to manage the attorneys working for the State more effectively. As I mentioned earlier, the management of lawyers who worked for agencies was shared between my office and the various agencies. It was not an ideal arrangement. I got legislation approved in the 1983 legislative session to consolidate management control over all the State lawyers in my office but the bill was vetoed by Governor Evans. I got a similar bill passed in the 1985 session but it was also vetoed by the Governor. We certainly worked hand in hand in the Swan Falls issue but that didn't mean we saw eye to eye on everything else. In any event, I got the veto overridden in the House and just needed all of the Republican Senators to support me in order to override the veto. The problem was that there was one Republican holdout, Senator Budge. Knowing it was going to be a hard sell, I went to speak with him but he wouldn't budge. I issued a press release on March 14, 1985, saying my "consolidation bill was approved by the Legislature but vetoed by Governor Evans on March 13. The House overwhelmingly overrode the Governor's veto. A veto override vote was not held in the Senate because there were not sufficient votes to accomplish an override of Evans' veto. Senator Reed Budge (R–Soda Springs, whose vote was essential to an override, had stated that he would not vote to support an override.)" Reed told the Associated Press, "It is in fact a political issue. I would certainly hate putting a Republican governor in the governor's chair and have him appoint the agency heads and not have them be allowed to name their own attorneys in the case where the attorney general is of the opposite party."[263]

The same day I put out my press release responding to Senator Budge's charges, I met with the Governor and Jim Bruce to discuss settlement possibilities. Following the meeting, the Governor said we had a good meeting and "things were looking up." However, one might not have gathered that from the newspaper headlines. The Times-News headlined its article, "Jones, Bruce exchange salvos."[264] The Idaho State Journal headline said, "Jones, Utility Chief Blast Each Other Over Water Rights."[265] My gripe was the ongoing advertising campaign, which I thought violated the agreement we made to tone down the debate. Jim Bruce was upset with the letter I wrote to Secretary Clark several weeks earlier and with the fact that we were looking into the pre-primary advertising campaign.

Since the Power Company was not going to honor any commitment to tone down the rhetoric, I made comments at a meeting of the Idaho Water Resource Board in Idaho Falls on July 25, along the lines that Reed Budge had touched on in

---

263   Associated Press. "Attorney general consolidation heads to governor." *Idahonian*, March 6, 1985.
264   Associated Press. "Jones, Bruce exchange salvos." *Times-News*, July 24, 1984.
265   Associated Press. "Jones, Utility Chief Blast Each Other Over Water Rights." *Idaho State Journal*, July 24, 1984.

his 1972 *Caribou Sun* article. The press release for the meeting read, "An expanded demand for energy in California is a major factor in the Snake River water rights fight. Idaho Power stands to gain hundreds of millions of dollars in revenues from out-of-state sales of surplus power if it wins the Swan Falls controversy." My press release continued:

The demand for electricity in Idaho has been abating in recent years but the Bonneville Power Administration predicts increasing demand in California. Idaho Power admits that it has a surplus of power to serve the needs of Idahoans and that the surplus will exist until the end of the century. Their purpose in trying to consolidate their hold on additional supplies of Snake River water is to more effectively serve the California market. Last year a power company official admitted that sales of surplus power were in the neighborhood of $60 million. Additional supplies of Snake River water could increase those sales well in excess of $100 million per year. Over the long haul their control of the Snake River could amount to billions of dollars. These sales would all come at the expense of growth, and quite possibly energy supplies, here in Idaho.

Idaho Power has launched a massive advertising campaign replete with half-truths for the purpose of duping the public into supporting this revenue enhancement project. The stakes are astronomical and the campaign is starting to be effective. However, people should ask why Idaho Power Company has suddenly become the champion of the ratepayers. If the company succeeds in its media blitz, future growth will be stymied in Idaho but the California economy will be greatly enhanced with our cheap electricity. One might characterize the Idaho Power effort as follows:

Support Idaho Power, send a kilowatt to California.

Governor Evans and I had proposed that each party to the Swan Falls controversy refrain from advertising and the public speaking circuit while negotiations were underway. However, Power Company officials rejected the idea, electing to carry on their media campaign. I do not intend to stand idly by while Idaho Power conducts its media campaign of deception and half-truths. People have a right to know what the real stakes are and what the power company's real motivation is. The company's stockholders would not be paying for this expensive campaign unless substantial benefits were to be reaped by the company.

I also told the Board about the Department of Interior's policy change on subordination and warned that Idaho Power could try to use it as leverage to get out of its subordination commitment at Hells Canyon.[266]

Jim Bruce fired back the next day, saying, "Not by the wildest stretch of the imagination could the company make billions of dollars selling electricity to California." He said he constantly finds himself having to respond to "inflammatory public statements from the Attorney General that cannot be left unchallenged."[267] In response to the rhetoric, the editor of the Idaho Statesman said we should "Get serious or stop talking on water rights."[268] The editor spoke of the exchanges between myself and the Power Company, saying we ought to tone it down and try to negotiate. This gave me a good opportunity to lay out our case in a guest opinion:[269]

266   Retallic, Ken. "Board sets limits on hydropower permits." *Post-Register*, July 26, 1984.
267   UPI. "AG accused of blocking settlement." *Idaho Press-Tribune*, July 27, 1984.
268   "Get serious or stop talking on water rights." *Idaho Statesman*, July 28, 1984.
269   "Idaho Power misleads in propaganda effort." *Idaho Statesman*, Aug. 5, 1984.

Although some of the points contained in The Statesman's editorial of July 28 are somewhat murky, the ultimate conclusion is right on point. That is, it is difficult to negotiate a solution to the Snake River water rights controversy in an emotionally charged atmosphere. When one party to the negotiations is utilizing tens of thousands of dollars extracted involuntarily from ratepayers' pockets (the Public Utilities Commission has required, at least, that the campaign be paid for out of the stockholders' share of power revenues) in order to frighten the public into supporting its side of the controversy, the negotiation process is not greatly benefited. In recognition of this point, Gov. John Evans and I have attempted to lower the profile of the public debate on the water rights controversy.

On July 23, Gov. Evans and I proposed that both sides refrain from publicly advertising or promoting their sides of the water rights controversy. This would include public speaking engagements and the current Idaho Power Co. advertising campaign. At that time I informed power company officials that I did not intend to stand idly by while they conducted an expensive and misleading propaganda campaign. Power company officials indicated that they would take the "cease-fire" or moratorium proposal under advisement. The next day, the power company negotiator advised my staff that the current ad campaign would continue unabated. Therefore, it becomes necessary to tell the other side of the story—that is, that Idaho Power is really more interested in enhancing its revenue picture than protecting the ratepayers.

Idaho Power Co. comes into its purported role as champion of the ratepayers at a very late stage of the game. This is the same Idaho Power Co. that requested that the ratepayers foot the bill for over $11 million in outlays made for the ill-fated Pioneer plant. This is the same Idaho Power Co. that has consistently obstructed the cogeneration industry that would be able to furnish lower-cost electricity through new cogeneration projects than Idaho Power is able to furnish under existing new construction projects or proposed projects. Apparently its monopolistic desire to stamp out competition takes precedence over its ballyhooed concern for ratepayers.

This is the same Idaho Power Co. that vigorously asserts that Gov. Evans should sign a contract to give it protection from the Public Utilities Commission for failing to protect what it asserts are its water rights on the Snake River. If Idaho Power Co. had rights on the Snake River that it did fail to protect, the company should be penalized through ratepayer relief for failing to protect those rights. That relief could amount to $50 million to $200 million but it would disappear if the contract were signed. Idaho Power would be gaining much at the expense of the ratepayers while giving up little, if anything, to upstream water users, who will probably prevail in court against Idaho Power Co.

Idaho Power purports to be the friend of the ratepayers, but the record does not support that widely advertised assertion. The record does support the fact that there is a power surplus which Idaho will be blessed with until the end of the century, and that our additional needs can be conveniently and reasonably provided for through cogeneration projects. The record shows that there is a growing power market to be served in California and that last year approximately $60 million worth of Idaho's cheap power was furnished by Idaho Power to California. More water would generate more surplus power for more out-of-state sales for more power revenues. Former power company President Tom Roach, a great Idahoan, would be saddened with the company's present policy.

There is no doubt in my mind that future growth and development can exist hand in hand with low-cost electricity. That end will be reached when the people of Idaho, not the private monopoly, have control of the state's most precious resource — the Snake River — as was the case from statehood until November, 1982. With the acquiescence of all parties, the state has had a subordination policy and, in fact, 80 percent to 90 percent of the power generated by Idaho Power Co. is generated at facilities which are unquestionably subordinated to upstream development. Wise new criteria are necessary under state law to protect the hydropower base so that unlimited growth does not infringe on the interests of existing ratepayers. We can and will have it all unless Idaho Power Co. is allowed to beat us into submission through its costly and persistent propaganda efforts.

Meanwhile, Governor Evans said he hoped to forge a "truce" between myself and Jim Bruce.[270] "Obviously, we're going to have to have a truce. We are hopeful that within the next couple of months, if we can lower the visibility, the difficulty created as a result of that heated debate, that we'll be able to come up with some answers to the problem."

The Power Company released the results of its customer opinion survey to the press at the end of July but the lead-in to the Associated Press report may not have been exactly what the Company wanted. It said, "Nearly three of every four Idaho Power Co. customers believe the utility should

---

270   UPI. "Evans hopes to forge 'truce' between Jones, Idaho Power." *Idaho Press-Tribune, July 29, 1984.*

give up at least a portion of its Snake River water rights to existing users, but be compensated for water rights turned over to future developers."[271] This is essentially expressing support for the Idaho Power contract legislation. However, the headline in the Blackfoot paper misfired a bit, saying "Idaho Power Co. contends customers back subordination."[272] This is probably not the headline they were hoping for.

The heated public debate appeared to be provoking some concern in the community, because my office received a call from a fellow who wanted to know what subordination was all about. He was currently a patient at St. Luke's Hospital in Boise. It turned out he was the kindly-looking gentleman who appeared along with his Levis in Idaho Power's advertising, expressing concerns about subordination. He indicated that he had been in the State for over a year when he was contacted at the Boise Veterans Home to see if he would do a commercial on subordination, which prompted him to ask, "What's subordination?" He was told by the advertising agent that he would be a natural with his distinctive voice, so he agreed to be in the ads. They proceeded to Robie Creek where the ads were filmed and photographed. He said that he talked to Larry Taylor at Idaho Power to find out what the deal was with subordination and wanted to get my side of the story too. He was a nice gentleman who was just trying to make a living but, at the same time, he was concerned about the message he was paid to give.

In the meantime, the Idaho Power ad campaign continued. On July 30, I wrote to Bob Hall, the executive director of the Idaho Newspaper Association, who questioned our inquiry into the Power Company's pre-primary advertising campaign. I said, "If this type of advertising campaign turns out not to be clearly included within the reporting requirements of the Sunshine Act, it may well be that corrective legislation

271   Associated Press. "Survey Shows Utility Customers Back Water Rights Compensation." *Idaho State Journal,* July 30, 1984.
272   Associated Press. "Idaho Power Co. contends customers back subordination." *The Morning News,* July 31, 1984.

is required."²⁷³ Hall responded that "further restrictions on 'issue advertising' could have a 'chilling' effect on groups who sponsor such ads." I thought it was interesting that the Newspaper Association spokesman was advocating non-disclosure of politically-oriented advertising, when openness and disclosure had been the holy grail of the media in the past.

When asked if Idaho Power was attempting to influence the election, Larry Taylor said, "absolutely not. It would be more believable if we said we were, but that sure was not the case." In response to an inquiry as to why the campaign increased in intensity as the primary election day approached, he responded that any time you launch an ad campaign, "you begin heavy to have an impact."

The exchange with Hall was precipitated by a letter he wrote to me on July 26, wherein he characterized the inquiry into the ad campaign as "a clumsy attempt to chill the free speech process." The Times-News article said, "Jones called Hall's letter 'bombastic,' and said he doubted that 'one scrawny attorney general' could strike fear into the hearts of Idaho Power executives."

Rick Shaughnessy followed up with a column the next day, noting that Hall's "chilling effect" concern seemed inconsistent with his action during the 1984 legislative session when he tried to censor copies of the Lewiston Morning Tribune that contained a Jim Fisher article that might adversely influence legislation to increase "the rates newspapers receive for 'legal' advertisements."²⁷⁴ Shaughnessy concluded, "Hall fits in well with the 47th Idaho Legislature which watered down the lobbyist disclosure section of the state's Sunshine Law. It appears Jones might help open-government advocates pick up some lost ground during the sessions of the 48th Legislature."

273   Bernton, Hal. "Jones seeking ad campaign disclosure law." *Times-News,* Aug. 2, 1984.
274   Shaughnessy, Rick. "Financial threats may obscure ideals." *Times-News,* Aug. 3, 1984.

The newspapers dwelled on the exchange of correspondence between myself and Hall for a few days. The Statesman had an editorial titled "Jim Jones is wrong to seek media's ad data."[275] The Press-Tribune headline read "Jones, media exec spar over disclosure law for Idaho Power-type ad campaigns."[276] In keeping with its head-in-the-sand posture, the Idaho State Journal had an editorial titled "Why This Crusade?"[277] The editorial writer was completely perplexed as to why I would begrudge the Power Company's campaign to take over the Snake River because it would deprive Idaho Power customers of their cheap electric power and harm the interests of Idaho Power stockholders. Apparently, it didn't occur to the editor that Idaho Power had filed two lawsuits against the State — one to get out of the Hells Canyon deal and the other to intimidate the holders of water rights junior to its rights at Swan Falls, nor that it had run what for Idaho was a massive advertising campaign designed to influence the primary elections. The Journal did, however, print a lengthy article two days later titled, "Attorney General Contends Utility's Ads Are Political."[278] The article included excerpts from what must have been the awfully long letter I wrote to Bob Hall about the advertising campaign and the need to have disclosure of politically-oriented advertising injected into election campaigns.

Bob Fick of the Associated Press wrote an article about the on-going conflict between myself and the Power Company that included some interesting comments by Senator McClure. According to the article:[279]

> McClure said he believed the controversy has to be settled one way or the other, although he maintained his formal neutrality in the fight.
>
> "We're probably not going to see any major devel-

275   *Idaho Statesman,* Aug. 2, 1984.
276   *Idaho Press-Tribune,* Aug. 3, 1984.
277   *Idaho State Journal,* Aug. 3, 1984.
278   *Idaho States Journal,* Aug. 5, 1984.
279   Fick, Bob. Associated Press. "Feud continues between Jones, Idaho Power." *Lewiston Tribune,* Aug. 3, 1984.

opments in Idaho until we can settle the question of water rights," the senior senator said. "This controversy is just going to keep us so uncertain."

Although Jones has asked the Interior Department to intervene in the dispute, McClure said there is no role for the federal government to play.

"I've spent my adult life trying to make certain that the federal government doesn't try to tell us how to manage our water," he said. "That's a state question to be settled on the state level and I just won't allow myself to get drawn into that question."

I certainly agreed with the Senator's position that federal government involvement in State water right issues was unwelcome. However, when the State and a private entity enter into a voluntary agreement that requires the parties to invoke federal authority to seal the deal, such as Governor Jordan and Idaho Power did when they agreed that three subordinated dams would be built in Hells Canyon, instead of one high federal dam, it is a different story. It appeared that Senator McClure's position was almost an exact counterpart of the new position of the Department of Interior — the State should not seek any federal assistance to get its water back and the Department of Interior should not give any assistance.

Charles Etlinger gave a good account of events to date in the August 13 issue of the Idaho Statesman:[280]

Idaho Attorney General Jim Jones recalls the fellow who came into his office "beet red, really livid that I would oppose the power company."

Jones has been enraging others lately, including those at the power company — Idaho Power Co. — with

---

280   Etlinger, Charles. "Subordination: What is it? A heated battle." *Idaho Statesman*, Aug. 13, 1984.

his barbed advocacy of subordination in the Swan Falls water-rights dispute.

Idaho Power also has perturbed Jones with its recent advertising blitz, to the point that he has begun an investigation into whether the ads violate the state's political expenditure reporting law.

In the process, Jones and Idaho Power have engaged in a statewide war of words.

Jones and Gov. John Evans have sought lower priority, or subordination, for Idaho Power's rights to Snake River Water upstream from Swan Falls Dam; agriculture and other uses would get higher priority. Their aim is to ensure that the state, not a power company, controls the river.

Idaho Power maintains that subordination would allow seizure of the water rights it now uses to produce cheap hydroelectric power, at great cost to consumers.

At stake is whether more development can occur along much of the Snake — it's now at a standstill — and the price Idaho Power customers pay for electricity.

After an inconclusive slugfest in the last two sessions of the Idaho Legislature, both sides settled down this summer to try to reach a compromise. But the verbal battle escalated recently.

The primary reason for the tough rhetoric, as gubernatorial legal counsel Pat Costello sees it, is the unwillingness of either side to risk losing ground in "the court of public opinion" should negotiations fail and the dispute erupt again in the Legislature.

Jones, a Vietnam War veteran, describes the conflict in terms of men under arms, in which each side "is trying to win the hearts and minds of the population."

He has accused Idaho Power of spouting half-truths, of being more interested in enhancing its revenues than protecting ratepayers, of beating the subordinators into submission with propaganda, of wanting to ship electricity to California.

Idaho Power President Jim Bruce has criticized Jones for not negotiating in good faith and of leading a "special-interest crusade," a role Bruce says it not appropriate to Jones' position as the state's top legal officer.

In one of the company's ads, a man is shown lifting a wallet from his back pocket, with the warning that rates could go up $200 a year.

The ad campaign has cost about $115,000, one-third of the utility's 1984 advertising budget, according to company spokesman Larry Taylor. The Idaho Public Utilities Commission will not allow the company to recoup the expenses from customers in the form of higher rates.

The last scheduled subordination ads ran Friday. Bruce said company officials plan to discuss Monday whether to continue them.

Some of the players in the subordination game say the rhetoric hasn't helped prospects for a compromise, and Evans has called for a lowering of the voices.

But Costello, who is one of the negotiators, said the heated exchanges have not caused problems in the negotiations—yet.

The three generals in the fray; Bruce, Evans and Jones—held two summit meetings in July. Costello said they have identified areas of agreement and isolated other areas to work out.

Hammering out possible solutions in another half-dozen meetings are three emissaries: Costello for the governor; Deputy Attorney General Pat Kole for

Jones, and Tom Nelson, a Twin Falls attorney, for Idaho Power.

"The thrust of the negotiations is to find a mutually acceptable way of protecting the hydropower base, while at the same time allowing for continued agricultural and other development," Costello said.

Early in the subordination dispute, both sides were confident they could win an all-out victory, but failed to do so in the Legislature, Costello noted. Now, partisans in both camps agree publicly that a compromise is in order.

That has not taken the issue out of the political arena, or at least has not eliminated what some participants see as possible political motivations in the rhetoric.

Some suspect that Jones hopes to win long-term political mileage — for a 1986 run at the 2nd Congressional District seat or for another political office — by arguing vigorously for a position many Snake River Plain residents support.

Idaho Power's Taylor, speaking for himself, suspects Jones thinks "he can get a political bounce" out of his position. If that's so, Taylor thinks Jones is mistaken. Taylor cites a recent Idaho Power survey showing that subordination is opposed by most customers, including those in the Magic Valley, from which Jones hails.

Jones denied that his rhetoric is motivated by personal political ambitions. He said he will take a strong look at running for re-election, although he would consider a 2nd District race.

"It doesn't help me to be fighting with the power company," he said, referring to Idaho Power as the most powerful political influence in Idaho. "They would be sort of a natural ally in any race."

Jones received $500 from Idaho Power for his 1982 race for attorney general.

"We'd like him to refund it," Taylor joked.

Jones maintained he is simply doing his job, like a bulldog, in representing the state, which is being sued by Idaho Power in Swan Falls litigation.

Politically, Jones figures his outspoken support of subordination might mean a trade-off. People who live upstream of Swan Falls (due south of Kuna) are generally happy with his position, but those downstream are more split, he reasons.

Costello, who is Ada County Democratic chairman, said the Republican attorney general simply believes his position is right, regardless of the political consequences.

Jones also has denied an accusation by Sen. Reed Budge, R-Soda Springs, of a conflict of interest because of a brother's water-right claim.

In anticipation of a possible "smear effort," Jones said, he long ago prepared a list of water permits and licenses in which he or his family might have an interest. He said family members would have been benefited by Idaho Power-backed legislation.

Jones said he is getting much positive reaction to his position, some of it from people who are pleased that somebody is standing up to Idaho Power.

At the same time, Idaho Power's intentions in mounting its ad campaign, the first salvo of which was fired before the May primary, are questioned by Jones and others.

Jones said part of the campaign was intended to help some legislative candidates, particularly two Magic Valley supporters of the company, Reps. John

Brooks, R-Gooding, and Gordon Hollifield, R-Jerome. But that backfired when the pair lost in the primary.

Jones said he suspects that influencing the fall elections is in the back of the minds of Idaho Power executives in running the ads.

Sen. Laird Noh, R-Kimberly, a chief legislative advocate of subordination, contended that through the ads, which appear on TV, over radio and in newspapers, the company is seeking to neutralize the issue in the election so it doesn't hurt some candidates who support the utility.

Noh said Idaho Power is making a "massive" political effort this year for candidates who favor its position.

Idaho Power Vice President Logan Lanham rejects such assertions by Jones and Noh about the company's political clout and motives as "a bunch of political rhetoric."

"Our ads don't have anything to do with elections," Lanham said. If water is diverted from the river, Idaho Power's 265,000 customers will have higher rates," he said. "Our desire is to inform them of that fact."

Lanham also minimized the company's political contributions as voluntary donations from employees. "There's not much of it anyway," he said.

The two sides have blamed each other for prompting continuations of the ads and pronouncements.

Jones considers the ads to be "totally deceptive," for example, by giving an exaggerated impression of how much subordination might cost consumers. He said he will not let the ads go unchallenged.

Similarly, Idaho Power officials were upset by statements Jones made, and continued the ads.

Idaho Power started putting together the ad campaign around the beginning of the year, Taylor said, after other means failed to clearly communicate to the public the threat of higher rates.

The management decided to hold off until after Evans vetoed legislation protecting the company from ratepayers' complaints that it had failed to protect water rights, Taylor said.

Bruce was concerned about "what the public reaction would be toward the company when the rates went up, on top of what they'll go up anyway," Taylor said. "Our customers, unless fully understanding what the cause was—they're going to blame Idaho Power, not the irrigators."

Idaho Power's stopping its ads might trigger a truce, Jones said. "I might make a few speeches here and there" in the event of a cease-fire, he said. "I don't want to go out on the rubber-chicken circuit."

Larry Taylor's remark about my use of the Swan Falls issue to build up political support for some other office was pretty wide of the mark. Picking a gratuitous fight with what was then the most influential player in Idaho politics was not exactly a good way to build up your political credentials. At that point I had no plans to seek any other office. The Governor's office did not appeal to me and, although I ran for Congress in the Republican primary in 1978 and 1980, that did not appeal any more either. I'm not sure why a person would give up a state-wide Attorney General position to run for Congress in a congressional district representing just half of the State. I was never too thrilled about the prospect of being a member of the House, even though I'd run for that office twice. It was an opportunity to get my foot in the political door and provide a springboard to an office I really wanted. My ambition since 1961 was to be a United States Senator.

As it turned out, I ran unopposed for reelection as Attorney General in 1986, and, unsuccessfully, for the Senate in 1990.

As a matter of fact, I was just doing what the Idaho Constitution required me to do—defending lawsuits brought against the State by Idaho Power Company and using every legitimate tool available to me, including the bully pulpit. If nothing else, I am tenacious and have been consistently so in my legal practice and political dealings. If one avenue toward the goal is blocked, I looked for every other possible alternate avenue. In the Swan Falls fight, I did not intend to give up until we prevailed or until every possible avenue for success was blocked. And, quite frankly, I did not think about the political fallout. I was in up to my neck and there was nowhere to go except straight ahead.

As strange as it may have sounded to some cynics, I was doing exactly what I thought was the right thing. My former boss, Len Jordan, had struck a wise bargain with Idaho Power in 1952, which provided for a balanced use of Idaho water. In an interview that took place a month later, Steve Green of United Press reported:[281]

> Jones asserted (Idaho Power) has used a paperwork loophole to disavow a promise made to former Gov. Len Jordan to subordinate all of its water to upstream users.
>
> "I really respected that man," said Jones, a former legislative aide for Jordan, who went to the U.S. Senate after he left the Statehouse. "I would really let him down if I didn't carry on the fight in his behalf."
>
> Jones claims the power company promised to subordinate all of its upstream water in return for Jordan's support of the company's effort to build its massive Hells Canyon hydroelectric complex.

---

281   Green, Steve. UPI. "Unique alliances develop over water." *Idaho Press-Tribune,* Aug. 30, 1984.

A letter written to Jones by the late Jordan's wife, Grace, supported the attorney general's contention that Jordan made an agreement with the power company to protect future upstream water consumption, Jones said.

"The letter told me I was on the right track," Jones said. "She was aware of all those agreements and negotiations."

Ever since hostilities had began in earnest early in the year, I got wind of various types of rumors circulating about me—conflict of interest, inconsistent positions, and so on. Compared with some of the other rumors, the claim that I was fighting the Power Company to enhance my credentials to run for some other office was actually fairly tame. But, it was a heated and nasty fight and I suppose one had to expect those kind of things. It did not make it pleasant, but I thought we were on the way to a win so that made it easier to take.

Bruce Newcomb called on August 9 to say that our public relations campaign was ready to go. That is to say, our bumper stickers were ready. I thought we should hold off on calling a press conference to announce our publicity campaign because I was told the Power Company brass was considering whether or not to end their ad campaign. We had heard, off and on, that there was somewhat of a struggle going on in the higher reaches of the Company. The rumor was that there was a hard-line faction that wanted to continue the fight and another faction that wanted to try to reach a settlement with the State. According to the political grapevine, Logan was involved with the hard-line faction that wanted to go for broke, while Jim Bruce was urging a settlement. Indeed, Jim publicly announced hopes of working out a settlement on several occasions. It did not appear that Logan was acting as much of a cheerleader for making a settlement. In any event, it seemed prudent to hold off a bit on our bumper sticker campaign to see whether the Power Company decided to stand down.

On August 12 the Idaho State Journal was kind enough to publish my response to its August 3 editorial questioning my "crusade." I could not resist writing,[282]

It is easy to understand why you are so confused over my efforts to prevent Idaho Power Company from taking over the main flow of the Snake River. Your paper has acted as chief apologist for Idaho Power in the water rights controversy. I suspect that the *Idaho State Journal* would like to see the Snake turned into a wild and free-flowing river at the expense of future growth in Pocatello, Bannock County and the rest of the portion of the Snake River plains east of Swan Falls. This type of no-growth attitude does little to serve your readership.

The answer for my involvement is simple — I was elected (without the support or help of your paper) to represent the people of Idaho. In 1977 Idaho Power Company filed suit against the State of Idaho seeking control over the main flow of the Snake River, as well as large monetary damages. That suit is known as the Swan Falls suit. The Attorney General is mandated to represent the interests of the State and I intend to vigorously resist that suit in the courts or in any other forum where Idaho Power Company decides to fight the battle. The power company has chosen to attempt to short-circuit the court processes by taking the fight to the legislature and the forum of public opinion and, because the outcome of the suit is so important to the future of Idaho, I have also entered those forums to

---

282   "Journal is 'Apologist.'" *Idaho State Journal,* Aug. 12, 1984.

inform the people and legislators of the other side of the issue — the State's side. As chief apologist for Idaho Power Company, you contend that Idaho Power has the unqualified right to utilize tens of thousands of dollars extracted from ratepayers to finance a massive and deceptive media blitz. You begrudge the Attorney General the right to make a few comments to indicate that there may be more than one side of the issue and that Idaho Power may be using the ratepayers' fears to get them to support the company's future growth and economic fortunes.

The letter continued with my talking points about the projected power surplus, Idaho Power's out-of-state sales, and the like.

Waldo Martens and Gary Robbins sent a letter to the Statesman, responding to its August 2 editorial that criticized me for inquiring into the Power Company's ad campaign. I decided to ignore the editorial, but as victims of the campaign, they wanted to have their say. This is what they wrote:[283]

The thinking in your Aug. 2 editorial is contradictory. You say that the Idaho Power Co. advertising campaign, which started May 10, 12 days before the primary election, was "obviously political in nature."

It was indeed a political advertising campaign, and we received the brunt of it during our primary election races against entrenched incumbents in the Magic Valley. Fortunately, despite the ad campaign, we both won.

It was very clear to us that the 12-day media blitz, which Idaho Power Co. conducted through election day, was designed to help our opponents and hurt us

283   "Political advertising." *Idaho Statesman*, Aug. 12, 1984.

in the election. John Brooks and Gordon Hollifield had supported Idaho Power right down the line in the Legislature. Idaho Power was glad to help them with political contributions from its political action committee and the large advertising campaign, which zeroed in on the hottest issue between us and our opponents in the election race.

In fact, Logan Lanham, the top lobbyist for Idaho Power, was escorting Gordon Hollifield around Minidoka County on May 21, the day before the primary election. The repetition of power company ads directed against us steadily increased on the radio and television and in the newspaper until they peaked out on election day.

The week before the primary election we called a press conference with other similarly situated candidates to demand equal time from the electronic media. We also called on the attorney general to look into what we thought was unfair political advertising directed toward helping our opponents and hurting us in the election.

Some of us complained to the Public Utilities Commission about this expenditure of ratepayer money. The bottom line is that the ad campaign was directed against us and in favor of our opponents and should have been reported under the Sunshine Act.

We would be very disappointed if the authorities did not pursue action against Idaho Power Co. for violating the Sunshine Law by failing to report these expenditures. Just because you are big doesn't mean you are exempt from the law.

We think the attorney general's request for information on the ad campaign is certainly justified, but the matter cannot be laid to rest there. If the evidence points toward an effort by Idaho Power Co. to influence the elections by making expenditures to support or oppose candidates, the Sunshine Act reporting requirement does come into play and appropriate action by the authorities should proceed. — WALDO MARTENS, Republican candidate for House Seat D, Legislative District No. 24, Jerome, and GARY ROBBINS, Republican candidate for House Seat A, Legislative District No. 22, Dietrich

When we received no word as to whether the advertising campaign would continue, I rattled my saber again, saying that I would resume my public speaking tour if we did not have word soon.[284] When contacted, Larry Taylor said that Company executives had not made a decision yet.

An editorial by the Press-Tribune that dealt with another issue caught my eye because it addressed the political aspiration concern that was expressed by Larry Taylor. The editorial started out, "Attorneys general in this state have traditionally used the position as a steppingstone to someplace else. A run for governor, Congress, whatever. As a result, when they are ever heard from it is usually on the side of a popular and/or non-controversial position. Not necessarily so with our current one, Jim Jones. He has shown no reluctance, no fear, of treading where his predecessors dared not to go for fear of the consequences. Currently, for example, the AG is fighting it out with Idaho Power over the water rights subordination question on the Snake River. And, a little more than a week ago, he told Idaho Fish & Game Department what it could do with a mailing it had sent out on behalf of a pro-wilderness sportsmen's coalition."[285]

The Department of Interior responded to my letter

---

284   UPI. "IP threatened again by AG." *Idaho Press-Tribune,* Aug. 14, 1984.

285   "Carrying water." *Idaho Press-Tribune,* Aug. 19, 1984.

to Secretary Clark, confirming what we thought the third paragraph of Hal Furman's letter meant. In an August 22 letter, Bob Broadbent, the Assistant Secretary for Water and Science, Furman's boss, wrote to say that Furman's letter "is a definitive expression of our policy. It is the positive intention of this Department and the Reagan Administration to recognize and support the primacy of State water rights except when in conflict with Federal law." The Department never answered our inquiry as to whether this policy applied to any river basin other than the Snake River. I suspected not but we had better things to do than to look into that issue.

Idaho Power had been claiming that the Idaho Public Utilities Commission was on record opposing subordination. This claim was asserted in print in an August 13 publication, the Idaho Power Update. The public information officer for the PUC wrote Larry Taylor on August 23 to say that neither the Commission nor the Commissioners had "gone on record opposing subordination." It is true that two of the commissioners, Conley Ward and Perry Swisher, expressed concerns about subordination but had not express opposition to the Evans-Jones legislation. The other commissioner, Dick High, may well have supported our position but I certainly wouldn't have pressed him on the issue. He was an outstanding person — smart, knowledgeable, and loaded with common sense.

Another individual who understood the importance of the multiple-use concept, as well as the historical setting of the Swan Falls fight, was Vern Ravenscroft. Vern wrote a letter to the editor of the Statesman, saying in part:[286]

> The silent issue in the Swan Falls debate is not Swan Falls at all. It is an attempt to avoid the existing subordination at Hells Canyon where nearly 1,400

---

286   "Swan Falls confusion." *Idaho Statesman*, Sept. 4, 1984.

megawatts of energy is installed. The Swan Falls plant, only 12 megawatts, represents less than one-half of 1 percent of Idaho Power Co.'s total capacity. Twelve megawatts could easily be replaced by raising the Swan Falls dam, or by building a new project down river at the American Freedom site, or by developing new storage facilities up river, or by purchase of alternative rights in the proposed Galloway (Weiser River) Project.

The power company has changed positions. In the heat of the Hells Canyon dispute, Idaho Power officials made promises to then Gov. Len Jordan and many other Idaho political leaders that upstream development must always come ahead of their power rights. The Hells Canyon projects were subordinated, and that action is spelled out in those licenses for all to examine.

I personally have testified before Congress on this issue. That testimony was invited by the power company.

Idaho Power has published brochures encouraging agricultural development in the entire Snake River Basin, and has provided valuable assistance to agricultural pumpers. This was done to create a market for the power they were generating. It was good business and created goodwill in the communities they are serving.

It is to the credit of the power company that they did not start the Swan Falls subordination fight. It is to their discredit that today, via their advertising program, they try to mask the fact that a change in position has actually taken place.

Steve Green of United Press wrote a good six-part series on the Swan Falls issue, giving a complete rundown of the history, the fight that was taking place between and among the parties, and the potential outlook for the State depending on who prevailed. His series was published in the Coeur d'Alene Press, the Idaho Statesman, and the Press-Tribune.[287]

The Idaho State Journal had an interesting editorial on September 7, regarding an advertising campaign in support of right-to-work legislation. The editorial writer bemoaned one-issue advertising blitzes in general, and the right-to-work campaign in particular, saying "the right-to-workers are the most strident, their political clamor often rising above that of Attorney General Jim Jones' noisy battle with Idaho Power over the subordination issue."[288] It appeared that my single-person blitz was more effective in Pocatello than the Power Company's massive advertising campaign because the editor seemed unaware of the Power Company's blitz. As I recall, I had not spent a thin dime on my noisy battle, compared to Idaho Power's reported $115,000 expenditure.

Speaking of that, Idaho Power announced on September 10 that it "halted its advertising on the Snake River water rights controversy and will not resume the messages unless negotiations with the state break down."[289] Larry Taylor made the announcement, essentially saying that the Power Company decided to give peace a chance. Hallelujah!

There is no doubt that the Power Company's image had taken a beating since the first of the year. The subordination proponents had aroused and energized the water-using community and shown that there was much more at stake than providing a band-aid to the defendants in Swan Falls II. People without an immediate stake in the fight also came to see that the outcome of the fight could have substantial effects on the future growth and development of the State. There is no doubt that the Power Company sustained significant damage in the fight, and its politically-oriented advertising

---

287   *Idaho Press-Tribune*, Aug. 27–Sept. 1, 1984.
288   "The One-Issue Blitz." *Idaho State Journal*, Sept. 7, 1984.
289   UPI. "Idaho Power stops advertising about water rights controversy." *Idaho Press-Tribune*, Sept. 11, 1984.

campaign did not help.

The Associated Press wrote an article that provided an assessment of Idaho Power's image problem and how it was adversely affected by its advertising campaign. I told the reporter, "Just because you provide cheap power doesn't mean that you can't provoke controversy. When the people of Idaho provide free water for the generation of power, there's no wonder it's inexpensive."[290] I said it was inappropriate for the Company to use money extracted from ratepayers to try to influence the outcome of legislative races.

---

290   Associated Press. "Idaho Power Co. fights image." *The Morning News,* Sept. 11, 1984.

BLESSED ARE THE PEACEMAKERS

Negotiations with the Power Company had been going on for some time and they intensified with the cessation of the advertising campaign. The negotiations continued with the three negotiators—Pat Kole, Pat Costello, and Tom Nelson. I met regularly with Pat and Clive to discuss the progress. Pat was a skillful negotiator while Clive was the water policy expert. It worked out pretty well. During September, Clive prepared and we released an in-depth position paper on the subordination issue, both with an eye toward the negotiations and for consumption by interested parties. Hal Bernton of the Times-News had a good article dealing with the negotiations:[291]

> Idaho Attorney General Jim Jones says an increase in the state-mandated minimum stream flows for the Snake River and some reforms in state water rights law are two key elements of a proposed negotiated settlement with Idaho Power to end the Swan Falls controversy.
> "The Snake River is going to have to be regulated on a minimum stream flow basis instead of on a basis of water rights and the magnitude of water rights at one dam or another," Jones said Tuesday.
> Despite some disagreements that still remain, both Jones and Idaho Power officials say that a final settlement could be reached soon, possibly by the end of the week.
> Negotiators are now meeting almost daily in an effort to reach a final settlement that could "resolve the biggest part of pending lawsuits relating to Swan

291   Bernton, Hal. "Swan Falls settlement seems near." *Times-News,* Sept. 26, 1984.

Falls," Jones said.

Draft copies of the proposed agreement have already been circulated among key legislators, Jones said.

State Sen. Laird Noh, chairman of the Senate Resources and Environmental Committee said he supports the proposed agreement.

"I am encouraged and pleased by what I have seen," Noh said. "It (the proposed agreement) has the possibility of turning what has been a bad situation into one that can benefit Idaho in the long run."

Jones said the agreement is likely to call for the state to set a minimum stream flow high enough to ensure the future integrity of Idaho Power's Snake River hydro base. In return, the company would have to agree to subordinate some of its Snake River water rights to the state, which would then allocate their use.

The minimum flows would include separate standards for winter and summer flows, Noh said.

Idaho Power officials declined to comment on the specifics of any proposed agreement, but company spokesman Larry Taylor confirmed that Jones remarks were a generally accurate summary of current negotiating points.

Jones says that negotiators have agreed that the use of Snake River water should be regulated by a minimum stream flow higher than the current 3,300 cubic-feet-per second flow level as measured at the Murphy gauging station below Swan Falls.

But just how much higher the flows should be set apparently remains unsettled.

Jones said the flow increases should be in only "moderate amounts above the minimum stream flow over the one now approved by the state." But he said the issue was still being debated by negotiators.

"We are not going to be satisfied with any agreement that does not put the state back into the job of administering the river and doesn't recognize the need for upstream growth," Jones said.

Jones said the Swan Falls agreement may also call for a reform of state water laws.

These laws were "drafted in a period of water abundance and it won't be long before we are in a period of scarcity," Jones said. The laws need to be updated in a manner that "allows for development to go forward but doesn't impinge on the hydro power base," he said.

Noh said the key water law reforms would probably result in an extension of the public interest doctrine already used by the state Department of Water Resources to allocate water rights. These reforms would have to be approved by the Legislature, he said.

Jones said the "specific issues" of the negotiations focused on "striking a balance between development and electric rates and updating water laws."

Jones said certain aspects of the agreement will probably have to be ratified by the Legislature, and that draft outlines of the agreement have been circulated to key legislators.

He said the negotiations which began in July, have at times been complicated by disagreements within negotiating teams.

The fine print details have also hampered attempts to reach a settlement.

Each time the negotiating teams come close to an agreement, new issues arise "that hadn't been thought of as crucial but suddenly become crucial," Jones said.

FERC finally acted favorably on the State's petition to intervene in the Swan Falls licensing proceeding. I announced the decision at a press conference on September 19, saying, "The action will substantially strengthen the state's hand in the entire water rights subordination issue."[292] I also advised the media that the Governor and I had "agreed on a 'reasonable compromise' offer to Idaho Power to solve some of the disputes over southern Idaho water rights." As of that time, we had not received a response from Idaho Power but we "expected to do so shortly." I said the Governor and I were "seeking to gain an agreement on water rights that will 'allow some farm growth upstream, and still protect low power rates.'"

On October 1, the Governor, Jim Bruce and I announced that we agreed upon a framework to settle the entire Swan Falls dispute. My press release that happy day read:

> The State of Idaho and Idaho Power Company have negotiated a framework which can be used as a basis for the state to again begin managing the Snake River for the benefit of all Idahoans. The framework lays the basis for allocating our precious Snake River water in a balanced, multiple-use manner. I believe the framework strikes a proper balance which will allow future growth and development by insuring additional supplies of water for consumptive uses, while protecting our low-cost power supplies. Most importantly, the framework places the state back in the position of making vitally important water allocation decisions.
>
> Jones, Governor John Evans, and Idaho Power Company Chief Executive James Bruce announced today that they had reached agreement on a negotiated package of measures to solve the Snake River water

---

292   Kenyon, Quane. "State Joins Swan Falls Suit." *Idaho State Journal,* Sept. 20, 1984.

rights controversy. The package calls for setting an increased minimum streamflow on the Snake River while freeing additional water for upstream growth and development. The framework calls for a new water allocation criteria, as well as court adjudication of the Snake River.

Under the negotiated framework Idaho Power would relinquish a large portion of its asserted Swan Falls water right so that southern Idaho residents will have the assurance of future growth and development. At the present time Idaho Power Company has a court-sanctioned claim to 8400 cubic feet per second of water at its Swan Falls Dam. This has effectively stymied state management of the Snake River and Snake River Plains Aquifer, while bringing upstream growth to a virtual standstill. Under the framework, the company's water right would be reduced to 3900 cfs during the irrigation season from April through October. During the remaining five months of the year Idaho Power would be entitled to a flow of 5600 cfs, which will result from inflows between Milner and Murphy. The parties have agreed to a zero flow at Milner, which would allow for the filling of present upstream storage facilities, as well as additional new water storage projects.

Since the historic summer low flow in the Snake River has been approximately 4500 cfs, the negotiated framework will free up a significant amount of additional water for upstream growth and development during the irrigation season. The levels agreed on for the minimum flows during the summer and winter will safeguard and protect Idaho Power Company's rate base so that Idaho citizens can continue to enjoy the benefits of low-cost hydroelectric power."

New water will be allocated under criteria which insure that sound, family-farm type projects can go forward. The framework frees up water for growth of upstream communities both by providing the necessary domestic water and by making water available for industrial and commercial enterprises which will provide economic growth, jobs and increased tax base.

One of the most important features is that water allocation decisions will be placed back in the hands of the state. That is where these important decisions should be made since state officials are more responsive to public demand than any private company would be.

The Swan Falls decision in 1982 placed southern Idaho's growth in a state of limbo and I am hoping that this negotiated framework can resolve that deadlock. There are still a number of mechanical matters which will have to be worked out in order to place the framework into effect and the general public and interested parties will have the opportunity to have their input into that process. If the process can be completed, we can get back about the business of managing the Snake River and southern Idaho's future without the necessity of more years of struggling through the courts.

Not everything in the negotiated package is to my liking but there were many areas of give and take during the negotiation process. Some of the more important considerations were bringing about an early settlement of the controversy which would allow for additional consumptive uses upstream, which would put the state back into the water allocation business, and which would protect the hydropower rate base. Additionally, each party had to assess the risks which might be involved in future litigation and I believe that from that standpoint the framework is a reasonable manner of resolving the controversy.

Jones noted that much additional work remained to be done in order to place the "framework" into operation. It will necessitate actions by the Legislature, the State Water Resource Board, approval by the Federal Energy Regulatory Commission, as well as additional negotiation on specific settlement language. In addition, there are a number of contingencies which could yet negate the entire process so we should continue to view the negotiated framework with cautious optimism.

A copy of the Framework for Final Resolution of Snake River Water Rights Controversy Framework, which was executed by the Governor, Jim Bruce, and me on October 1, is attached as an Appendix.

With the agreement on the Framework, I was not particularly disturbed when I received a letter from Assistant Secretary Broadbent, signed by someone lower in the Interior Department, indicating that the Department would not intervene in FERC licensing proceedings for Swan Falls, Upper Salmon, Shoshone Falls, and Twin Falls. The letter was dated October 4 and it made mention of the agreement the Governor and I reached with the Power Company. The Interior Department must have been monitoring the situation. My thought was, "go fly a kite."

Immediately upon our announcement of the settlement Framework, most of the usual suspects began denouncing it. Ken Robison claimed the agreement would "cost ratepayers as much as $150 million a year in electric rates, about $3 billion over the next 20 years."[293] Al Fothergill echoed Robison's claims "and questioned the need for further agricultural

---

293   Bugger, Brad. "Critics Attack Swan Falls Settlement Framework." *Idaho State Journal*, Oct. 2, 1984.

development." They labeled the agreement a "multi-million dollar raid" on the pocketbooks of ratepayers. Harold Miles joined in, claiming the agreement would endanger upland game birds, have a negative impact on water quality, and be "devastating" to fish populations. The agreement called for a general adjudication of the water rights in the Snake River Basin, something that was absolutely necessary to quantify and prioritize water rights in the Basin and something that had to be done sooner or later. The Water Resource Board had estimated previously that adjudication would cost about $28 million to complete. Water users were rightly concerned as to how that cost was going to be paid and whether they were going to be assessed with part or all of the cost.[294] I pointed out that the Framework did not specify how the adjudication would be financed, which was something the Legislature would have to decide in its upcoming session.

Governor Evans said that the agreement "establishes a 'more realistic' minimum streamflow for the Snake that will allow for low-cost hydropower, as well as agricultural development and industrial and commercial needs."[295] For my part, I said the agreement "lays the groundwork for a balance in the use of a resource that will increasingly become more scarce." Jim Bruce said the claims by Robison and Fothergill "about the possible increase in electric rates have been 'vastly overstated.'" He indicated he could not say how much rates will go up, "but under the public interest criteria in the agreement, I don't anticipate any major impact, and I repeat 'major impacts,' with respect to electric rates. There will be some over the course of the years, but just how much I can't say." Ken Robison fired off a guest opinion to the Post-Register claiming the sky was falling. The headline read, "Wildlife interests sold down the river by Jones."[296] Apparently, Robison was not aware that two other individuals

294   Associated Press. "Criticism mounts against Swan Falls plan." *South Idaho Press,* Oct. 3, 1984.
295   Retallic, Ken. "Water will be shared." *Post-Register,* Oct. 2, 1984.
296   *Post-Register,* Oct. 4, 1984.

participated in putting the framework together, although he did say the "Evans-Jones policy is one of new irrigation at any price — any price to conservation or the consuming public."

The Statesman editorialized that "the proposed settlement to the Snake River water rights controversy appears to be an equitable solution to a complex problem."[297] The editor correctly stated, "The package, worked out by Gov. John Evans, Attorney General Jim Jones, and the utility, would bring a direction to water planning more sweeping than any the state has had."

The Governor, Logan Lanham, and I appeared before a Water Resource Board meeting in Pocatello on October 5 to explain the agreement.[298] The newspaper stated, "Jones and Lanham, who exchanged a series of vitriolic personal attacks last spring, were all smiles Friday as they lined up beside Evans to tout the new agreement." It is true that the knife wounds were starting to heal. However, we were not necessarily out of the woods yet.

At its Pocatello meeting, the Water Resource Board announced that it would be holding a series of six public information meetings in communities along the course of the Snake River in late October to inform the public about the agreement. The three principal negotiators — Tom Nelson, Pat Costello, and Pat Kole — would participate to explain the details of the deal. I assured the Board that, "Once the people know all the details and all of the mechanics involved, they will say it was a reasonable agreement and they will realize they can live with it."[299]

The principals to the agreement were busy on the speaking circuit to explain and sell the Framework to the

---

297   "Swan Falls plan offers solution to thorny issue." *Idaho Statesman,* Oct. 5, 1984.
298   Bernton, Hal. "Board to explain water agreement." *Times-News,* Oct. 6, 1984.
299   Miller, John. "Swan Falls pact won't come cheap." *The Morning News,* Oct. 6, 1984.

public. Jim Bruce told the Pocatello Rotary Club on October 11 that Idaho Power had not sold out its ratepayers.[300] He said, "There has been an outcry from some consumer groups that we have sold out the ratepayers. But I couldn't find them (the consumer groups) when I needed them. For two years, there's been a very strange silence."

Senator Risch expressed his support for the agreement, saying, "It's about as fair a compromise as you can get. I will support it, although I was on the side of not subordinating the water right."[301] Tom Stivers, who had opposed subordination, also expressed support for the agreement.

The most important part of the Framework dealt with how the 8,400 cfs Swan Falls water right would be subordinated. The State Water Plan had previously established a minimum streamflow of 3,300 cfs at the Murphy Gage, which was located immediately below Swan Falls. As stated in the Framework, "The best available hydrologic data indicate that existing uses result in a potential irrigation season low flow of approximately 4,500 cfs at Murphy Gage on an average daily basis." It was agreed that the minimum streamflow during irrigation season would be set at 3,900 cfs, the midpoint between 3,300 cfs and 4,500 cfs. The Framework set the non-irrigation season flow at 5,600 cfs. It was agreed that the minimum streamflow would be set at 3,900 cfs from April 1 to October 31 and 5,600 cfs from November 1 to March 31, and that Idaho Power's water right at Swan Falls would be unsubordinated up to those new minimum streamflows. The water right would be subordinate and subject to depletion by future upstream consumptive uses over and above those new minimum flows. Of course, any new water right application would need to meet the new public interest criteria.

The Framework contemplated that a settlement agreement would be prepared, spelling out the details of the

300   Bugger, Brad. "Utility Didn't 'Sell Out' Ratepayers." *Idaho State Journal*, Oct. 12, 1984.
301   UPI. "Top lawmakers back Swan Falls plan." *Idaho Press-Tribune*, Oct. 15, 1984.

agreement and how it would be performed. Pat and Clive prepared and circulated a proposed agreement that would subordinate the Swan Falls water right over and above the new minimum streamflows, effective upon fulfillment of the conditions in the agreement—enactment of the legislative package and approval by the Public Utilities Commission, the Idaho Water Resource Board, and the Federal Energy Regulatory Commission.

Unfortunately, Idaho Power had a substantially different view as to how the water right would be subordinated. The Power Company's concept was that it would retain its water right over and above the 3,900 cfs minimum streamflow and that the right would be gradually subordinated as new water rights were approved and granted above Swan Falls. In other words, we differed as to whether there would be an immediate subordination or whether the subordination would gradually occur over an extended period of time. The dispute was whether the water right was to be "subordinated" or "subordinatable."

We had called this conflict to the Governor's attention and urged that the State require that the water right be subordinated immediately upon fulfillment of the conditions. The Power Company was insistent on the subordinatable language and drafted a document containing that language. We got word back from Pat Costello that the Governor was inclined to go with the draft proposed by Idaho Power in order to get the dispute resolved.

On October 17, I wrote the Governor to express my concern about a subordinatable right and about the timing of the signature of the 1180 Contract. I wrote:

> Enclosed, as per your request, are several copies of the Snake River water rights agreement between the State of Idaho and Idaho Power Company. The con-

tract has been prepared for your signature on behalf of the State of Idaho and for the signature of Jim Bruce on behalf of Idaho Power Company,

The contract is drafted in accordance with the matters negotiated between the State and Idaho Power. While the agreement represents a balanced and equitable settlement of the water rights dispute and while it accurately represents the items negotiated between the parties for the most part, I cannot advise you to sign it in its present form for two reasons.

First, it does not resolve the Senate Bill 1180 problem. That is, it does not address the timing for the signature between you and Idaho Power of the contract authorized pursuant to the Senate Bill 1180 legislation. That contract, as revised, is an integral part of the agreement and it should be executed but only at such time as the enclosed contract has been fully performed by the fulfillment of other contingencies. I think it would be a potentially disastrous mistake for you to sign the Senate Bill 1180 contract until the other contingencies have been met. It is my understanding that you intend to consult with me and with your task force before signing the Senate Bill 1180 contract and I would strongly advise that you not sign the contract until such time as the contingencies in the enclosed contract have been fulfilled. In my estimation it is a grave mistake not to address this situation in the enclosed contract.

Second, I believe it would be a serious mistake for you to sign the enclosed contract with the present definition of Idaho Power Company's water right as outlined in paragraph 7.B. I have strongly advised you to adopt the language prepared by my staff which makes the power company's water right above the new increased minimum streamflows a "subordinated" right instead of a "subordinatable" right. I see great potential for legal difficulties with the language as drafted and cannot in good conscience recommend that you sign the contract with that language. With the "subordinated" language I think we have clearly achieved the objective that we have been working for in the lawsuit and in the negotiations. With the "subordinatable" language, I think we may achieve the same end but with potentially serious legal difficulties which I would not be willing to accept.

Although I do believe that the agreement can accomplish what we have been striving for — a balanced approach toward usage of Snake River waters and control of Snake River waters by the State of Idaho — I do have these two strong and serious reservations. My strong recommendation is that the contract not be signed in its present form without addressing these two vital concerns. As the State's Governor, you are certainly entitled to pursue your own course with regard to these two problems and you certainly have the discretion to disregard this advice, but I strongly believe that the advice is the correct advice and that I have the obligation to voice it to you.

One additional point that should be made regards the rush preparation of the enclosed agreement. My staff has done the best job they can of reviewing all documents to insure that they are correctly and properly drafted. However, with the time frame we have been given to operate within, I cannot absolutely guarantee that everything is letter perfect or that all possible problems have been fully evaluated. We have done the best job we could under the tight time frame and, quite frankly, I think my staff has performed a near Herculean task.

I circulated copies of the letter to the coalition supporting subordination—the Committee of Nine, the Idaho Water Users Association, Senator Noh, Representative Chatburn, and our legislative supporters, as well as our group of water attorneys and others to let them know the problems with the draft as proposed.

Of the two problems I addressed in my letter to the Governor, the 1180 Contract was the lesser concern. There was absolutely no need for that contract because the provisions contained in the Framework addressed each and every issue. Idaho Power's insistence that the 1180 Contract had to be signed as part of the deal was more about saving face than accomplishing anything. The Power Company had made such a big deal of the 1180 Contract over the last two years that I think the bigwigs felt that it just had to be signed.[302]

The subordinated–subordinatable problem was clearly more troubling. We thought it essential that the Power Company's water right over and above the new minimum flows be subordinated immediately so that no dispute could later arise regarding the status of Idaho Power's Snake River water rights. When the 1952 deal had been struck between Len Jordan and Idaho Power, everyone knew what the agreement was. However, with the passage of time, the State's institutional memory became fuzzy, the Water Resources records were not adequately documented, and a dispute arose. Thus, it was essential to clearly resolve the status of the flows over and above the new agreed minimums immediately, rather than leaving ownership of the rights in Idaho Power and allowing them to be subordinated over an extended period of time.

I was scheduled to speak to the Gooding Chamber of Commerce on October 18 and took that opportunity to publicize the problem. We had gotten word that the Governor

---

302   Because the 1180 Contract utilized different terminology and dates than the Framework and subsequent settlement agreement, it created numerous implementation problems in subsequent years.

was planning to sign the draft I was concerned about, so drastic action was required. The Times-News headline read, "Attorney general drops support for Swan Falls document."[303] I thought Pat Costello had been too accommodating in the negotiations in order to get the settlement wrapped up. Because of that and so as not to get the Governor riled up by directly criticizing him, I told the Chamber that Pat was a loose cannon. Hal Bernton's report said:

> Idaho Attorney General Jim Jones has abruptly dropped his support for a final legal document drawn up by state and Idaho Power Co. officials to resolve the Swan Falls water rights dispute.
>
> His surprise announcement at a Gooding County Chamber of Commerce luncheon Thursday was accompanied by a sharp attack on the negotiating techniques of Pat Costello, Gov. John Evans' representative in the Swan Falls talks.
>
> Jones charged that Costello was a "loose cannon rolling around the deck making concessions before they have to be made. If he would step out of the negotiations, we would be a lot better off."
>
> Holding up a draft copy of the still unreleased legal document, Jones said "it contains elements that I cannot in good conscience sign off on."
>
> Costello was "out on the range" in Malad Thursday afternoon, briefing Evans on the progress of the Swan Falls talks, said Evans' press secretary Jean Terra. The Times-News was unable to reach him for comment.
>
> Jones said he would not support a clause in the draft document, calling for a gradual subordination of Idaho Power's Swan Falls water rights as new water permits are issued by the state Department of Water

---

303   Bernton, Hal. "Attorney general drops support for Swan Falls document." *Times-News, Oct. 19, 1984.*

Resources.

Instead, Jones said once the agreement is finalized, Idaho Power should agree to full subordination of these Snake River water rights down to the 3,900 cubic-feet-per-second level at the Murphy gauge near Swan Falls.

Without the protection of immediate subordination, Jones said court challenges and other legal maneuverings could prevent the state from regaining control over allocation of Snake River water.

Peavey was at that meeting and expressed strong disagreement with my call for immediate subordination. He said, "It's critical that we subordinate (Idaho Power's Swan Falls water) right as it is used—not all at one shot. Otherwise, we could lose all that we have been fighting for all these years." Quite frankly, I think the two of us had been fighting to achieve completely different goals.

Needless to say, my unwillingness to agree to the Idaho Power language caused quite a stir. At a press conference in my office the next day, I advised the press of my October 17 letter to the Governor and said the proposed Idaho Power version of the settlement contract with its subordinatable language "contained a potential 'Trojan horse' favorable to Idaho Power Co."[304] I took the opportunity to suggest that Senator Peavey prompted Pat and the Governor to sign the contract immediately in order to boost Peavey's reelection chances, as he was in a certain amount of trouble in the general election for his anti-subordination stance. Jim Taney of Idaho Power said the Company "insisted the 'subordinatable' language be inserted in the contract because using 'subordinated' would immediately allow the river to be drawn down for irrigation—regardless of whether the diversion benefitted the state." My response was that the "subordinated" wording would not

---

304   UPI. "Jones tells Evans not to ink Swan Falls pact." *Idaho Press-Tribune*, Oct. 19, 1984.

allow unlimited pumping from the Snake because of the new public interest criteria that was called for in the agreement.

Governor Evans, who was in Lava Hot Springs at the time, expressed surprise about my concerns. He said Pat Costello had done a fine job in negotiating and was displeased that I had injected partisan politics into the matter.[305] However, he said he thought it was still possible to reach agreement to resolve the controversy.

My comments produced one interesting result: The antique cannon located on the lawn in front of the State Capitol sported a sign a few days later, that read "S.S. Costello." I should say, however, that Pat Costello was a decent person and all of us were working on a crash basis to finalize an agreement. As I indicated in my letter to the Governor, the subordinatable language may have eventually produced the same result as the subordinated language, but at that point it was a matter of trust and I did not have a great reservoir of trust remaining after the contentious fight. By leaving title to the excess water in the Power Company's hands, it seemed that the State was taking an unnecessary risk. With paper title to that water, there would be great temptation to make a grab for it. Therefore, it was unacceptable to not have the Power Company's priority to the excess water divested immediately upon satisfaction of the conditions in the agreement.

My concerns were shared by others. Laird attended an emergency meeting on October 20 at the Governor's regional office in Pocatello to discuss the disagreement. According to his note taken of the meeting, Kent Foster, Ray Rigby, Roger Ling, Representative Al Johnson, Representative Dwight Horsch, and Pat Costello, were present. Laird's note recited:

> The meeting was to discuss the disagreement with the Attorney General over language in the Swan Falls

---

305   Associated Press. "Attorney general surprises Gov. Evans." *The Morning News,* Oct. 20, 1984.

"contract" agreement. All of us came on strong for AG's position and the importance of getting him back on board for a united front.

The question is whether Idaho Power should maintain full ownership over 100% of asserted right or subordinate to the State the right down to 3900 cfs [flow] proposed. All there are highly suspicious that Idaho Power will find some way to upset the agreement or maneuver to get all of the water in the future if they have that extra leverage.

* * *

Rigby is most vocal in arguing for concept of State being trustee of water until granted to others.
Costello is worried about consumer groups and he and Gov. think Idaho Power won't give on the point.

* * *

Gov. makes no commitment but I sense they will try to get Jones back on board.

Laird's note referred to a concept that would eventually prevail to resolve the dispute—that the title to the water would be held in trust by the State of Idaho.

The dispute was aired at an informational meeting of the Department of Water Resources held in Pocatello the evening of October 23. Pat Kole and Ben Cavaness discussed the subordinated/subordinatable controversy and explained that the subordinatable language was unacceptable. Journal reporter Bill Francis wrote:[306]

Under the "subordinated" concept, the State of Idaho would be in complete control of the disputed water rights (above a certain minimum stream flow) at Swan Falls. But using the "subordinatable" concept,

---

306   Francis, Bill. "Jones: 'Swan Falls Agreement Hitch May Be Worked Out.'" *Idaho State Journal*, Oct. 24, 1984.

Idaho Power would retain those rights at Swan Falls until people applied for them and could show their use would be in the public interest. This agreement would allow the utility to hold those rights in trust until developers could meet that criteria.

But it would also give Idaho Power incentive to protest each application, according to Jones, so the joint title concept was proposed. Under this concept, the state would hold the disputed water rights in trust and allow Idaho Power to use them until developers met public interest criteria.

"I strongly object to leaving ownership of that water with Idaho Power," Jones said, explaining that Idaho Power is "probably not keen on" the new proposal, but that it is "in keeping with the whole tenor and intent of the negotiations. I never intended on Idaho Power retaining control over the water."

Jones said the difference in the draft agreement submitted by Idaho Power and the settlement negotiated by the three parties was "whether they (Idaho Power) would be giving up unequivocal control of the water, or whether they're keeping it. I see that as the difference on whether we prevailed in our negotiations or not."

The trust concept mentioned in the article — that title to the subordinated Snake River flows over and above the new agreed minimum flows would be held in trust by the State — was the brainchild of Ray Rigby. Ray had the trust and confidence of both the Governor and myself and his proposal came along just at the right time. Things were getting tense between the Governor and me — he even threatened to sign the contract without my approval. Ray's solution was just what we needed to get things back on track.

Ray's concept was that "the water rights Idaho Power will give up in the agreement be held in trust by the state until decisions are made on how to use the water."[307] That is, instead of Idaho Power retaining the excess flow as a subordinatable water right and instead of the excess water being immediately subordinated, the State would hold the water in trust for the benefit of future water right applicants. The trust water concept was satisfactory with me, the Governor liked it, and the Power Company reluctantly agreed that it would not oppose the State placing the water rights in a legislatively-created trust. So, everybody kissed and made up, the contract was signed by all three of us on October 25, and everybody was more or less satisfied, if not happy.[308] Despite my misgivings, the Governor also signed the 1180 Contract at the same get-together, but that was clearly the lesser of the two concerns I expressed.

The water users had been meeting to work out a plan to apportion the costs of the Snake River Basin Adjudication and they reported to the Water Resource Board on October 24 that they agreed to a plan. The projected cost of the adjudication was $27.5 million, which discounted to a July 1, 1986 value of $19 million. It was agreed that hydropower generators would pay $6.5 million, irrigators would pay about $5.5 million, the State would pony up $3 million, and the remaining money would come from municipalities, fish farmers, the federal government, and others.[309] This was a significant development because it paved the way for favorable action on the bill in the legislative package calling for the adjudication. Incidentally, the cost estimate for the adjudication was actually about one third of what it eventually would cost.

Although there were concerns about the settlement agreement and the implementing legislative proposals

307   Zellar, Ron. "Evans, Jones, Idaho Power sign Swan Falls plan." *Idaho Statesman*, Oct. 26, 1984.
308   Associated Press. "Officials initial Swan Falls pact." *Post-Register*, Oct. 25, 1984.
309   Bernton, Hal. "Water users OK adjudication compromise." *Times-News*, Oct. 25, 1984.

among water users, it appeared that there was somewhat of a consensus developing for passage of the legislative package. Some groups were announcing their intention to amend the legislation, which could well undo the entire agreement. The agreement was specifically conditioned upon passage of all of the legislation and approval by the various governmental entities. The Idaho Conservation League announced on December 1 that it would "seek inclusion of fishery considerations in laws that carry out a proposed settlement of the Snake River water-rights dispute."[310] I told the reporter that existing law already provided for protection of fisheries and that any change in the bill establishing new public interest criteria for approval of water permits would likely scuttle the agreement. The agreement did, in fact, provide additional protection for fish and wildlife. It increased the minimum streamflow from 3,300 cfs year-around to 3,900 cfs during the irrigation season and 5,600 cfs during the non-irrigation season. The new public interest criteria also allowed for consideration of all competing demands for Snake River waters.

At a meeting of the Food Producers of Idaho on December 10, I said that the settlement agreement "was arrived at after much tough negotiating, heated debate, hard-fought legislative wrangling, and protracted litigation. If changes are made in some of the essential provisions of the agreement, we will be back in court, and possibly the Legislature, fighting the same winner-take-all struggle that began with the 1982 Swan Falls court decision."

As the 1985 legislative session began, Harold Miles sent out a guest opinion to a number of papers, claiming the settlement agreement was "badly flawed" and constituted "larceny" of Idaho water.[311] Later, he filed suit against the State,

---

310   Zellar, Ron. "ICL fears water pact would leave fish high and dry." *Idaho Statesman,* Dec. 2, 1984.
311   "Proposed Swan Falls Agreement Would be 'Larceny.'" *Idaho State Journal,* Jan. 15, 1985.

challenging the statutes enacted pursuant to the agreement. He lost both in the district court and in the Supreme Court.[312]

The Idaho Water Users Association voted to support the settlement agreement on January 17.[313] This was an important endorsement because the members of the Association constituted the backbone of the subordination effort.

The House passed the package of Swan Falls bills on February 18 under Vard's leadership.[314] Vard observed, "This isn't the legislation that I would have liked to have had two years ago when we in the House voted to subordinate Idaho Power's water rights. This is a compromise, the best we can come up with." The bills passed with an overwhelming vote.

The Senate sent the legislative package to the Governor on February 20, again by an overwhelming vote. During consideration of the bills in the Senate, two significant things happened. First, Laird recorded the proceedings of the hearings on the bills in order to preserve a record should it be needed in the future. Second, Senator Mike Crapo insisted on a statement of legislative intent to accompany the bills. The Senate Resources and Environment Committee prepared a six-page statement laying out the intent and purpose of the legislation. With regard to the new Idaho Code section 42-203B, which provided that the "portion of the water rights for power purposes in excess of the [agreed minimum flows] shall be held in trust by the state of Idaho," the statement read in part:

> Any portion of such water rights above the established minimum flows will be held in trust by the State of Idaho, by and through the Governor.... Hydropower rights in excess of such flows will be held in trust by the State and are subject to subordination to, and to depletion by lawful beneficial uses.... As applied to the

312   *Miles v. Idaho Power Co., 116 Idaho 635, 778 P.2d 757 (1989).*

313   Zellar, Ron. "Water Users Association backs Snake River rights agreement." *Idaho Statesman,* Jan. 18, 1985.

314   Kenyon, Quane. Associated Press. "House passes Swan Falls package." *Times-News,* Feb. 19, 1985.

agreement between Idaho Power Company, the Governor and the Attorney General, this trust arrangement results in the State of Idaho possessing legal title to all water rights previously claimed by Idaho Power Company above the agreed minimum stream flows and Idaho Power Company holds equitable title to those water rights subject to the trust.

In 2007, when the State's ownership of the trust water was challenged in court proceedings, these records proved invaluable in turning away the challenge and supporting the State's ownership of the waters over and above the minimum flows established in the settlement agreement.

It was a great relief to receive the Legislature's approval of the measures called for in the settlement agreement. Because of the sometimes messiness of lawmaking, that seemed to be the biggest hurdle for implementation of the agreement. My press release upon Senate passage of the legislation read:

> Attorney General Jim Jones has praised the Idaho Legislature for its "expeditious action" on five bills to implement the Swan Falls settlement agreement. The Idaho Senate today gave final legislative approval to the last of five measures designed to implement the Snake River water rights settlement between the State of Idaho and Idaho Power Company. "The Legislature's prompt action on these important bills has moved the State of Idaho much closer to a settlement of the complicated water dispute. In addition, passage of the bills insures a wise and balanced water policy for the State of Idaho which will serve us well long into the future."
>
> The Senate today gave overwhelming approval to a measure authorizing the adjudication of water rights

on the Snake River. An adjudication proceeding quantifies the amount of water held by a water rights holder and prioritizes water claims. "This legislation will set out the priority and quantity of each person's water right on the Snake River, giving each water right holder a greater measure of protection. In addition, it will lay the ground work for Idaho to better resist any future efforts by other states to lay claim to Idaho's water."

"The Legislature's expeditious action on the Swan Falls settlement bills is a major milestone in Idaho's water policy. The legislative action was a most essential element for implementation of the Swan Falls settlement agreement. I expect that the other elements, approval by the State Water Resource Board and the Federal Energy Regulatory Commission, will be forthcoming in the near future. This will give us the ability to put the complex and divisive Snake River water rights fight behind us and to embark on a wise, balanced water policy for the future. The agreement provides additional water for continued growth and development in southern Idaho while preserving low electric rates."

Jones praised the efforts of Senator Laird Noh (R-Kimberly) and Representative J. Vard Chatburn (R-Albion), chairmen of the Senate and House Resource Committees. "Senator Noh and Representative Chatburn were very helpful throughout the entire process. Their input into the settlement negotiations was tremendously helpful. They did a careful job of reviewing the legislation and expedited its consideration. The people of Idaho owe a great debt of gratitude to them and to the members of their committees."

Jones also praised the efforts of several southern

Idaho water lawyers. "Ray Rigby of Rexburg, Kent Foster of Idaho Falls, Ben Cavaness of American Falls, and Roger Ling of Rupert, provided invaluable legal advice and assistance during the negotiating process. Their counsel and assistance was generously and freely supplied to the state. They have provided a great service to the people of Idaho."

On March 1, with Jim Bruce and myself looking on, Governor Evans signed the Swan Falls legislative package. He said the passage of the package puts Idaho "on the threshold of a new era in water-resource development and management of the Snake River."[315] That certainly was true. That same day, the Idaho Water Resource Board amended the State Water Plan to reflect the streamflow and other requirements in the settlement agreement. The Public Utilities Commission approved the agreement on April 12.

After the dust settled on the contentious fight, I held a press conference in Twin Falls on May 10 to publicly thank a number of individuals who worked hard for subordination and played an instrumental role in bringing about the settlement agreement. Dean Miller of the Times-News said:[316]

> Five Magic Valley residents were honored Friday by State Attorney General Jim Jones for their contributions towards the settlement of the controversial Swan Falls water rights conflict.
>
> Those honored at an afternoon news conference were Bill Lanting of Hollister, a member of the State Water Resource Board; Rep. Vard Chatburn (R-Albion), the chairman of the House Resources and Conservation Committee; State Senator Laird Noh (R-Kimberly); Jerome farmer Elaine Martin, organizer and

---

315   Associated Press. "Evans inks bill, heralds water pact." *Idaho Statesman,* March 2, 1985.
316   Miller, Dean. "Jones pays homage to Swan Falls help." *Times-News,* April 15, 1985.

secretary of the Idaho Water Rights Defense group, which is composed of the water users named by Idaho Power Co. in a lawsuit that spurred the negotiations; and Jerome farmer and rancher Forrest Hymas, another member of the water rights group.

Jones said the people he honored, who were named special water advisers, should be given credit for their expertise and advice more than any other group in the state. His staff often would make "frantic" calls to them, soliciting their comments about the Swan Falls dispute.

The Swan Falls agreement was the result of a negotiation between the Idaho Power Co. and the state about Snake River water rights. The package of bills passed last session to enact the agreement included, among many other items, regulations on the use of water in southern Idaho and minimum flow at Swan Falls.

Bruce Newcomb of Burley and Roger Ling of Rupert also will be honored with certificates for their contributions. Those attorneys who provided legal help will be named honorary deputy attorneys general, Jones said.

In presenting certificates, Jones said Noh was a leader in the effort to resolve the water rights dispute.

Hymas, who Jones praised for his bringing the issue before the public, was one of the defendants named by Idaho Power Co. in its claim that water users were compromising its water rights. After the suit was filed, he took six months to research the historical aspects of the controversy involving Swan Falls.

"The more involved I became, the more fascinating it became," Hymas said. He began to give presentations on the history of the conflict and helped organize a group of defendants to work together.

Martin, another organizer, said she has worked almost full-time with the group since November 1983.

Although the state laws that enacted the agreement have been passed, a lot of work remains, Jones said. Part of the Swan Falls agreement included a 10-year adjudication to determine water rights. The logistics of the process have yet to be determined, Jones said.

At a peaceful settlement conference held in Boise on April 30, I had the opportunity to do a postmortem on the Swan Falls fight. The often mean-spirited battle over Snake River flows was probably not the poster child for a peaceful settlement, although it did eventually end up that way. I told the group that the Power Company's hard-liners refused to budge from their position at first, apparently believing that they had the edge both in the Legislature and the arena of public opinion. Recognizing that we had an uphill fight, both the Governor and myself stepped up our involvement, primarily using the bully pulpit to explain the consequences of allowing Idaho Power to control the Snake River. Additionally, we intensified our efforts in administrative and court proceedings, both in State court and before the Federal Energy Regulatory Commission. Doing that kept us from coming out badly in the 1984 legislative session. Idaho Power made a miscalculation when it launched its $115,000 advertising campaign just before the 1984 primary election. That effort backfired, giving the subordination effort a boost in public opinion. As a result, the forces of moderation in Idaho Power, particularly Jim Bruce, realized that a negotiated settlement was the way to go. Idaho Power's public image was sustaining substantial damage and there were settlement alternatives that both sides could agree upon and benefit from. It did not hurt that Jim was planning to retire and wanted to get the matter resolved before he left the Company. I told the group that were it not for a Democrat governor and a Republican attorney general working hand-in-hand throughout the fight that the subordination side would likely have lost the fight in the Legislature. Quane Kenyon, one of my favorite reporters, did a nice piece on the discussion.[317]

About a month after the settlement agreement

317   Kenyon, Quane. Associated Press. "Jones: Utility initially re-fused to negotiate over water rights." *Times-News*, May 1, 1985

FROM MERE FORMALITY TO NEAR DISASTER

was signed, Idaho Power filed a petition with the Federal Energy Regulatory Commission to obtain its approval of the agreement. With the fight having been resolved, it did not appear that there would be any difficulty in getting prompt approval from FERC. Unfortunately, it didn't work that way. FERC acted even more slowly than its usual glacial pace, the path was fraught with unanticipated perils, and the proceedings almost took a disastrous turn.

Several months after the petition was filed, I was in Washington, D.C. for a meeting with some of the FERC Commissioners and staff. I was the chairman of the Energy Committee of the National Association of Attorneys General and the Committee had conveniently arranged a meeting with FERC to discuss the issue of state government input into hydropower licensing proceedings. At our meeting on March 26, 1985, we told the FERC officials that the states were entitled to more participation in hydropower licensing proceedings and that greater weight should be given to their input in those matters. I took the opportunity to point out that the State of Idaho was requesting the Commission to approve the Swan Falls settlement agreement with Idaho Power. The FERC officials seemed to be receptive but indicated they would have to review the pertinent documents.

As time passed, we did not hear a peep from FERC regarding the petition to approve the settlement. The agreement called for the parties to "meet on May 15, 1985, to determine if the contract shall be continued or terminated." Logan, the Governor, and I met on that date and we all signed a document titled, "Affirmation of Continuation of Agreement," which acknowledged that all conditions of the agreement had been satisfied, save and except approval by FERC, and that the agreement was to be extended until FERC approval was received.

The Idaho Wildlife Federation had been raising concerns about the adequacy for the minimum flows called for in the agreement and had indicated it might seek intervention in the FERC proceeding to assert those concerns. Because the utility and the State were both in support of the petition, this possibility was not particularly worrisome. However, in September we received a courtesy copy of a letter written to FERC by the Boise field office of the U.S. Fish & Wildlife Service. The letter indicated that the Service believed there was a federal reserved water right for the Deer Flat National Wildlife Refuge on the Snake River extending below Swan Falls that was "obviously greater than 5,600 cfs." According to the Service, higher flows were necessary to protect "ground-nesting birds like Canada geese...from mammalian predators such as coyotes, farm dogs, and foxes." In other words, if the flows dipped below 5,600 cfs, the coyotes would be able to get to the nesting birds and eat their eggs. We recognized that a claim for a federal reserved right for Deer Flat would be a serious problem for the State, with or without subordination, and were making preparations to deal with it in the proper venue—the upcoming Snake River Basin Adjudication.[318] In our view, the on-going FERC proceeding was not the proper time or place to have the issue raised. We were able to make an agreement with the Interior Department to defer the issue to the adjudication negotiations. However, the Idaho Wildlife Federation did follow up with a petition to intervene in the FERC proceeding, as did the National Marine Fisheries

318   The Deer Flat reserved right claim was later considered and decided in the Snake River Basin Adjudication. The claim was denied. *United States v. State of Idaho*, 135 Idaho 655, 23 P.3d 117 (2001). It appeared that the predation was caused by raccoons swimming to the islands, rather than by coyotes, and that flow was not a deterrent for the raccoons.

Service, the Idaho Natural Resource Legal Foundation, and the Golden Eagle Audubon Society. These intervention petitions likely slowed down the FERC proceeding.

When no FERC action had been taken on the petition for another ten months, I wrote a memorandum to Jim Goller, Senator McClure's Idaho fix-it man, to broach the subject of Congressional action. The August 27 memo read:

> As you know, the Swan Falls settlement agreement resolves the water rights conflict between Idaho Power Company and the State of Idaho. All elements required to complete that settlement agreement have fallen into place, with the exception of approval of the agreement by the Federal Energy Regulatory Commission. A petition filed by the state and Idaho Power Company with FERC has been pending for about a year and half and we have no idea when final action might be taken by FERC. One of the problems has to do with a claim by the Fish and Wildlife Service for a federal reserved flow right in conjunction with the Deer Flat Wildlife Refuge. We suggested to the Fish and Wildlife Service that the claim can and should be considered in the adjudication proceeding and that completion of FERC action on the petition to approve the Swan Falls settlement agreement would not prejudice any rights of any water claimant, including the Fish and Wildlife Service. Fish and Wildlife, through the Secretary of the Interior, agreed with our position to defer this issue to the adjudication negotiations. However, the Idaho Wildlife Federation has petitioned FERC to intervene in the case alleging that the agreement will impact the federal reserved water right at Deer Flat. Therefore, we are still encountering some resistance which has helped to delay FERC action on the Idaho Power and

state petition for approval.

One way to hasten a conclusion to this matter would be to obtain passage of federal legislation granting approval of the Swan Falls settlement agreement. This would be an appropriate exercise in federalism, i.e. giving federal blessing to a compromise agreement entered into for the purpose of resolving an intra-state water controversy. (similar to the dissolved oxygen issue)

A draft of some proposed legislation is attached. While it approves the agreement (which would finalize action to put the agreement into place), it makes it clear that federal rights and claims would not be affected. Quite frankly, I have a hard time believing that anyone would object, except the environmental extremists who speak for a very limited viewpoint and constituency.

If Senators McClure and Symms were to introduce this legislation, I think it would be a welcome piece of news for Idaho Water Users and others who want to close the chapter on the Swan Falls controversy. It would even be better if it could get final congressional approval during the remainder of this session. I have checked with Phil Reberger and he seems to be willing to cooperate in getting the legislation into the hopper. If Senator McClure is willing to do likewise, it might be appropriate to make a joint announcement of our intentions at a fairly early date. Please let me know what you would like to do on this matter.

Following the memo to Jim Goller, I met with both Idaho senators to see if they could get something done before the end of the year. They both seemed to be supportive. On September 11, Senator Symms announced that he would be introducing legislation to either force FERC to act or to simply give Congressional approval to the agreement. Steve introduced his legislation on September 30, with the co-sponsorship of Senator McClure. Senator McClure announced on October 9 that he was going to try an end run around FERC for federal ratification of the agreement. Senator McClure, who then chaired the Senate Energy and Natural Resources Committee, indicated he had negotiated on the matter with Representative John Dingell (D–Mich.), chairman of the House Energy and Commerce Committee, to get the legislation moving. McClure said that the Symms-McClure proposal would be added to the National Appliance Energy Conservation Act, which was scheduled for Senate action within several days.

The House considered the Conservation Act on October 15 and, with the support of Representative Richard Stallings of Idaho's Second Congressional District, the Swan Falls rider passed as a part of that legislation. The Senate acted upon the legislation the same day, sending it to President Reagan. This was all very impressive. Who would have thought that Congress could act so quickly?

On October 16, I issued a press release commending the senators for their quick action, noting that I contacted them on August 27 to suggest the passage of federal legislation and that they were able to accomplish it in less than two months. I wrote, "Passage of the legislation will allow the state to fully implement the Swan Falls settlement agreement so that we can finally be in a position to go about the important business of managing and conserving our precious Snake River water," noting that the legislation required FERC to approve the settlement agreement within 90 days.

On October 30, I followed up with another press release indicating that Senator Symms received word from FERC that very day saying it would act to approve the agreement within the time frame called for in the legislation. I noted, "There was always a serious possibility that the settlement agreement could have been unraveled at any time before it was approved by the federal authorities. Approval was necessary so that there would not be an inconsistency between federal and state law with regard to the power company's water rights at its Snake River Dams."

As far as I could tell, everyone involved was pleased with the Congressional action and we were glad to have the struggle behind us. However, Randy Stapilus, who was then working at the Idaho Statesman, wrote an article on October 31 that caused a cloud of doom to appear. The headline read, "Reagan may veto bill with Swan Falls pact."[319] That was an unwelcome Halloween surprise. According to the article, "the Office of Management and Budget, Justice Department, Federal Trade Commission, and Council of Economic Advisors asked Reagan to veto the bill, because they oppose the appliance-efficiency standards it requires manufacturers to meet." The threatened veto did not have anything to do with the Swan Falls provision but, rather, with the Conservation Act to which it was attached. The Congressional delegation pleaded with the President to refrain from vetoing the legislation but to no avail. On November 1, the President vetoed the bill and with it the requirement for FERC to approve the settlement agreement.[320] We were back to square one with FERC.

On November 3, I issued a press release saying that the veto of the legislation "should create no major problem." President Reagan made a commitment to ensure a prompt and favorable resolution of the Swan Falls issue, so it didn't look like we would have any trouble. Also, Martha Hesse, the FERC chairman, had committed on October 30 to consider the Swan Falls settlement agreement within 90 days. On November 3, the Secretary of Energy, John Herrington, told

319   Stapilus, Randy. "Reagan may veto bill with Swan Falls pact." *Idaho Statesman*, Oct. 31, 1986.
320   Essex, Marilyn. "Reagan vetoes Swan Falls pact bill." *Idaho Statesman*, Nov. 2, 1986.

the press that he supported the objective of our settlement agreement and would seek its implementation, noting the President's support for the agreement. Unfortunately, all of this happy talk did not result in FERC action.

The Times-News ran an article on November 9 titled, "FERC mum on Swan Falls."[321] According to the paper, "No one in Washington who is familiar with the issue seems to know precisely what is going on inside the Federal Energy Regulatory Commission on Swan Falls nor why, after two years, the pact between Idaho Power Co. and the state has not received federal approval." A spokesman for Representative Stallings told the paper "there is a dispute going on within FERC's staff about whether the agency should get involved in the Swan Falls agreement." Representative Stallings indicated that "FERC is saying Swan Falls would put a new wrinkle in federal water law, and the agency is reluctant to get into this."

Representative Stallings announced in December that he would introduce legislation to approve the Swan Falls agreement and that Representative Larry Craig agreed to co-sponsor it.[322] He said, "I don't see any land mines in this. I don't see any problems with it right now.... I don't think the bureaucrats at FERC want to take the responsibility of this kind of precedent. I think they're going to do nothing and wait until Congress directs them to accept the settlement."

While everyone was waiting for Congress or FERC to do something, the newspapers continued with their after-action articles regarding the Swan Falls fight. The Times-News ran two articles in its December 21 issue. In one article, Governor Evans said that the Swan Falls agreement was the "hallmark" of his administration and a "magnificent document."[323] The Governor was leaving office and former

321   *Times-News,* Nov. 9, 1986.
322   Stapilus, Randy. "Swan Falls legislation planned." *Idaho Statesman,* Dec. 12, 1986.
323   Pratter, Mark, and Robison, Jane. "Only Evans happy with

Governor Cecil Andrus, who he succeeded, would take the governorship once again. Had Governor Andrus been in office when the Swan Falls fight occurred, the outcome may well have been quite different. Andrus supported Idaho Power's position, would likely have signed the 1180 Contract, and certainly would not have vetoed the two Idaho Power bills in 1984. Governor Evans was blessed with a clear vision of what best served Idaho's long-term interests and he stuck with his guns. Without that, it would have been extremely difficult to achieve the favorable outcome.

The other article in the Times-News had some interesting tidbits. Ben Cavaness said Idaho Power "was stonewalling from the start. They said, 'We think we have the muscle to make it work (in the Legislature).' From what I gather, the reason we had a settlement was (IPC chairman) Jim Bruce. He could see it was best for everybody. If some other officer was involved in negotiations besides Bruce, the outcome would have been different."[324] I was reported as saying that Logan Lanham "tried to shoot holes in the agreement, at least until he saw the handwriting on the wall. Bruce was retiring and wanted to leave a legacy. Lanham felt the company had given up too much." Logan said part of his concern was that not enough water was being preserved for domestic, commercial, municipal and industrial uses but he would "not comment more fully on disagreements within the company." Vard Chatburn said, "I have never been up against such a formidable adversary in 30 years in the Legislature. They were in there (the chamber) early enough to catch the fellows as they came in. There wasn't a person they missed. Some fellows told me (they were) even threatened, 'We'll (IPC) see you're not re-elected.'"

Getting back to Congress, Senator McClure announced on January 28, 1987, that his committee sent Swan Falls

---

pact." *Times-News*, Dec. 21, 1986.
324   Pratter, Mark, and Robison, Jane. "Utility gains more control over Snake." *Times-News*, Dec. 21, 1986.

legislation to the Senate floor.[325] Rocky Barker of the Post-Register reported that the new legislation was a stand-alone bill requiring FERC approval within 90 days. According to McClure, "The President, in his (veto) message last year specifically gave approval to the Swan Falls language. As far as I know it has full administration support." In mid-February, "McClure said he and Idaho Power lobbyist Logan Lanham have questioned whether to proceed by legislation or to push for a FERC decision, choosing the former."[326] Apparently, they had been conversing on the issue.

On March 13, the Times-News reported that the Swan Falls legislation "stalled in the U.S. House Energy and Commerce Committee because of objections by several national environmental groups to its effect on the Deer Flat National Wildlife Refuge."[327] The article noted that the McClure–Symms bill in the Senate had passed on February 19. The Times-News reported on May 23 that the Idaho Wildlife Federation dropped its opposition to the Swan Falls settlement agreement.[328] According to a Federation spokesman, "We don't feel Swan Falls is a good agreement biologically, but it is politically inevitable." The Federation indicated that language added to the bill by Representative Stallings made it more acceptable. On June 2, Representative Stallings was reported to have said that "he had the votes to get the Swan Falls water rights agreement passed despite environmental objections. However, he says he wanted to incorporate changes to satisfy the environmentalists. Representative John Dingell, D–Mich., the key committee chairman on the bill in the house, will support the modified bill."[329]

325   Barker, Rocky. "Swan Falls legislation advances." *Post-Register,* Jan. 28, 1987.
326   Associated Press. "Swan Falls destiny unclear." *Post-Register,* Feb. 16, 1987.
327   Pratter, Mark. "Accord on water hits snag." *Times-News,* March 13, 1987.
328   Pratter, Mark. "Wildlife group dropping Swan Falls protest." *Times-News,* May 23, 1987.
329   Pratter, Mark. "Stallings thinks history will be the judge of Rea-

This was a bit concerning. We had no idea what changes he had in mind.

Shortly thereafter, on June 19, Clive Strong marched in to the State district court in Twin Falls to file an historic petition to commence a general adjudication of the Snake River Basin. This, of course, was one of the conditions of the Swan Falls agreement. The adjudication was estimated to take approximately ten years to complete with an estimated cost of $28 million. Our estimate on the time was about 20 years short and the cost estimate was around $70 million short. Without the outstanding work done by Clive, it would have cost more and extended much longer.

Ken Dunn and I put out a joint press release, that read in part:

> "The adjudication represents an opportunity for the state to resolve all existing conflicts over the use of the waters in the upper Snake River Basin and develop a complete and accurate list of those rights," A. Kenneth Dunn said. Dunn, director of Idaho Department of Water Resources said, "Upon completion of the adjudication, the state will be in a position to administer all state and federally created water rights."
>
> The director said the general adjudication of all uses is also necessary to ensure the state meets its obligations arising from the Swan Falls agreement.
>
> Attorney General Jim Jones said, "Although a number of water users have concerns about the adjudication process, it is a necessary step to insure protection of all water rights in the Snake River Basin. Completion of the adjudication will give water users solid protection for their water rights and prioritize all water claims. This process will make Idaho less vulnerable to

gan." *Times-News*, June 2, 1987.

claims from out of state interests."

When we finally learned of the changes in the bill that Representative Stallings mentioned in his June 1 Times-News interview, we were astounded. The bill, as amended, would essentially give FERC the unprecedented ability to set minimum streamflows higher than those agreed to in the Swan Falls settlement agreement, based on environmental grounds. Clive immediately contacted Representative Stallings' office to say the bill was completely unacceptable and that we would vigorously oppose it. Stallings' staff was caught somewhat off-guard, apparently not realizing the effect of the changes requested by the environmental groups. It was agreed that the proposed changes needed to be discussed and Stallings' office indicated that it would try to arrange a meeting of the parties with Representative Dingell's staff person, David Finnegan, who was largely responsible for drafting the changes.

Clive and Pat Kole, along with representatives of Governor Andrus and Idaho Power, among others, attended the meeting with Finnegan and came away thinking that the language problems would be remedied. We received a revised draft of the legislation in mid-September but it, again, was totally unacceptable. I faxed Representative Stallings a letter on September 24, saying:

> Thank you for providing me with an opportunity to review the revised draft of H.B. 519 prepared by Mr. Finnegan on behalf of Mr. Dingell. I have carefully reviewed the proposed changes and find that the new draft is radically different than what I had been led to expect following the meeting with Mr. Finnegan. The changes will undermine the Swan Falls agreement and are a clear departure from existing law. Unless some fundamental changes are made, this legislation should

not see the light of day, as it poses serious dangers for Snake River water users. Perhaps a review of the negotiations will help to put this matter into perspective.

Idaho Power Company and the State of Idaho initially filed a petition with FERC as required by paragraph 12(B)(ii) of the Swan Falls agreement. The filing was made to obtain assurances that the Company would not later be subject to a challenge that it had wasted project property resources. The purpose was to protect both the State and Idaho Power against later challenges to the agreement before FERC. After 24 months of inaction by FERC, it became clear that it would be prudent to seek a legislative solution in order to close this long-standing controversy.

The proposed legislation had the limited purpose of insuring that FERC could not later upset the agreement by finding that Idaho Power Company's actions were: (1) inconsistent with the terms and conditions of Idaho Power Company's licenses concerning project property or the utilization thereof; or (2) imprudent for purposes of the Federal Power Act (FPA). In fact, in our earlier filings with FERC, when agencies of the federal government feared that we sought broader protection, the parties to the agreement consented to offers of settlement that clarified the intent of our request. We likewise agreed to committee language that made it clear that we sought nothing in the legislative proposal that would be inimical to fish and wildlife interests.

After the veto of H.R. 5465, environmental groups and the parties to the agreement met in Washington at your request. At that time, the major sticking point was the fear that the federal government would not adequately protect federal interests in the Snake River adjudication. Two actions have been undertaken to address this concern. First, the state and the federal government are meeting and negotiating on federal reserved water rights. Already a stipulation regarding cooperative technical studies has been agreed to for the Deer Flats refuge, one of the main concerns of the environmental groups. I am enclosing a copy for your use. Second, the parties agreed to examine and include language either in the committee report or as to an amendment to H.R. 519 to place a high priority on funding for the necessary technical studies for federal agencies to negotiate or litigate federal reserved water rights.

The changes that are now proposed go far beyond any concern that has previously been raised. As we read the substitute bill, it no longer is neutral on the state/federal water right issue. It now explicitly expands FERC's jurisdiction to allow federal intervention into state water law through the setting of streamflow conditions. This cannot be tolerated. The state can accept a bill that neither expands nor restricts FERC authority to establish conditions consistent with existing law. What is wholly unacceptable is a bill that overreaches and seeks to establish FERC authority to set minimum streamflows on the river where I believe no such authority exists.

The letter outlined three pages of proposed changes, together with an explanation of why they were necessary.

The FERC proceeding and the proposed legislative remedy had drawn the attention of downstream interests that saw an opportunity to assert control of Snake River water. The Columbia River Intertribal Fish Commission (CRITFC), the Confederated Tribes of the Umatilla Reservation, and the State of Washington had filed petitions for intervention in the

FERC proceeding, claiming that the Swan Falls agreement did not set adequate streamflows for anadromous fish migration. We learned that even though the State had entered into an agreement with the Fish and Wildlife Service to defer its Deer Flat claims to the adjudication for resolution, some staff members of that agency were assisting the downstream interests. Thus on September 28, I wrote to Don Hodel, who was then Secretary of the Interior:

> I have been most impressed with the cooperative, straight-forward manner of dealing you have brought to the Department of Interior. Your intervention was instrumental in working out a compromise on the federal quiet title issue and I believe your assistance was helpful in working out a settlement between the Department of Interior and the State of Idaho in the on-going FERC proceeding involving Idaho's Swan Falls settlement agreement. I am enclosing a copy of the referenced stipulation in case you need it to refresh your memory.
>
> Based on fairly solid information, it appears to my staff that certain personnel of the Fish and Wildlife Service and regional solicitor's office may not understand that this matter has been resolved between the Department of Interior and the State of Idaho. We have good information to indicate that some of your personnel in Portland have been assisting other parties, including the Columbia River Intertribal Fish Commission and certain members of Congress, in actions before FERC and Congress which would undermine the spirit, if not the letter, of our stipulation. I would very much appreciate it if you would have someone look into this matter and, if my information is correct, convey to employees in the Portland office of the Fish and Wildlife

Service and the Regional Solicitor's Office that they are acting without the authority of their superiors when they assist other parties with efforts to undermine those matters agreed to in the stipulation.

By October 5, Pat and Clive were able to remove the most obnoxious provisions of the amended House bill, which I reported in a press release that same day:

Attorney General Jim Jones said today that federal Swan Falls legislation has been "defanged so that it is now only mildly obnoxious instead of being a serious danger for Idaho." Jones was referring to legislation pending before the U.S. House Committee on Energy and Commerce. The proposal is designed to give limited federal approval to the Swan Falls settlement agreement entered into in 1984 between the State of Idaho and Idaho Power Company.

Legislation to approve the Swan Falls agreement was passed by the Senate earlier this year. The measure is awaiting action before the Energy and Commerce Committee.

"During the last several weeks my staff and representatives of Congressman Stallings, Governor Andrus and Idaho Power Company have been working with members of the House Committee staff to develop compromise language for the legislation. Because representatives of certain environmental groups and the Columbia River Intertribal Fish Commission have seen this legislation as an opportunity to leverage Idaho into environmental concessions, it hasn't been an easy task. Those groups have attempted to use the legislation as a means of gaining flow concessions which they are not entitled to under the law and which would upset the Swan Falls settlement agreement."

"In a negotiating session last week we were able to remove or tone down several provisions in a House Committee draft of the legislation which posed serious dangers for Snake River water users. The draft would have extended unprecedented control by the Federal Energy Regulatory Commission over Snake River waters. It would have required the State of Idaho to fund and participate in studies designed to increase streamflow levels agreed on in the Swan Falls agreement. The draft would have significantly expanded federal intrusion into the state's ability to administer its waters."

"We were able to remove the most obnoxious provisions from the draft legislation, including one which would have given the Federal Energy Regulatory Commission new power to impose environmental regulations on the management of Snake River waters. We also removed a provision requiring Idaho to fund certain studies which other parties intend to use later as a means of upsetting the Swan Falls settlement agreement. In addition, we were able to gain a concession which will secure final federal approval to the Swan Falls agreement."

"The legislation still contains some obnoxious features but they are not so bad as to require state opposition to the bill. When all is said and done, passage of the legislation may be slightly better than the alternate course of obtaining needed federal approval through the Federal Energy Regulatory Commission. I don't have a great deal of confidence in FERC since we have been waiting almost three years for that agency to take action. Almost everything FERC has done to date has been of disadvantage to the State of Idaho. This legislation would essentially require FERC to give its approval to the Swan Falls agreement."

Jones said that while he was not enthusiastic about the legislation, he would probably support it. "It took a lot of effort to fight back the efforts of the House Committee staff, CRITFC, and certain self-proclaimed environmentalists, and I suspect we would have to contend with their efforts to undermine the Swan Falls settlement in FERC proceedings if the legislation were not approved. The legislation provides a mildly obnoxious, but known, solution in lieu of what could be a long-delayed and more obnoxious resolution at the hands of FERC."

During the negotiations, Pat and Clive had tried to obtain language that would further limit the scope of the environmental studies, but were unable to get support from Gary Ellsworth, who represented Senator McClure. He essentially told Clive and Pat that this was the best deal they were going to get. That being the case, we felt that we had been able to eliminate the most serious threats posed by the amended bill and that we could deal with the resulting language, provided that the committee report accompanying the bill remained strictly neutral.

I wrote Representative Stallings on October 6 to say that the legislation was now only "mildly obnoxious" but that he should be on the alert to make sure the committee report that accompanied the legislation did not contain harmful language. "Because of the fact that committee report language could erode some of the concessions we gained in the negotiating sessions last week, I think it is critical that my staff be able to have input into the drafting of the committee report. Additionally, we would be happy to assist you in putting together a floor statement on the legislation. Because of the ambiguity in certain areas of the legislation, it may well be that committee report language and floor statements have to be looked to in future years to determine legislative intent."

Later in October, the State filed objections with FERC to the petitions by the State of Washington and others to intervene in the proceedings there. We pointed out that the last day for filing a timely motion to intervene was August 30 of 1985 and that the intervention petitions were late, coming more than two years after the deadline. We fully anticipated having environmental concerns raised and considered with respect to Snake River flow conditions but the appropriate forum for that was in the Snake River Basin Adjudication. The State had already begun negotiations with the Fish and Wildlife Service over the federal reserved water right for Deer Flat. I found it somewhat odd that the State of Washington, apparently acting on behalf of its ocean fishery, and CRITFC were positioning themselves as champions of Idaho-origin salmon and steelhead when they had often authorized over-fishing on depleted fish runs. I issued a press release on October 2, saying in part:

> It is passing curious that CRITFC and the State of Washington, which have consistently sanctioned the harvest of Idaho-bound wild steelhead below accept-able levels, should now launch this frivolous litigation. After years of insensitivity to the needs of Idaho's wild salmon and steelhead stocks, it is strange that they should now try to interject themselves into Idaho wa-ter issues out of purported concern for anadromous fish. My office has had a strong commitment to rees-tablishment of anadromous fish runs in the Snake and Columbia river systems. We will take whatever actions are prudent and necessary for protection of Idaho-or-igin wild fish stocks. However, actions must be taken in the appropriate forums, and the Swan Falls proceed-

ing before FERC is not one of them.

CRITFC and Washington are aware that the state has just instituted an adjudication proceeding for the Snake River Basin. That is the more appropriate forum to consider questions of allocation of water for specific purposes. The National Marine Fisheries Service and Federal Fish and Wildlife Service became involved in the Swan Falls proceeding before the Federal Energy Regulatory Commission early on but withdrew objections to approval of the Swan Falls agreement because they understood that the adjudication proceeding was the appropriate forum to assert those claims. The federal agencies representing fishery interests have no difficulty in approval of the Swan Falls settlement agreement, making it difficult to fathom why CRITFC and Washington should launch this last minute spoiling effort.

What I referred to in the press release was ongoing litigation regarding the anadromous fish runs in the Snake and Columbia River systems. One case, *U.S. v. Washington*, dealt with the ocean fishery for salmon. The other was *U.S. v. Oregon*, which dealt with the anadromous fish runs in the rivers. In 1985, my office had sought intervention in both cases because CRITFC and the States of Oregon and Washington seemed to be more interested in catching fish than in conserving the fish runs.

Disputes between Idaho and downstream fishery interests had a long history. One of the skirmishes broke out during the spring of 1985. On April 17, 1985, I issued a press release saying that the downstreamers had made a "backroom deal" to conduct a fishery on the spring chinook run that year even though the anadromous fish runs "have been dangerously low in recent years as a result of dams and over-fishing." Idaho learned of the deal only a week earlier and we went to court in *U.S. v. Oregon* on April 19 to seek a conservation closure of the fishery. I said, "It is indeed unfortunate that the downstream fishing interests have been so insensitive to the compelling need to exercise prudent conservation and management practices with respect to anadromous fish. They have consistently ignored Idaho's requests to properly manage the anadromous fish runs, as well as our requests to participate in the meetings where important management and allocation decisions are made."

Unfortunately, we were not successful at the U.S. District Court level and by the time our appeal was heard by the U.S. Ninth Circuit Court of Appeals in July of 1986, the case was ruled moot, despite our arguments that the downstream fishery interests would repeat the over-fishing of the runs. This was just one skirmish in the ongoing struggle with the downstreamers' blasé attitude toward the health of Idaho-origin salmon and steelhead. It was interesting that they were demanding a seat at the table in the FERC proceeding when they had done everything possible to exclude Idaho and ignore the State's interests in the anadromous fish litigation. I think they considered Idaho to be a fish farm, to be operated solely for their benefit.

The downstreamers' implication that Idaho was not concerned with the well-being of Idaho-origin anadromous fish was also irritating, to say the least. During my tenure in office, Idaho took quite a number of actions to protect and enhance the anadromous fish runs. During the time that Washington, Oregon, and CRITFC were seeking intervention in the FERC proceedings and attempting to influence the House committee report, my office was engaged in proceedings with the Bonneville Power Administration to protect Idaho's anadromous fish from injury that was threatened by the BPA's plan to expand its electrical transmission intertie's capacity to carry electric power from the Pacific Northwest to California. BPA planned to substantially expand the carrying capacity of the intertie in order to dramatically increase its sale of surplus power to California. In making those plans, it failed to take into account the impact on anadromous fish — the more water that was used to generate power, the less there would be at the right times to facilitate migration of fish.

Idaho Fish and Game Director Jerry Conley and I worked for months to convince BPA that it needed to study the effects of the expansion of intertie capacity on wild and natural fish runs and to determine what mitigation measures might be necessary to protect them. When we made no headway and concluded that we were going to continue to be stonewalled, it became apparent that a lawsuit was necessary. The State filed suit against BPA in November of 1986 to force the issue. I announced the suit in a November 26 press release saying, "By squeezing the maximum amount of power out of Snake and Columbia River flows for surplus power sales to California, it is very likely that Idaho's wild fish runs would suffer. By ignoring these concerns, BPA has left the State no alternative but to institute legal proceedings."

BPA issued a draft environmental impact statement, which we criticized as woefully inadequate for the protection of our anadromous fish. The downstream interests then pitched in and eventually we reached a settlement of the suit in April of 1989. In an April 10 press release, I announced settlement of the BPA suit, which provided additional water spills to facilitate fish mitigation over a ten year period. The value of lost power production resulting from the spills was estimated to be $40–70 million over the life of the agreement. This was the type of action that would actually protect anadromous fish.

Back on the Congressional front, we were still waiting for a draft of the House committee report. When nothing had been forthcoming by November 3, I sent Representative Stallings a letter indicating it was critical for my staff to review the House committee report before action was taken on the bill, that it appeared the committee report was being drafted in secrecy, and that if the language in the report attempted to gain concessions for the downstream interests, it might be best to kill the bill altogether. When we had no word back by November 6, I faxed another letter to Representative Stallings, saying

> I am quite concerned with the manner in which the staff of the House Energy and Commerce Committee is handling the committee report on the Swan Falls bill. My office has received information to the effect that the committee report language has been finalized and that the draft report is 40 pages or more in length. Although we had asked for an opportunity to review and comment upon the report prior to its finalization, we received word back that Mr. Finnegan, a staff attorney, would not accede to this request. We have received information that an attempt may be made to bring the legislation to the House floor for a vote as early as next week.
>
> These developments are very unsettling. It is difficult to understand why the drafting of the committee report should be handled in a seemingly clandestine manner. Although we are not able to independently verify the length or content of the committee report, it is curious that such a simple piece of legislation should entail such a lengthy committee report. It is curious that the matter seems to be taking on a good deal of haste after the legislation had languished in the committee for such a considerable period of time. My concern is heightened by the adversarial attitude dis-

played by Mr. Finnegan against the interests of Idaho when the bill language was being negotiated. Since he is the one in charge of the committee report drafting effort, it may well be that there is cause for concern by Idahoans about the effect of the committee report language on Idaho water interests.

Because of the number of ambiguities in the language negotiated for the bill, the language in the committee report becomes very critical. In the event of litigation, the courts will probably look to the committee report language for resolution of uncertainties.

If the report language does not affect the letter or spirit of the compromise bill language, there is no problem. However, with the apparent secrecy and haste involved in developing the report language and the reported length of the final draft, I am concerned that the committee staff may be trying to recover some ground that it compromised away during the negotiations on the bill language. If so, the legislation could be more harmful than beneficial to the state's interests.

As it stands, the legislation is only marginally beneficial to the state, given the concessions that had to be made to the committee staff in order to obtain their approval for movement of the bill. Unfavorable report language could well make the bill unacceptable from the state's standpoint. If the committee staff has drafted the report to grant additional advantages to the Columbia River Intertribal Fish Commission, the environment groups, or others, I would be inclined to urge its defeat since we could well be in a better position to fend off their demands through the litigation process.

It is absolutely essential that my staff and I have an opportunity to review the committee report before the bill comes up for consideration in the House. Please

use every available means to hold off floor consideration of the bill until the parties to the Swan Falls
agreement have an opportunity to review and consider the effect of the language used in the committee report. If the committee report language imposes additional requirements and restraints on the state, it may
well be that the state's best interests would be served
by opposing the bill.

The legislation passed the House on November 9, even
though the committee report was not available in final printed
form at that time. We had received a draft copy of the report
and it was bad news. I issued a press release that day, which
read:

Attorney General Jim Jones said today that "language dangerous to Idaho water users has been approved by a committee of the U.S. House of Representatives." The language is contained in a report issued
by the House Energy and Commerce Committee on
the Swan Falls bill. A vote is scheduled on the legislation today.
"The House committee report could seriously jeopardize Idaho's control over the Snake River," Jones
said. "The report language urges unprecedented federal control over Snake River waters, including the
ability to set minimum streamflows above those determined to be prudent by the state. The report language
is contrary to the intent of the bill, as agreed on among
committee staff, the state, and Idaho Power."
"The parties carefully worked out language for the
Swan Falls bill during tough negotiating sessions with
the House Energy and Commerce Committee staff. The
state asked for the opportunity to review the language

of the committee report on the bill, as the report may be very critical in determining the intent of the legislation. However, we were denied that opportunity and the reason is now obvious. The report attempts to gain back federal controls over the Snake River which were conceded away by the committee staff in the negotiations. This is an underhanded effort to renege on the negotiated agreement." Jones said that the committee staff person responsible, David Finnegan, had been adverse to the state's interests during the negotiating sessions. "Finnegan was clearly in the corner of the Columbia River Intertribal Fish Commission and environmental groups who were attempting to secure stronger federal control over Snake River waters, including flow conditions. Those groups had input into the committee report while the state was denied that opportunity. We were only able to get our hands on a draft of the report Friday and the bill is scheduled for passage on Monday. The report was drafted clandestinely and held back from state officials so that the bill could be hastily pushed through the House without alerting Idahoans as to the dangers it posed."

Jones said that he had notified Congressman Richard Stallings and Congressman Larry Craig of the dangers posed to Idaho control over its waters. "I have asked them to take action to strike the committee report so that it will not be a millstone around the state's neck. If that is not possible, the bill should be killed. With the committee report it is a dangerous piece of legislation. It will cause much more harm than good."

Jones said that Craig expressed a willingness to enter a statement in the floor debate expressing the state's concerns about the report language. It is not clear what Stallings intends to do. He had been directly involved in working with the House committee staff.

Jones said that acceptable alternatives to the legislation are available. "The matter can be handled in proceedings before the Federal Energy Regulatory Commission without congressional action. Alternately, the parties to the Swan Falls agreement can agree to forego FERC approval of the agreement without doing violence to the settlement. As it presently stands, with the report this legislation is worse than no solution."

To his credit, Representative Stallings did make a floor statement trying to place the proper legislative interpretation on the bill but a statement by one congressman would not take precedence over floor statements by the floor manager of a bill nor the contents of a committee report. The floor manager, Representative Sharp of Indiana, said, "The committee amended this bill to give solid environmental protection to the fish and wildlife in the Snake River habitat. The bill in its present form is now supported by the Audubon Society, the Friends of the Earth, the Indian tribes with water interests there, the federal fish and wildlife agencies, the Governor of Idaho (Andrus) and the Idaho Power Co. (The bill) would direct the licensee and interested agencies to negotiate an agreement to protect fish and wildlife resources located in and around the Snake River. Of particular concern is maintaining adequate river flows for the Deer Flat National Wildlife Refuge." Thus, it was clear that the legislation intended to increase the streamflows above what the parties agreed to in the Swan Falls settlement agreement and that the Snake River Basin Adjudication was to be preempted as the forum for deciding these issues. That should be readily apparent from the list of entities that endorsed the legislation. The bill, when considered in the context of the late-surfacing committee report, was poisonous from the standpoint of the State.

Recognizing that we would need to undo the damage caused by the House committee report through Senate action, I sent a fax to Senator McClure that same day to put him on notice of the problem and to seek his help. I wrote:

> The committee report prepared on the House version of the Swan Falls bill is extremely troublesome for the State of Idaho. It purports to grant the federal government unprecedented control over the operation of the Snake River. Unless significant damage control efforts are made in the Senate, this legislation will pose significant dangers for Idaho's water interests.
>
> The language of the bill itself, while it is not particularly desirable from the state's standpoint, is tolerable. There are a number of ambiguities in the language, however, which the state agreed to as a matter of necessity in order to prevent a more obnoxious form of legislation from being approved by the House committee. We were convinced that the ambiguities would be resolved in our favor if litigation ensued. These dealt primarily with the level of authority which the Federal Energy Regulatory Commission has to impose environmental controls on the Snake River and the legal effect of the studies which are to be conducted pursuant to the legislation. We were convinced that the language used in the bill was sufficient to protect the state's interests.
>
> However, the House committee staff has attempted to gain back ground which it conceded in the negotiations on the bill language. The committee report is stacked heavily in favor of the environmental and downstream interests. With this kind of language guiding the interpretation of the bill, the state's inter-

ests are severely jeopardized. The bill purports to give the Federal Energy Regulatory Commission the ability to affect the outcome of the Snake River adjudication and to require that environmental concerns raised in the studies be implemented by mitigation measures which would be the responsibility of the parties to the Swan Falls agreement, among other things.

In light of the dangers posed by this legislation, it is critical that the Senate take appropriate action to mitigate the effect of the committee report language. That can be done by amending the bill to clarify the existing ambiguities or by a strong committee report outlining the state's side of the arguments raised in such a one-sided manner in the House committee report. I do not believe that a floor colloquy would be sufficient to remedy the damage.

I would strongly urge that no action be taken on the legislation before our staffs have the opportunity to get together and work out some language which will prevent the federal government from unwarranted intrusion into the operation of the Snake River. Unless this is done, the state's water interests will be seriously jeopardized and the Swan Falls agreement significantly undermined at least from the state's point of view.

I thought this letter would resonate with Senator McClure because of his strong opposition to federal involvement in state water issues.[330] I wrote an identical letter to Senator Symms, who had been fully supportive of our efforts.

It was becoming increasingly apparent that we were in serious trouble. I had absolutely no ability to directly affect what happened in Congress, particularly in the House. We

---

330   Fick, Bob. Associated Press. "Feud continues between Jones, Idaho Power." *Lewiston Tribune*, Aug. 3, 1984.

had a hostile committee chairman, Representative Dingell, with a hostile staff. I suspected that Logan, either freelancing to gain back what he lost in the Swan Falls settlement agreement or acting on behalf of the Company, was working behind the scenes to obtain the ability to increase the agreed-upon streamflows through FERC proceedings. He certainly had more influence with Representative Stallings and Senator McClure than I did. He had shown himself adept at working with the environmental groups in the events leading up to the settlement agreement and we were pretty sure that the same thing was happening in the Congressional proceedings. At this point, I no longer had a supportive person in the Governor's office because Governor Andrus was clearly on Idaho Power's side and was also supporting the efforts of the downstream environmental groups. Things were looking bleak. The only strategy at hand was to raise the profile of the issue as much as possible and to get the water users activated to put as much pressure on the Congressional delegation as possible. It helped that many elected officials seemed to regard a state attorney general as one who is using his office as a perch to run for some other office. Holders of federal offices seemed to believe that AGs were constantly lusting for their position. That certainly wasn't my intention at the time, but I figured that rattling some cages might incline some of the Congressional office holders to come around, if nothing else as a defensive mechanism.

On November 10 I sent out a packet of information to a large group of addressees—the members of the Water Resource Board, the attorneys who had been involved in the state proceedings, our friends in the Legislature, and other individuals who played an active part in the Swan Falls fight—alerting them to the dangerous turn that had occurred in the Congressional arena. I wrote:

Although the bill language is tolerable from the state's standpoint, the House committee report language poses serious problems for Idaho's water users. As an interpretative tool in FERC or other administrative or judicial proceedings, the language could be used to upset the compromise reached in the Swan Falls settlement agreement. It is absolutely critical that those concerned about the legislation immediately communicate with Senator McClure to request damage control measures. A committee report in the Senate, outlining the state's view and concerns, would be very helpful. An amendment to the bill would cure the problem but I doubt that Idaho Power would permit the bill to be amended. A floor colloquy between Senator McClure and Senator Johnston, chairman of the Energy Committee, would be helpful but would not fully remedy the problem posed by the House committee report. Unless the damage is repaired, I think we would be just as well off if the legislation died but I do not believe that Idaho Power will permit that to happen. In any event, I would urge you to contact Senator McClure to outline any concerns you have on this matter and to request that he take action to control the damage.

The next day, I was practically driven up the wall by an article that appeared in the November 10 issue of the Morning News.[331] It was titled "Stallings expresses joy" and read:

Rep. Richard Stallings, D–Idaho, was a very happy man after the historic Swan Falls legislation breezed through the House of Representatives here Monday.
The House voted unanimously, 393–0, to endorse leg-

---

331   Miller, John. "Stallings expresses joy." *The Morning News*, Nov. 10, 1987.

islation mandating federal approval of the Idaho agreement which settled a lengthy battle for what amounted to control of the Snake River.

"There was not a negative vote. Not one," a jubilant Stallings said in a telephone interview from his Washington, D.C., office Monday night, just after the legislation was passed after 10 minutes of debate.

The measure now goes to the Senate, which, Stallings said, should pass the measure easily.

"They've already passed their own version of the measure," he said. "I'm sure our senators will support it all the way."

He said he expects the legislation to be on the president's desk before the Christmas break.

There were some hitches before the measure went up before a House vote. Stallings said Indian tribes raised some concerns and the state of Washington interceded at one point.

Stallings and Rep. Larry Craig, R–Idaho, urged their fellow representatives to support the measure, which requires the Federal Energy Regulatory Commission to approve the 1984 agreement between the state of Idaho and Idaho Power Co.

Stallings looked at Monday's vote as a tremendous victory.

"I've presented some commemorative legislation before, but this was the first piece of legislation with major substance," he said. "It's a tremendous feeling."

As for the bill's chances in the Senate, Stallings said, "I don't see any obstacles."

Here was a man trying to put lipstick on a pig. I was astounded by the naiveté displayed by the man. He had failed to heed our warnings about the real possibility that dangerous language would be inserted into the House committee report. Now, a truly obnoxious piece of legislation had been approved by the House and he was crowing about his remarkable work. I simply could not let him get away with it, so I gave him both barrels in a November 11 press release:

> Attorney General Jim Jones said today that Congressman Richard Stallings has "willingly participated in an effort by downstream interests and environmentalists to extend federal control over the Snake River." Jones said that, "Stallings failed to lift a finger to protect Idaho's water interests when Swan Falls legislation was before the Congress on Monday." Jones said that as a result of Stallings' actions, the Federal Energy Regulatory Commission (FERC) "may be in a position to exercise unprecedented control over Idaho water."
>
> The Swan Falls bill, originally designed to give federal approval to the water rights settlement agreement negotiated between the State of Idaho and Idaho Power Company, was approved in House action on Monday. On Monday morning, prior to the afternoon vote, Jones disclosed that a committee report which had just surfaced posed serious dangers to Idaho's water sovereignty. Today Jones released copies of letters he had written to Stallings warning of the possibility of such problems. Jones said, "Mr. Stallings failed to respond to my warnings regarding the dangers posed for Idaho in the committee report. He didn't lift a finger to try to remedy the damage. If FERC imposes higher minimum streamflows on the Snake River in the future as a result of dangerous language contained in the committee report, Idaho's Second District Congressman can be thanked."
>
> "My staff sent Mr. Stallings a detailed outline of the

problems and potential dangers of the committee language by telefax on November 8. Yet, he did absolutely nothing to try to remedy the situation. In fact, we had been warning him for weeks of the possibility that the committee report could undermine the legislation and yet nothing was done to respond to our concerns or even check them out. He didn't even make a comment on the House floor raising the concerns or stating that the report language in any way varied from his understanding of the bill negotiations. It is rather apparent that Mr. Stallings is quite comfortable with the concessions made in the report language to the environmentalists and downstream interests."

Jones revealed today that he had written Stallings on October 6 to urge that the state have input in drafting committee report language on the Swan Falls legislation.... Jones said that he had received no reply to his October 6 letter.

Jones said that he had telecopied a letter to Stallings on November 3 reiterating the critical need for state input in the committee report. Jones said, "With the apparent secrecy involved in developing the report language, I am concerned that the committee staff may be trying to recover some ground that it compromised away during the negotiations on the bill language. If so, the legislation could be more harmful than beneficial to the state's interests. Jones' letter continued, "The legislation is only marginally beneficial to the state at this point, given the concessions that had to be made to the committee staff. Unfavorable report language could well make the bill unacceptable from the state's standpoint. If the committee staff attempts to gain additional advantages for CRITFC (the Columbia River Intertribal Fish Commission), the environmentalists or others, I would be inclined to urge its defeat since we could well be in a better position to fend off their demands through the litigation process."

On November 6 Jones telecopied a letter to Stallings urging that he "use every available means to hold off floor consideration of the bill until the parties to the Swan Falls agreement have an opportunity to review and consider the effect of the language used in that committee report." Jones pointed out that he had learned the committee report was over 40 pages in length and had been drafted in secret. Jones said that he was concerned that the report was being drafted by David Finnegan, a staff member of the House Energy and Commerce Committee. "My concern is heightened by the adversial attitude displayed by Mr. Finnegan against the interests of Idaho when the bill language was being negotiated. Since he is in charge of the committee report drafting effort, it may well be that there is cause for concern by Idahoans about the effect of the committee report language on Idaho water interests."

Jones' November 6 letter continued, "However, with the apparent secrecy and haste involved in developing the report language and the reported length of the final draft, I am concerned that the committee staff may be trying to recover some of the ground that it compromised away during the negotiations on the bill language."

"It appears that Mr. Stallings caved in to the downstream fishery interests and environmental interests at the expense of Idaho water users. In a news report earlier this year, he contended that he had the votes to get the bill out of the committee but that he was holding up action to accommodate the concerns of environmentalists. If this is indeed the case, he has sold Idaho water interests down the river."

Jones said that the bill passed the House Monday on the consent calendar. "Any congressman could have stopped the legislation dead in its tracks. Mr. Stallings did not avail himself of this opportunity or make the slightest effort in his floor comments to do any damage control. We can only hope that the Senate is able to repair some of the damage. As a result of House action the bill turned into a Frankenstein's monster and must either be modified or mercifully killed."

"Idaho Power was treated very well in the legislation. The environmentalist groups and downstream fishery interests got much of what they hoped for in the bill. All of these parties were clamoring for immediate passage of the bill and they got it. Much of what they have got will be at the expense of Idaho. I anticipate seeing the committee report language used against the State of Idaho in future FERC proceedings, in the Snake River adjudication, and possibly in court proceedings involving the interpretation of the Swan Falls bill."

"Even though he is not from the Second Congressional District, Congressman Larry Craig was willing to make some statements on the House floor calling attention to our concerns. This will be the only legislative history in the House to indicate that Congress did not intend to extend federal control over Snake River waters."

The press release was issued in conjunction with a press conference I held in Idaho Falls that day. Rocky Barker reported me saying "the bill should die a merciful death," unless the Senate could remedy the damage done by the House committee report.[332] I could also have said that Representative Stallings was stretching things a bit with his claim of a 393-0 vote. The bill passed on the consent calendar, which means that nobody objected so it just passed without a recorded roll call vote. And, generally, there are few people present on the floor at such a time.

Also on November 11, Mark Pratter reported in the Times-News that Representative Stallings "said he may be willing to make changes in Swan Falls water rights legislation to satisfy objections of Idaho Attorney General Jim Jones."[333] He told the Times-News that if my "objections proved to be legitimate, a statement can be added to the committee report saying that the report won't jeopardize the State's traditional control over the Snake River." However, the report had already been issued and there was almost no chance that it could be amended. Indeed, no action was ever taken to amend it. Stallings said that he and Representative Craig "got the opinions of Idaho Power Co. and (Governor Cecil) Andrus' office that they did not share Jones' concerns." But, of course, they wouldn't because the House committee report nicely served their purposes.

Stallings followed up with a press release on November 12, claiming my criticism of the House-passed legislation was "provocative and short-sighted." He said "other attorneys involved in drafting the agreement, do not share Jones' concerns." What he did not mention was that those other attorneys included the House committee staff, Idaho Power's attorney, Governor Andrus' attorney, and attorneys representing the downstream interests. Stallings correctly said that my staff had been involved in negotiating the language of the legislation, but that is not what we were concerned about. It was the language in the committee report,

---

332   Barker, Rocky. "Jones: Kill Swan Falls bill." *Post-Register*, Nov. 11, 1987.
333   Pratter, Mark. "Stallings willing to change water rights bill." *Times-News*, Nov. 11, 1987.

which only had input from the downstream interests and was clearly one-sided.

That same day, I sent a letter to Chairman Dingell to bring his attention to the fact that the report language drafted on his behalf by Finnegan "attempts to resurrect and endorse certain non-germane conditions advanced by environmental and downstream fishery interests which were laid to rest by the negotiators. Much of the language contains a one-sided gloss on the important issues in the bill, thereby giving a strong anti-Idaho bias to the legislative history—a bias which is contrary to the negotiations resulting in the bill language." I asked that he respond to let me know what could be done to remedy the errors in the committee report but I did not intend to hold my breath waiting for an answer.

On November 13, I sent out a guest opinion to practically every daily and weekly newspaper in southeast and south central Idaho:

> Environmentalists and downstream fishery interests are trying to use the Swan Falls legislation in Congress as a means of gaining greater federal control over the Snake River. With the aid of a staff member of the House Energy and Commerce Committee, those interests have placed Idaho's water in jeopardy. The House committee report on the Swan Falls bill, which just emerged from secrecy on November 6, contends that the Federal Energy Regulatory Commission should have unprecedented control over the Snake River, including the ability to increase streamflows above those agreed on in the Swan Falls agreement.
>
> The committee report was not printed in final form nor available for consideration by House members when the bill was voted upon on November 9. The secrecy and haste of the proceedings is understandable

when one reads the committee report and realizes its distasteful implications for Idaho water users. Despite agreements to the contrary when the language of the bill itself was negotiated, the report implies that federal authorities have the jurisdiction to set streamflow conditions on the Snake River. It contends, contrary to the clear understanding of the negotiators, that the Federal Energy Regulatory Commission can require the state to observe and perform recommendations of certain environmental studies which will include participation of environmentalists, fishery interests, and other out-of-state parties. Despite repeated requests for review of and input into the drafting of the committee report, the House committee staff refused to allow the state's participation. The report was finally pried out of the committee just one working day before the bill was voted upon by the House.

The damage caused by the House report, which will be looked to by courts and administrative agencies to interpret the Swan Falls legislation, must be cured in the Senate. The Senate can prepare its own report, outlining that the settlement agreement does not have adverse environmental consequences, as the state has correctly contended all along. It can also negate the implication that federal authorities have the ability to affect streamflow conditions on the Snake River or that they can require implementation of any recommendations resulting from environmental studies conducted under the bill. Quite frankly, it would be better to have this legislation killed, since the state would be better off litigating these issues before the Federal Energy Regulatory Commission. Concerned citizens must immediately make their views known to Senator Mc-Clure so that remedial action can be taken. The issue is too important for citizens concerned with the future of Southern Idaho to stand silent.

Clive quickly prepared some proposed committee report language for the Senate to counter the language in the House committee report. The language made it clear that FERC had no ability to affect the terms of the settlement agreement or to alter the streamflows provided in the agreement. The proposed language indicated that the State would not have to participate in any study, would not have to share in the costs of any study, and would not have to implement the findings or conclusions of any study. I sent that proposed language to Senator McClure on November 13, noting that a meeting had been arranged between the two of us to discuss it on November 14.

My meeting with Senator McClure on November 14 went quite well. I summarized the results of the meeting in a letter I wrote to the Senator on December 17:

As we discussed and agreed on November 14, the House committee report issued in conjunction with the House-passed Swan Falls bill poses serious dangers for Idaho's water sovereignty. As you stated at that time, effective measures would have to be taken to negate the adverse legislative history contained in the report. At that time I wholly concurred in your statement that a floor colloquy in the Senate would not be sufficient to remedy the damage. As we discussed, changes in the bill language are necessary in order to effectively remedy the problem. As you indicated at the end of the meeting, it would be best to kill the legislation as opposed to letting it move forward without necessary damage control measures.

Members of the Committee of Nine swung into action

on November 13, faxing a signed statement to my office, the Congressional delegation, and others, expressing grave concern about the House-passed legislation. The statement said:

> From the legislation and its accompanying committee report, it is apparent that the legislation calls for a broad federal study of the Snake River. The express purpose of the study is to evaluate the adequacy of flows in the Snake River for protection of fish and wildlife. The express harm to be studied is the alleged insufficiency of agreed minimum flows on the Snake River. Jurisdiction to implement and enforce the study is given to the Federal Energy Regulatory Commission (FERC). The State of Idaho is prohibited from participating in negotiations to implement the study unless it waives certain rights, the extent of which is unclear from the wording of the legislation and the committee report.
>
> This unprecedented action by the House of Representatives could result in major new inroads of federal control over the Snake River to the detriment of state sovereignty. Although proponents of the legislation claim it does not expand the jurisdiction of FERC over the Snake River and that there has been no determination that the Swan Falls Agreement is harmful to environmental concerns, the legislation and committee report raise serious questions:
>
> —Why should the legislation, which passed last year as a simple two-page measure and did not expand or limit environmental concerns, now be amended to force a full scale federal environmental evaluation of the Snake River?
>
> —Why should the federal government insert itself

into the management of flows of the Snake River in this manner?

— Why should FERC be given jurisdiction in this legislation to enforce this study unless the intent is to give FERC increased authority to set or manage in-stream flows on the Snake River?

— Why must the State of Idaho be precluded from participating in the study unless it agrees to be bound by the agreement of the negotiating parties?

— What impact will the new environmental study have on the existing state-controlled adjudication of water rights on the Snake River?

The undersigned water users are concerned that critical principles which traditionally have governed management of water rights in Idaho have been ignored or undercut by this legislation. The State of Idaho, not FERC or any other federal agency, is sovereign and entitled to adjudicate the status of water rights in the State. The adequacy of the flows of the Snake River can and should be determined by the state courts under existing state and federal law in the pending adjudication. FERC has not had authority in the past and should not be given the authority now to enforce or insert itself into management of minimum flow regimes on the Snake River.

When I opened my Idaho Statesman on November 14, I saw this headline, "Andrus: Jones is 'out there by himself' on water rights."[334] The article read in part:

Democratic Gov. Cecil Andrus has entered the fray over a document supporting congressional legislation mandating federal approval of Idaho's water-rights

---

334   Associated Press. "Andrus: Jones is 'out there by himself on water rights." *Idaho Statesman,* Nov. 14, 1987.

settlement. Not surprising, Andrus again is on the other side of the fence from Republican Attorney General Jim Jones.

The bill was approved unanimously by the U.S. House on Monday amid warnings from Jones that language in a supporting document would undermine Idaho's control over its water if the provision is not changed in the Senate.

But after talking with other water-rights attorneys, including those for Idaho Power Co., Andrus said he has not been able to find another lawyer who sides with Jones.

"I can't find anyone who takes the same view as the attorney general," Andrus said. "He seems to be out there by himself....Everyone else wants it behind us and approved."

Apparently, the Governor didn't look very hard for attorneys from whom to seek an opinion. It is not surprising that any attorney for Idaho Power would have said everything is fine and dandy. Most of the other water lawyers involved in the Swan Falls fight fully supported my view—Ray Rigby, Kent Foster, Roger Ling, Senator Ringert, and Ben Cavaness, as well as Senator Mike Crapo. The Governor was apparently unaware that members of the Committee of Nine had seen the House committee report and fully agreed with my view. A group of eastern Idaho legislators met with myself and others on November 17 and, according to a report by Rocky Barker, shared my concerns about the legislation.[335] Senator Con Mahoney of Idaho Falls "expressed the feelings of most of those at the meeting. 'No legislation is preferable to legislation that jeopardizes Idaho's water.'"

The Idaho Statesman reported that politicians and interest groups were choosing sides between myself and

---

335   Barker, Rocky. "Legislators echo Jones' Swan Falls misgivings." *Post-Register*, Nov. 18, 1987.

Representative Stallings.[336] Representative Stallings received the support of Idaho Power, four Columbia River Treaty fishing tribes, Idaho Steelhead and Salmon Unlimited, and Friends of the Earth. Logan was quoted as saying he expected quick approval of the bill in the Senate "despite Jones' eleventh-hour politicking." On the other hand, Laird Noh "said in a statement issued (November 17) that he and Sen. Mike Crapo, R–Idaho Falls, fully support Jones' move to 'neutralize language' in the House bill." I thought my side was more representative of Idaho's water interests.

On November 20, I issued a press release saying that actions taken by Representatives Dingell and Stallings "will not be effective to remedy dangers posed to Idaho by the Swan Falls bill. However, it is good that they are starting to recognize those dangers." I was referring to a letter purportedly written to me by Dingell and a statement made by Representative Stallings in the Congressional Record. I wrote, "This bill is still a Trojan Horse which could leave Idaho high and dry in the future. The dangers posed to Idaho's control over its water cannot be alleviated by an after-the-fact statement inserted in the Congressional Record or by a letter written by a Congressman."

Dingell's letter did not address why downstream interests were allowed to have input into the drafting of the committee report while we were excluded. His letter claimed that nothing in the bill would be hurtful to Idaho's water interests. However, he went on to say that he, his committee, and the environmental organizations "have not been entirely satisfied.... to leave the matter of fish and wildlife, including anadromous fish, and the Deer Flat National Wildlife Refuge solely to the vagaries of State forums." That was my exact concern—that his committee report was intended as a

---

336   Associated Press. "Support lines up in Stallings–Jones dispute over Swan Falls." *Idaho Statesman*, Nov. 18, 1987.

directive to FERC to set higher streamflows for the Snake River. He apparently did not understand that the state judge in the Snake River Basin Adjudication would have to apply federal law in setting the federal reserved rights that applied to Snake River waters and that the State forum would by necessity be fair to federal interests.

Another troubling thing about Dingell's letter was that I never received it. As I noted in my press release, "It is instructive, however, to note that the letter was being passed around by Idaho Power Company's lawyer in Twin Falls Thursday (November 19) at a court proceeding on the adjudication. One can only wonder how non-addressees are brandishing the letter before the person to whom it is purportedly addressed has even received it." This certainly didn't alleviate my concern that Dingell and others in Congress were rubbing elbows with Logan.

I followed up with a press conference in Idaho Falls on November 21 saying that, "In order to prevent the federal government from gaining new control over the Snake River, both houses of Congress will have to act."[337] As Rocky Barker reported, I said that unilateral action by the U.S. Senate would not be sufficient to satisfy my concerns about the House report.

That same day, Senator McClure had a guest opinion in the Post-Register saying that he was "sufficiently concerned about the report language in the House-passed bill to take a much closer look....The basic issue is too important to be pushed into quick approval of bad legislation."[338]

On November 22, Mark Pratter reported that Ray Rigby "and other prominent water lawyers such as Roger Ling of Rupert and Kent Foster of Idaho Falls back Jones." Ray Rigby said, "I really believe his cause is just."[339] Pratter

337   Barker, Rocky. "Dingell calls Swan Falls report worries insignificant." *Post-Register,* Nov. 22, 1987.
338   "Swan Falls water legislations takes cool heads, work." *Post-Register,* Nov. 22, 1987.
339   Pratter, Mark. "State politicians battle over pact." *Times-News,*

correctly observed:

> There are two items to keep in mind about the Stallings, Andrus and IPC position.
>
> First, higher river flows to benefit fish and wildlife would also help IPC because there would be more water to generate electricity, Rigby says.
>
> Stallings' bill calls for studies of the fish and wildlife question that could one day lead to recommendations for higher flows.
>
> Second, Stallings and Andrus and their staffs are relative newcomers to the Swan Falls process compared to Jones and his staff.
>
> Stallings, now in his second term, stands to reap statewide prestige and political points with IPC if he can bring the Swan Falls issue to resolution. Indeed, last May when the Swan Falls bill was hung up in committee over environmental issues, Stallings wrote a handwritten postscript in a letter to Rep. John Dingell, D–Michigan, chairman of the House Energy and Commerce. It said, "This is so very important to me and to my future. Please do what you can."

Pratter made a further observation that left me a bit puzzled. He wrote, "Jones' bluntness and independence makes him popular with reporters and he is a politician who likes to court the press."

Actually, I had made an effort to forge a good relationship with the media, particularly the political reporters. At that time, when the public actually relied on the papers for their news, most of the daily papers had experienced political reporters on board. I learned early on in my political campaigns that earned or free media was practically worth its weight in gold. Without it, the pro-subordination side would

Nov. 22, 1987.

have had a difficult time matching Idaho Power's firepower. So, yes, I did work hard to maintain credibility and a good relationship with the press and I believe it was very helpful in bringing about the Swan Falls settlement.

During the time that he was considering what to do with the Swan Falls bill in the Senate, Senator McClure suggested that the rhetoric be toned down a bit, and everybody, including myself, took the hint. It seemed to me that things were moving in the right direction because practically every southern Idaho water lawyer had contacted all of the members of the Congressional delegation to urge support for my position. At the same time, the comments that I had made about Representative Stallings' failure to protect Idaho water interests were making the rounds in Republican circles and there were a lot more circles that were Republican than Democrat in the Second Congressional District. He would be coming up for reelection in less than a year and he was well aware that he would have to deliver results on the issue to the water-user community.

On November 25, I sent out a press release saying that the Committee of Nine, acting through its chairman Dale Rockwood, wrote to Senator McClure asking that the bill either be amended or killed. My press release also pointed out that Congressman Ron Wyden of Oregon said on the House floor, "This bill will also allow Idaho, the Indian tribes, downstream States like Oregon and Washington, and interested agencies like the Northwest Power Planning Council to have input into a study that will help make water allocations on the river." The press release observed, "Oregon Congressman Wyden certainly contemplates that the bill will make additional Idaho water available for usage in Oregon and Washington. It's no wonder that the out-of-state and downstream interests are pushing hard for passage of this bill."

Senator Ringert sent a fine letter to Senator McClure on

December 7, saying that "the concerns expressed by Attorney General Jim Jones are valid and merit careful consideration." He said, "the federal agencies involved in this situation will not hesitate to use any means available to expand their control over resources and activities in Idaho." He concluded by urging action "to eliminate from the legislative history the effects of the House Committee Report." Apparently, Senator Ringert was not swayed by Representative Dingell's assurances that Idaho would be well served to have FERC set Snake River streamflows to please the downstream interests.

Things came to a head on Thursday December 17. I got word that the Senate was going to act on the legislation that day or the next day. First thing in the morning, I faxed Senator McClure a letter recounting our discussion of November 14 and saying:

> I hope that we can count on you to do what is necessary to remedy the problem. We are advised that the Columbia River Intertribal Fish Commission has met several times with representatives of the two federal agencies involved to discuss the scope of the study required under the legislation. As indicated in Congressman Dingell's letter of December 7 (copy enclosed), it is contemplated that the study will have far-reaching effects (much beyond the immediate environmental effects of the Swan Falls agreement on fish and wildlife). With the committee report language authorizing and directing FERC to require implementation of the study recommendations, the bill poses extreme dangers to Idaho's control over Snake River waters.
>
> I should point out to you that the legislation is not required in order to protect the interests of those who have applied for water rights. Nothing is said in the Swan Falls agreement about confirming federal legis-

lation. The legislation was seen as a convenient vehicle to obtain quick action from the Federal Energy Regulatory Commission. There is no reason why the state cannot move forward with processing of water applications. The enclosed article from the February 5, 1987, issue of the Statesman clearly indicates this to be the case.

I should point out that virtually all of the southern Idaho water law experts who have reviewed the legislation agree with me as to its dangers (except those beholden to Idaho Power Company.) I enclose an article from the Times-News outlining Ray Rigby's views, a copy of a press release issued by Mike Crapo and Laird Noh, and a copy of a letter written to you by Bill Ringert. Roger Ling, Ben Cavaness, and Kent Foster, the other people with long experience in Idaho water law, concur with my view regarding the dangers posed by the bill. Please use your best efforts to amend it and, if that is not possible, to kill it.

Shortly thereafter, I called to speak with the Senator. For some reason I kept my AT&T bill for that time. It says that our call lasted 22 minutes. We discussed what was possible and he was not encouraging. When I said it was absolutely essential that the bill be amended by both Houses, he said it couldn't be done. Representative Dingell would not permit it under any circumstance. I said if it could not be done, then the bill had to be killed. He said that could not be done. As I said in my letter, killing the bill would not be the disaster that Stallings, Logan, and a few others suggested. But he insisted he could not do it. I then said that the only alternative was to have the bill amended by both Houses. We had already sent him an amendment that would negate the language in the House committee report. I told the Senator I knew that he could do it and concluded the call in a somewhat less than diplomatic fashion. I said, "If you don't get the bill amended, I will call a press conference in the morning and blast your _____ from heck to breakfast." From what he had observed of me, I have no doubt that he believed I would do just that. Although I don't recall it, Clive, who was in the room at the time of the call (but not listening in), claims that I was practically shouting into the phone and making threats to appear on the steps of every county courthouse in the State to denounce the Senator for selling out Idaho's water interests.

We were surprised and delighted to learn that the bill had been amended and passed by both Houses on December 18. Senator McClure had gotten the bill amended and passed without any opposition. Not only that, he inserted into the Congressional Record written questions to, and answers from, Representative Dingell laying to rest our concerns that FERC would have any ability to require that Idaho implement any recommendations coming out of any study.[340] Section 3(a)(4) of the bill provided, "The evaluations and studies and the report thereof required by this subsection shall be made available by the Federal parties to the public and the Commission and shall be considered by the Commission in accordance with existing and applicable law." The amendment we had written was inserted here and it read, "Nothing contained in this Act requires the Commission to take any action pursuant to such consideration, or authorizes or grants the Commission any authority to take any action, based upon the findings, recommendations, results, or conclusions of the study required by this section." Senator Symms made a fine statement in support of the legislation and commended Senator McClure and myself for our "efforts to resolve the very troublesome ambiguities created by language in the House report."

That very same day, the House approved the amended Senate version of the bill. Rocky Barker wrote a fairly

---

340   Congressional Record, Dec. 18, 1987, pp. S18443–S18451.

balanced article explaining how this came about:[341]

> When the Swan Falls marathon turned into a sprint late last week, the two major participants found themselves helping each other over the finish line.
>
> The legislation that gave federal approval to the 1984 water rights agreement between the state and Idaho Power Co. breezed through the Senate and House Friday and awaits President Reagan's signature.
>
> Sen. James McClure, R–Idaho, pressured hard by irrigators and Attorney General Jim Jones to offset potential threats in the legislation to Idaho water rights, decided it must be amended. Had he done that alone successfully, it would have presented serious political problems for Rep. Richard Stallings, D–Idaho, who sponsored the House legislation, which included a fish and wildlife study that rankled irrigators.
>
> Under usual circumstances, McClure would have called on his old friend Rep. John Dingell, D–Mich., chairman of the House Energy and Commerce Committee, and worked out a deal. But Dingell was not in a mood to hand his Republican friend the kind of political plum he often provided in the past.
>
> Jones had targeted Dingell's committee report as the "great Satan" for Idaho water interests. Jones' attacks on the report hardened Dingell's opposition to any change in the Swan Falls bill he already had pushed through the House.
>
> So McClure took the extraordinary step of asking for Stallings' help. They had worked together on legislation before but never so openly.
>
> If McClure needs Stallings' clout to pass legislation

---

341   Barker, Rocky "Swan Falls tiff endangers non-partisan effort." *Post-Register,* Dec. 20, 1987.

in the House, it gives at least tacit support to the Rexburg Democrat's claim it helps Idaho to have a Democrat in the delegation.

But McClure said that Jones' very public efforts to blast Stallings and Dingell's version of the Swan Falls bill made a bipartisan effort necessary.

I think that's fair," McClure said Friday. "I think it's fair to say he (Dingell) wasn't going to play into the middle of a partisan fight."

However, it was that loud, persistent campaign by Jones and irrigators against the House-passed bill that convinced McClure and even Stallings that the change was necessary. As late as Wednesday, McClure's plans were to allow the bill to pass without an amendment.

Then he wouldn't have needed to cajole Dingell. And he could have solved most of Jones' problems with Dingell's committee report with a competing Senate committee report, he said.

But what he couldn't do was reconcile the concerns of the Committee of Nine. The panel of eastern Idaho canal company representatives oversees Water District 1 and represents virtually all of the irrigators in the Snake River Basin above Twin Falls.

They told McClure that they opposed the legislation as long as it had a study of the effects of the Swan Falls agreement on fish and wildlife. Such a study could not do anything but threaten their interests.

State Sen. Mike Crapo, R–Idaho Falls, went to Washington last week as an attorney representing the committee. He worked with McClure's staff to try and find an acceptable solution. He came back, he thought, empty-handed.

Jones said McClure made his decision after a frank phone call with him (Thursday).

"I had a discussion with Senator McClure on the importance of the amendment, and he agreed with me," Jones said.

McClure said Jones had slightly different interests than the irrigators, noting that he originally agreed to the fish and wildlife study. It was ultimately the irrigators' concerns, "and the opinions of a variety of attorneys whose opinions that I respect," that made him go for the amendment, said McClure.

The study would be performed by Idaho Power, the U.S. Fish and Wildlife Service, the state and the National Marine Fisheries Service. If the parties fail to agree on the scope of the study, the Federal Energy Regulatory Commission could authorize its own study.

The amendment makes it clear that FERC cannot take any action based on the study. That was enough to please the Committee of Nine, though it still has reservations about the study.

"One of the messages this delivers is that from now on (the Committee of Nine) is going to be one of the players in these things," said Crapo.

The Swan Falls agreement set a minimum stream flow of 3,900 cubic feet per second at Idaho Power's Swan Falls Dam near Murphy. That provides the power company with enough water to operate its Snake River hydroelectric system while providing the state with water for further development on the Snake River Plain.

The congressional legislation was designed to meet the agreement's requirement for FERC approval. It was first passed without a study in 1986, but President Reagan vetoed the bill to which it was attached.

McClure pushed similar legislation through the

Senate early this year but conservation groups had Dingell add the study to the bill in the House after negotiating with the state and the power company.

The state's concern over the legislation is due to a basic difference in opinion between the state and FERC over control of river flows. Idaho argues that FERC has no control over Snake River flows, while FERC argues that it does have some authority due to its authority to license power dams.

For that reason the Swan Falls legislation was written to be neutral on the issue. Jones contended that Dingell's committee report tipped the scale in FERC's favor in future lawsuits.

"For southern Idaho water is life," said McClure. "Who controls that, controls our life."

Thursday morning McClure met with Stallings and solicited his aid in convincing Dingell to reconsider the bill with the amendment.

"I went to the chairman and he was not very happy," Stallings said. "Some of the statements the attorney general made about him deeply offended him."

McClure also met with Dingell and finally the two Idaho lawmakers were able to change his mind.

"We both explained that this was not to help the attorney general, it was something our state needed," Stallings said.

Once on board, Dingell overcame the even greater objections of his committee staff. He even strengthened the language that McClure, offered, Stallings said.

McClure easily got the bill through the Senate Friday evening.

When Dingell delivers, he pulls out the stops. Although Stallings predicted it would be Sunday or even Monday before it could get through the House, Dingell got it approved less than two hours after the Senate approved it.

Apparently, Representative Dingell dispensed with his patronizing attitude and decided to change the legislation, which he had declared he would not do, in order to get Representative Stallings out of the hot water he was in. Neither of them was very happy with me but things worked out fine for the State. The Swan Falls agreement became finalized and the studies provided for in the bill did not pose any danger to the State. They would likely be used to support the Federal reserved water rights claims in the Snake River Basin Adjudication and that was fine. Something similar would have been done in any event.

I didn't actually bear any ill-will toward Congressman Stallings. In my estimation, he did a fairly good job of representing his constituents on other matters. On the Swan Falls legislation , I think he was just in way over his head. He was listening to Logan and others who wanted Snake River streamflows increased, rather than to his constituents. Like so many others who think they become experts on almost every subject by being elected to Congress, he failed to listen to people who knew what they were talking about on this complicated issue.

On December 23, I dropped Senator McClure a letter saying:

> Many thanks for your good work on the Swan Falls legislation. My staff and I have reviewed the floor statements and have concluded that they should be helpful to the state in any future litigation involving the interpretation of the legislation. You certainly pulled a rabbit out of a hat by gaining congressional approval of our amendment and I want you to know that we very

much appreciate your efforts.

Steve Hartgen of the Times-News wrote a kindly editorial on the matter, which I immodestly reprint:[342]

Who should get credit depends on which side of the political fence you sit, but it seems to us that Attorney General Jim Jones and his deputy, Patrick Kole, have done Idahoans a favor in their determined, 11th-hour, and ultimately successful clarification of the Swan Falls agreement.

Final legislation on Swan Falls was whisking through Congress in November when Jones raised a number of questions about both the language of the law itself, as well as the "committee report" from which Congressional intent could be inferred in later years. Jones' reading of these was that the legislation left state control of the Snake River water very much up in the air; he asked for clarification.

The first response was, not to worry. Neither Rep. Richard Stallings, nor Gov. Cecil Andrus, nor Idaho Power Company saw any problem with the language.

But Jones persisted, turning up the heat on the issue in a series of public forums.

Others took a closer look at the language and expressed reservations too, including Southern and Eastern Idaho irrigators; Sen. Laird Noh, R–Kimberly, who chairs the Idaho Senate Natural Resources Committee; and U.S. Sen. James McClure, the ranking Republican on the Senate Interior Committee.

The result of that attention were changes in the language which, Jones says, will better protect the state's water, particularly for future agricultural use. But

342   "Jones served us well on Swan Falls issue." *Times-News,* Dec. 22, 1987.

without the scrutiny and visibility Jones gave the issue at the last moment, the changes probably wouldn't have occurred.

We have several interesting points in this event.

One, Idahoans should take a lesson from the fact that, once an "agreement" gets to Washington, all bets are off. Jones, as Idaho's lawyer, read the fine print.

Two, Idaho Power Company, which has its water right protected under the agreement, didn't seem very concerned about the language protecting others' rights for non-hydro use. Nor did Andrus' office.

How, we should all ask, has either served us by effectively signing off on the previous language?

Three, political considerations are never very far below the surface. It took Jones leaning on McClure, to get the latter's clout and threat to hold up the legislation to get the language changed. As politics is a game of compromise, we should watch now to see who traded what for this.

Four, Jones' outcry won't reflect well on Stallings, who perhaps should have given the matter closer attention.

Fifth, there is a lesson in Jones' approach. The feisty Attorney General isn't ever likely to miss a chance to bash a few Democrats if he can, and he beat up on Stallings more than a little in this incident.

But political hay aside, Jones raised important questions and spoke out for the state's interest at a time when others weren't. That's an appropriate role for Idaho's attorney general and staff.

President Reagan signed the legislation and it became Public Law 100–216 on December 29, 1987. Len Jordan would

EPILOGUE: All's Well That Ends Well

have been pleased.

Despite the prolonged proceedings involving FERC approval of the settlement agreement, the parties worked to implement and observe the terms of the agreement from the date it was signed. Following the 1985 legislative session, everything had been put into place except FERC approval. Strangely enough, the sky has not fallen since that time. Electric rates have not skyrocketed, fish and wildlife have not suffered a massive die-off, and the State has not handed over water in massive amounts to every Tom, Dick, and Harry.

Even after 30 years of living under the agreement, with minor tweaks here and there from time to time, things appear to have worked out well under the new water provisions implemented under the settlement agreement. It is true that salmon and steelhead faced substantial problems during that period of time, but those problems were not a result of the settlement agreement.

It is also true, as I had predicted, that Idaho Power would raise electric rates, but the rate increases were the result of factors other than river flows resulting from the agreement. Indeed, at about the same time that the State and Idaho Power entered into the extension agreement on May 15, 1985, acknowledging the accomplishment of everything except FERC approval and extending the agreement until such approval was forthcoming, Idaho Power announced its intention to seek a rate increase.[343] It had last received a rate increase of 15.3 percent in September of 1982. Neither increase had anything to do with Swan Falls or Snake River water rights. Rather, they were primarily motivated by the

---

343   "Idaho Power plans to seek rate increase." *Idaho Statesman,* May 18, 1985.

Power Company's desire to place an additional component of a coal-fired plant into its rate base.

The Power Company followed up the announcement with a request to the Public Utilities Commission to increase its power rates by 27.4%. On September 6, 1985, the Company requested an increase of $84,169,669 per year. Three days later, I moved to intervene in the proceeding to represent the interests of the State and other Idaho Power customers. In a press release issued that day, I wrote, "If an increase of this magnitude is granted, it will have a very severe impact on Idaho consumers, businesses and farmers. With the depressed nature of Idaho's economy, the prospect of $84 million in additional electric costs is indeed grim."

Robert O'Connor, who was then CEO of the Company, told Idaho Public TV that he was "shocked" that I would seek intervention in the case.[344] "I am amazed that the attorney general would decide to enter this case at this time in history. No attorney general has ever done that." I believe Bob was correct in this regard but at the time I wondered why the Attorney General should not intervene in a proceeding that would substantially impact the State, as well as ratepayers generally. We calculated that the rate increase would cause the State's electric bill to increase by about $1 million per year, residential rates would increase by about $35 million, and irrigation rates would rise by about $11 million. The PUC granted our petition to intervene and my staff participated in the proceedings before the PUC. We presented three expert witnesses, who focused in on the rate of return to shareholders, the Power Company's effort to put the new plant (Valmy II) into the Company's rate base, and a contract with another utility to operate the new plant. We contended it was unwise for the Company to build additional capacity in light of the energy surplus in the Pacific Northwest.

---

344   Associated Press. "Idaho Power president is surprised at attorney general's intervention." *The Morning News,* Sept. 14, 1985.

In a press release dated May 13, 1986, I commended the Power Company for reducing its rate hike request from $84.2 million to $66.2 million but argued that the remainder of the rate request was unwarranted. On July 11, the PUC issued its decision, granting Idaho Power less than $1 million of its $66.2 million rate request. In a July 16 press release, I congratulated the PUC for its decision, noting that the PUC acted favorably upon testimony submitted by my experts by reducing Idaho Power's rate of return to stockholders from 15% to 12.75% and refusing to place the Valmy II plant into rate base until it became useful to Idaho customers.

The Power Company appealed the PUC decision to the Idaho Supreme Court. I was not completely satisfied with the PUC's briefing to the Court and, therefore, sought to submit an amicus curiae brief and to present argument on appeal. Idaho Power opposed my efforts but the Court allowed me to submit briefing and oral argument. I personally decided to argue the case, explaining to the Associated Press that, "This is an important case, not only because large sums of money are at stake for ratepayers, but also because of the legal principle involved. When a utility makes an imprudent decision on building surplus capacity, ratepayers should not have to pay the tab. It is extremely unfair to ratepayers to automatically require an unneeded generating plant to be placed into the rate base."[345]

At the hearing before the Supreme Court on December 2, 1987, I contended that the Valmy II plant was a "white elephant" that would not be needed to serve Idaho customers until 1993 at the earliest and that it therefore should not be placed into the Company's rate base.[346] As reported by the AP's Quane Kenyon, the argument stretched almost three hours. That was a little unusual, but a lot of money was at stake. I was a little bit surprised because Chief Justice Allan Shepard, who

---

345   Associated Press. "Idaho Power to ask court for rate hike." *Lewiston Morning,* Nov. 22, 1987.
346   Kenyon, Quane. Associated Press. "Utility claims punishment." *Times-News,* Dec. 3, 1987.

had written the Swan Falls decision and previously served as Idaho Attorney General, seemed quite unhappy with me for being involved in the case. His face was red and his questions were hard edged. Unfortunately, he suffered a heart attack later that day, a fact that I learned in the newspaper the next morning. I hoped that our interchange during the argument had not contributed in any fashion.

When the Supreme Court finally acted upon the case a year later, it provided for an 8.8% hike in electric rates, which translated to an increase of about $28.4 million.[347] My office and others filed a request for rehearing, which the Court granted on January 18, 1989. The Power Company and PUC then got together and reached an agreement for a 5.1% increase in electric rates.

I decided not to challenge the compromise agreement, telling the press that, "Although I am not thrilled by the compromise agreement, it presents fewer risks for ratepayers than the other possible outcomes of the case. The compromise reduces the rate impact on Idaho Power customers by a couple of million dollars, as compared to the Supreme Court decision. In addition, Idaho Power has agreed not to ask for another rate increase for three years."[348] The Supreme Court withdrew its opinion in the case, based on the settlement.

Although the studies called for by the FERC legislation ran into some problems, those were overcome. The first problem surfaced on February 19, 1988, at a meeting in Boise to determine the scope of the studies. Representatives of the U.S. Fish and Wildlife Service and National Marine Fisheries Service presided and made it clear at that time that Idaho would not be allowed to participate unless the State agreed to share the costs of the studies and be bound by the terms of a FERC order as to the scope of the studies. We sought relief from Interior Secretary Don Hodel, who had been responsive

---

347   Miller, Bill. "Court Oks Idaho Power rate hike." *Idaho Statesman*, Dec. 10, 1988.
348   Associated Press. "AG Jones won't oppose rate settlement." *The Morning News*, Feb. 9, 1989.

on other issues, and got relief, which I announced in a March 13 press release. It said that "the studies were going to range far beyond the potential impact of the Swan Falls agreement on fish and wildlife." I noted that myself, the director of Water Resources, and Sheryl Chapman, executive director of the Idaho Water Users, met with Secretary Hodel to discuss our concerns and that he took the matter to heart and appointed the head of the Fish and Wildlife Service to participate directly in the scoping negotiations and to limit them in accordance with the amended version of the legislation. Things worked out from the State's standpoint.

Swan Falls I and II, neither of which served any further purpose, were dismissed by the Ada County District Court on August 29, 1989. The suit that Harold Miles had brought against the State and Idaho Power, challenging the constitutionality of the Swan Falls agreement, was dismissed by the Idaho Supreme Court on August 8, 1989. That disposed of all of the pending Swan Falls litigation.

Starting in 1994, Idaho Power made a number of attempts to roll back provisions of the settlement agreement in legislative and court proceedings but those efforts ultimately proved unsuccessful. In order to reduce the likelihood of future disputes and misunderstandings, the parties entered into a further agreement on March 25, 2009, titled, "Framework Reaffirming the Swan Falls Settlement."

The Snake River Basin Adjudication proceeded apace for almost three decades. Although it was not fully and finally concluded by then, the Court, the State, and many attorneys and parties held a ceremony on August 25, 2014, to mark the conclusion of the adjudication. By that time, the Court had adjudicated 158,591 claims, making it one of the quickest and most successful adjudications in U.S. history. As Clive noted in The Advocate, the Idaho State Bar's publication:[349]

---

349   *The Advocate*, Nov./Dec. 2014, p. 28.

Idaho's accomplishment becomes even more impressive when compared to the current status of other state general stream adjudications. The only other states to have completed stream adjudications are Wyoming and Washington. In both instances, however, these adjudications were smaller and took more time to complete. Wyoming adjudicated the water rights of approximately 25,000 claimants, and Washington adjudicated 3,000 claims. Each adjudication took 37 years to complete. Montana, Arizona and New Mexico commenced their general stream adjudications before the SRBA, and all are years from completion.

In that same article, Judge Eric Wildman, the SRBA Judge, estimated that the Final Unified Decree exceeded 275,000 pages. Over the course of the SRBA, the court handled 43,822 contested cases; the Idaho Supreme Court issued 36 opinions; and the United States Supreme Court issued one opinion. Although a number of issues remain to be resolved, for all intents and purposes, the adjudication has been completed.

I attended the celebration and saw a number of the people who made major contributions toward settlement of the Swan Falls controversy. Of course, Clive was there and I mentioned in my remarks that he was the primary reason the adjudication went so smoothly. He successfully negotiated a myriad of federal claims, including Tribal claims, worked out numerous controversies between and among competing claimants, and was largely responsible for developing critical procedural and substantive rules and mechanisms. Laird Noh was present at the celebration, as was Bruce Newcomb. During his tenure in the Legislature, particularly as Speaker of the House, Bruce had been very effective in working out snags that developed from time-to-time with regard to carrying out the intent of the Swan Falls agreement. The only unfortunate thing about the celebration was that Governor Evans and Jim Bruce were not there to see the successful completion of their work. Both had passed away earlier in 2014.

Mention should be made about the role John Peavey played in the Swan Falls drama. In January of 2015, Steve Stuebner, a former reporter for the Idaho Statesman, who now engages in writing, marketing, and public relations, called to ask if I would be in a video he was preparing about John Peavey and the role that he played in water issues. After giving some thought to the request, I agreed to do so and gave John some deserved credit for precipitating action to put Idaho's water house in order. I said that although I cussed John at times while the Swan Falls fight was on-going, his action in filing the complaint with the PUC, which got the ball rolling in Swan Falls I, caused the State to revamp its water laws before matters reached crisis proportions. He deserves credit for waking the water community up so that matters could be addressed in a timely fashion. I viewed Steve's video on the website, Life on the Range, and found it to be well done.

One final matter deserves mention. Following the conclusion of hostilities over Swan Falls, I had an okay relationship with the folks at the Power Company. We did not see eye-to-eye on the Company's $84.2 million rate request or on its handling of cogeneration issues. However, I had a congenial relationship with Bob O'Connor, who succeeded Jim Bruce as CEO, relative to the intertie dispute with BPA. We corresponded and spoke several times during that proceeding. For its own reasons, perhaps because it, too, was involved in selling surplus power to utilities in California, the Power Company pretty much sided with the State. In any event, I found Bob to be a good person. At one point I met with him to discuss an issue and, to be quite frank, I cannot remember the subject matter. In searching over my appointment records, I note that I met with "Idaho Power" on December 2, 1987. That date would have fit for a discussion on the intertie case. In any event, I recall having a pleasant discussion with Bob.

However, I will never forget a comment Bob made as I was leaving his office. He said, "Jim, you really hurt the Company on Swan Falls. You really hurt Idaho Power." I can't remember what I said in return, but when I closed the door behind me I have to admit that I felt pretty darn good — not that I had hurt the Power Company but that this was a recognition that the State had driven the Company to a good deal. And, I felt it was a good deal for all concerned — the Company, the State, the ratepayers, the farmers and other consumptive users, and the environmental community. It was a balanced arrangement that would allow for multiple use of Snake River water. The Snake would truly be what Senator Jordan called it "a working river."

There are so many people who made this book possible. Many of them have already been mentioned — the five to

ACKNOWLEDGEMENTS

whom the book is dedicated, the legislators who supported the subordination efforts in 1983 and 1984, those who lobbied, those who litigated, those who advised, and those who played many other roles. I do not intend to list them all here because it was such a massive effort to bring about the Swan Falls agreement and there were so many who played instrumental roles. I do want to mention three people, however.

Clive Strong is certainly at the top of the list. Without his hard work and sound counsel, the job could not have been done as well as it was. Clive was also kind enough to read my work and make suggestions, just as he did when I was Attorney General. I can't thank him enough.

I owe a great deal of gratitude to my trusty assistant and good friend, Tresha Griffiths. I hired Tresha as legal secretary for my law practice in Jerome in June of 1976. She had just received her certificate for the legal secretary program at College of Southern Idaho in Twin Falls. She has been with me through thick and thin ever since—from my private law practice, to the attorney general's office, back to private law practice, and then to the Supreme Court in January of 2005. She weathered through and supported me in political campaigns for U.S. Congress, Attorney General, and U.S. Senate. She has played a major role in any success I have had and has been a staunch supporter and friend.

The third person to whom I owe so much is my wife, Kelly. Being an author herself, she has given me much advice and assistance and has been kind enough to read my manuscript and offer suggestions. I must say, it was with some trepidation that I asked her to perform this task because she is a wonderful writer, whereas my writing is much more technical, to the point, and perhaps a bit dry. Thanks, Kelly, for all of your support and assistance.

APPENDIX

FRAMEWORK FOR FINAL RESOLUTION

OF SNAKE RIVER WATER RIGHTS CONTROVERSY

INTRODUCTION

The litigation concerning water rights on the Snake River and its tributaries has focused public attention on the relationship between hydro-power generation at facilities such as Swan Falls dam, and upstream water use and development which impacts the availability of water for power generation. While the litigation has been costly to the Idaho Power Company, other water users, and the State of Idaho and has resulted in uncertainty over future availability of water, it has served to stimulate much-needed dialogue and study concerning prudent management of this vital natural resource.

However, Governor John Evans, Attorney General Jim Jones and Idaho Power Chief Executive Officer James Bruce believe we have reached the point of diminishing returns in pursuing further judicial resolution of this water rights controversy. Achieving a proper balance among competing demands for a limited resource such as water in the Snake River system is a fundamental public policy question. Litigation is not the most efficient method to resolve complex public policy questions. Moreover, adversary proceedings may not necessarily yield solutions which reflect the broad public interest as well as the interests of the proceeding's participants.

2

In order to resolve the controversy and settle the pending litigation, we have identified a series of judicial, legislative and administrative actions which we agree should be taken in the public interest, and which would resolve the outstanding legal issues to our mutual satisfaction.

1. THE MINIMUM STREAMFLOW IN THE STATE WATER PLAN SHOULD BE ADJUSTED TO 3,900 CUBIC FEET PER SECOND AT MURPHY GAGE DURING THE IRRIGATION SEASON AND TO 5,600 CUBIC FEET PER SECOND DURING THE NON-IRRIGATION SEASON.

The State Water Plan currently provides for a minimum streamflow of 3,300 c.f.s. on an average daily basis at Murphy Gage (below Swan Falls Dam). The Plan itself acknowledges that 3,300 c.f.s. is "less than the amount identified as needed for fish, wildlife and recreational purposes at Swan Falls or downstream." The best available hydrologic data indicate that existing uses result in a potential irrigation season low flow of approximately 4,500 c.f.s. at Murphy Gage on an average daily basis. By raising the irrigation season minimum streamflow, the state will be able to assure an adequate hydropower resource base and better protect other values recognized by the State Water Plan such as fish propagation, recreational and aesthetic interests, all of which would be adversely impacted by an inadequate streamflow. Conversely, by setting the irrigation season minimum flow at 600 c.f.s. below the current actual minimum, the state can allow a significant amount of further development of water uses without violating the minimum streamflow.

3

Non-irrigation season flows are of critical importance to the preservation of a low-cost hydro base, and to the ability of the Idaho Power Company to meet the needs of its customers. Therefore, the State Water Plan should be amended to recognize a seasonal differential in flows.

Implementation of an irrigation season (April through October) minimum flow of 3,900 cfs at the Murphy gage would result, under similar assumptions, in a low flow of 5,600 cfs in the non-irrigation season (November through March). The non-irrigation season minimum flow should be set at that level. While new storage projects which use non-irrigation season flows may serve to make more water available during the summer irrigation season, they may adversely impact generation capacity during winter months. Therefore, the state water plan should be amended to require that before new storage projects are approved by the state, we should require that existing storage facilities be fully utilized. After such time, new non-irrigation season storage in the reach below Milner dam and above Murphy Gage should only be authorized if it can be coupled with provisions which mitigate depletions such storage would cause in hydro-power generation.

The actual amount of development that can take place without violation of these minimum streamflows will depend on the nature and location of each new development, as well as the implementation of new practices to augment the streamflow.

4

Development of new domestic, commercial, municipal and
industrial (DCMI) uses should proceed without further impediment
because of their minimal effect on total water supply. Availability of an assured water supply for those purposes is
essential for the orderly development of all the State's
resources. Therefore, the State Water Plan should be amended to
reserve a block of water for future consumptive DCMI development. This will both assure its availability and avoid the
necessity of numerous eminent domain cases to acquire water for
such uses.

2. BECAUSE ADDITIONAL WATER USE DEVELOPMENT POTENTIAL IS
LIMITED, EACH NEW DEVELOPMENT SHOULD BE CAREFULLY SCRUTINIZED
AGAINST EXPRESS PUBLIC INTEREST CRITERIA.

The right to develop the remaining water resources on the
Snake River system should be allocated in a manner which will
maximize long-term economic benefit to all sectors of society.
Priority should be given to projects which promote Idaho's
family farming tradition and which will create jobs. Because
maintenance of inexpensive hydropower resources contributes to
a positive economic climate for the creation of new jobs for
Idahoans, future water rights allocation decisions should weigh
the benefits to be obtained from each development against the
probable impact it will have on the Company's hydropower
resources.

5

To this end, the settlement of the pending Swan Falls litigation should be structured in a way which will allow the State to utilize Idaho Power Company's asserted water right to augment the State's existing and proposed legal authority to promote beneficial development and to reject proposed development which it deems to be detrimental to the public interest. This authority should extend to pending undeveloped permits as well as new applications.

In addition, legislation should be adopted which will enunciate state policy regarding the types of water resource development which are deemed to be beneficial, and which expressly recognizes hydropower generation benefits as an element of such public interest determination. The public interest criteria should also address the timing of new development.

The legislation should also clarify the authority of the Department of Water Resources to impose and lift moratoriums on the granting of new water rights permits. The parties envision that the Department can resume processing of pending water rights filings upon adoption of regulations implementing such legislation.

3. THE STATE SHOULD COMMENCE A GENERAL ADJUDICATION OF THE ENTIRE SNAKE RIVER BASIN IN IDAHO.

The key to effective management of the Snake River lies in a comprehensive determination of the nature, extent and priority of all of the outstanding claims to water rights.

6

Only through a general adjudication will the state be in a position to effectively enforce its minimum streamflow rights, protect other valid water rights, and determine how much water is available for further appropriation. A general adjudication will also result in quantification of federal and Indian water rights which until now have been unresolved. A further benefit of adjudication is that it will enable the establishment of an efficient water market system, which will encourage the highest and best use of our water resources.

Because a general adjudication will take many years to complete, it is essential to initiate the process as soon as possible so that it will be completed before an even more severe water rights crisis is upon us. The costs of the adjudication will be substantial, and legislation should be passed which equitably distributes those costs among water users, ratepayers and other taxpayers. The parties consulted with representatives of affected interests, and will recommend an equitable cost-sharing formula as part of a joint legislative package.

4. THE STATE SHOULD ENCOURAGE THE ESTABLISHMENT OF AN EFFECTIVE WATER MARKETING SYSTEM.

If the actions outlined in this document are taken there should be a significant amount of water available for appropriation in the Snake River Basin. However, such appropriations should be on the terms and conditions referred to in #2 above. The day is also approaching when there will be no further water

7

available for traditional appropriation. Therefore some provision must be made to enable people to acquire water rights outside of the appropriation process, over and above the amount reserved for DCMI. Private condemnation proceedings generally involve transaction costs which make it an unattractive alternative. The State should make it easier to get willing sellers together with willing buyers, and to facilitate approval of changes in the place of use. Conjunctive use and managment of ground and surface water should also be explored.

5.   THE STATE SHOULD FUND HYDROLOGIC AND ECONOMIC STUDIES TO DETERMINE THE MOST COST-EFFECTIVE AND ENVIRONMENTALLY SOUND MEANS TO IMPLEMENT THE STATE WATER PLAN AND TO AUGMENT FLOWS IN THE SNAKE RIVER.

The State Water Plan is the cornerstone of the effective management of the Snake River and its vigorous enforcement is contemplated as a part of the settlement. Much additional information is needed to permit informed management and planning decisions.

A number of methods have been suggested to enhance streamflows in the Snake River, which would benefit both agricultural development and hydro-power generation. Among them are new in-stream storage and aquifer recharge projects. These and other methods deserve study to determine their economic potential, their impact on the environment, and their impact on hydro-power generation.

8

6. LEGISLATION SHOULD BE ENACTED TO CLARIFY THAT PROCEEDS FROM UTILITY SALES OF HYDROPOWER WATER RIGHTS WILL BENEFIT RATE-PAYERS.

Concern has been expressed that current law could permit a utility to sell its water rights to others. An additional concern is that the proceeds of such a sale would go to stockholders. The parties will propose legislation to address these concerns. Legislation in a draft form has already been discussed at a staff level and should be ready for inclusion in the joint legislative package.

CONCLUSION

The focus of discussion of settlement of the "Swan Falls Controversy" has necessarily been on the claims of right and authority at that site. However, the settlement of those issues necessarily involve putting in place legislation and policies which will govern the rest of the Snake River and other watersheds also.

The ultimate benefit will be to allow informed state policy decisions on future growth and protection of hydropower generation. The definition and implementation of a known and enforceable state policy will make the Swan Falls controversy an asset in the history of the state.

9

IMPLEMENTATION TIMETABLE

The nature of the controversy surrounding this issue is of such dimensions and affects the actions of so many citizens that the parties have agreed to an implementation timetable to assist the public in understanding when actions may be expected However, it must be emphasized that the nature of the issues raised in this matter are complex and changes should be expected. Every effort will be made to keep the public informed concerning actions of the parties that could affect their interests.

October 1...Release Framework and Public Interest Criterion.

October 15...Execute Settlement Agreement, S.B. 1180 Contract and Stipulation.

November 1...Proposed amendments to the State Water Plan, and proposed legislation providing public interest criteria, authority of the Department of Water Resources to impose moratoriums on new permits, funding for adjudication of the Snake River, establishment of an effective water market system, funding for hydrologic and economic studies to augment Snake River flows and clarifying allocation of proceeds on sales for hydropower water rights released for comment.

November-December...Meetings with legislative committees for briefing and comments on proposed legislation.

January 15, 1985...Presentation of legislative package to State Legislature.

10

DATED this _____ day of October, 1984.

Governor   Attorney General   Chairman of the Board
State of Idaho   State of Idaho   & C.E.O., Idaho Power
John V. Evans   Jim Jones   Company
                                                        James E Bruce

INDEX

Numbers

1180 Contract. *see also* Evans-Jones bill; Evans-Jones bill (new); Swan Falls Decision; Swan Falls II litigation
amendment to, 98–99
compromise to, 187–189
constitutional challenge to, 53
impact on ratepayers, 45–46
impact on Swan Falls Decision litigation, 58
implications of, 79–80, 94
lack of public awareness of, 48
provisions in, 50–51
support for, 68, 92, 93, 94, 185
veto of, 157–158
7500 Suit, 37

A

ad campaigns
increase in use of during primary campaign, 56, 191–195, 198–199, 227–229, 243
inflammatory tone of, 223–226, 231–232, 236–238
moratorium agreement on, 253–254, 260
adjudication. *see* settlement; Snake River Basin Adjudication
agriculture
as economic powerhouse of Idaho, 2
impact of Swan Falls Decision on, 31–32
infringement on Idaho Power Company's water rights, 31, 33–34
anadromous fish, 33, 304, 308–311

Andrus, Cecil (governor of Idaho)
appointment to Secretary of Interior, 16
opposition to purchase of Swan Falls, 41
support for 1180 Contract, 298
support for House Energy and Commerce bill, 331–332
support for Idaho Power Bill, 158
Attorney General. *see also* guest opinion articles; Jones, Jim
and conflict of interest in Swan Falls fight, 233–234
consolidation bill, 235–236
on control of the Snake River, 74–78
disagreements with settlement terms, 273–275
involvement in primary election by, 170–171, 183–184
legal services provided by, 49–50
relationship with Idaho Power Company, 52, 70
relationship with the press, 335–336
response to House Energy and Commerce Committee report, 312–316, 317–318, 320, 322–325, 329
on settlement of Swan Falls, 285–289
withdrawal of settlement support by, 277–278

B

Bell, Maxine, 170–171
Bonneville Power Administration, 8, 56, 237, 310–311

addition of language to House
Energy and Commerce report
by, 308–316
amendments to Swan Falls settlement by, 301–303
delay in approval of settlement
by, 291–292
implied mandate for subordination in federal power licenses,
213–215, 221–223
insubordination clause for Swan
Falls and, 34, 41–42
procedures to license dams and,
55
removal of subordination provisions and, 63–64, 68–70
Twin Falls relicensing and, 141
Finnegan, David, 301, 315, 324, 327
FMC Corporation, 102–103, 112
Freedom of Information Act,
221–223

G
grassroots support, 91–94, 111–113,
148–149
guest opinion articles
a case for state control of Snake
River, 239–241
effect of subordination on water
exportation, 189–191
impact of non-subordination
on Southern Idaho's economic
growth, 136–138
on passage of House Energy
and Commerce Committee bill,
327–329
public understanding of Swan
Falls fight, 75–78
subordination of water rights at
Hells Canyon, 105–108

H
Hansen, Reed, 178, 184, 203
Hells Canyon dams
conditions required for construction of, 13
licensed as "one complete project," 8
relicensing strategy for, 143–144
Hollifield, Gordon (Idaho Congressman), 134, 152, 168, 170, 195
Home Below Hells Canyon (book), 13
House Energy and Commerce
Committee report, 312–316, 320,
329

I
Idaho Cattle Association, 139
Idaho Consumer Affairs, 60
Idaho Irrigation Pumpers Association, 151, 185
Idaho National Engineering Laboratory, 71
Idaho Potato Growers Association,
135
Idaho Power bill
as alternative to 1180 Contract,
55–56
passage of by House, 110
passage of by Senate, 155
veto of, 157–158, 169
Idaho Power Company
customer opinion survey,
232–233, 241–242
employees as ambassadors for,
90–91, 115
expansion of water rights by, 60
financing of ad campaigns by,
209, 217, 227–228
Idaho Supreme Court decision
and, 1–12
immunity proposal and, 32

Jim Jones is an Idaho native, who grew up on his family's farm in Eden. He graduated from the University of Oregon in 1964 and received his law degree from Northwestern University School of Law in Chicago in 1967. Jim served as an artillery officer in the U.S. Army, including a 13-month tour in Vietnam. He served as legislative assistant to former U.S. Senator Len B. Jordan for three years, commencing in 1970. He started a law practice in Jerome in 1973 and maintained it until he was elected as Idaho Attorney General in 1982. Jim served two elected terms as Attorney General. He received the Idaho Water Statesman of 1990 Award from the Idaho Water Users Association. Following the completion of his second term, he established a private law practice in Boise, which he maintained until being elected to the Idaho Supreme Court in 2004. He was re-elected in 2010. Jim served as Chief Justice from August 2015 until his retirement from the Supreme Court in January 2017. He is married to Boise author Kelly Jones. They have three children and eight grandchildren.